EARLY CHILDHOOD EDUCATION SERIES

NANCY FILE & CHRISTOPHER P. BROWN, EDITORS

ADVISORY BOARD: Jie-Qi Chen, Cristina Gillanders, Jacqueline Jones,
Kristen M. Kemple, Candace R. Kuby, John Nimmo,
Amy Noelle Parks, Michelle Salazar Pérez, Andrew J. Stremmel, Valora Washington

Emotionally Responsive Teaching: Expanding
Trauma-Informed Practice With Young Children
TRAVIS WRIGHT

Rooted in Belonging:
Critical Place-Based Learning in Early Childhood
and Elementary Teacher Education
MELISSA SHERFINSKI WITH SHARON HAYES

Transforming Early Years Policy in the U.S.:
A Call to Action
MARK K. NAGASAWA, LACEY PETERS,
MARIANNE N. BLOCH, & BETH BLUE SWADENER, EDS.

Music Therapy With Preschool Children on the
Autism Spectrum: Moments of Meeting
GEOFF BARNES

On Being and Well-Being in Infant/Toddler Care
and Education: Life Stories From Baby Rooms
MARY BENSON MCMULLEN

Principals as Early Learning Leaders: Effectively
Supporting Our Youngest Learners
JULIE NICHOLSON, HELEN MANIATES, SERENE YEE,
THOMAS WILLIAMS JR., VERONICA UFOEGBUNE,
& RAUL ERAZO-CHAVEZ

Resisting the Kinder-Race:
Restoring Joy to Early Learning
CHRISTOPHER P. BROWN

Reshaping Universal Preschool:
Critical Perspectives on Power and Policy
LUCINDA GRACE HEIMER & ANN ELIZABETH
RAMMINGER, WITH KATHERINE K. DELANEY, SARAH
GALANTER-GUZIEWSKI, LACEY PETERS,
& KRISTIN WHYTE

Pre-K Stories: Playing with Authorship and
Integrating Curriculum in Early Childhood
DANA FRANTZ BENTLEY & MARIANA SOUTO-
MANNING

Ready or Not: Early Care and Education's
Leadership Choices—12 Years Later, 2nd Ed.
STACIE G. GOFFIN & VALORA WASHINGTON

Teaching STEM in the Preschool Classroom:
Exploring Big Ideas with 3- to 5-Year-Olds
ALISSA A. LANGE, KIMBERLY BRENNEMAN,
& HAGIT MANO

High-Quality Early Learning for a Changing World:
What Educators Need to Know and Do
BEVERLY FALK

Guiding Principles for the New Early Childhood
Professional: Building on Strength and Competence
VALORA WASHINGTON & BRENDA GADSON

Leading for Change in Early Care and Education:
Cultivating Leadership from Within
ANNE L. DOUGLASS

When Pre-K Comes to School: Policy, Partnerships,
and the Early Childhood Education Workforce
BETHANY WILINSKI

Young Investigators: The Project Approach in the
Early Years, 3rd Ed.
JUDY HARRIS HELM & LILIAN G. KATZ

Continuity in Children's Worlds: Choices and
Consequences for Early Childhood Settings
MELISSA M. JOZWIAK, BETSY J. CAHILL,
& RACHEL THEILHEIMER

The Early Intervention Guidebook for Families and
Professionals: Partnering for Success, 2nd Ed.
BONNIE KEILTY

STEM Learning with Young Children:
Inquiry Teaching with Ramps and Pathways
SHELLY COUNSELL ET AL.

Courageous Leadership in Early Childhood
Education: Taking a Stand for Social Justice
SUSI LONG, MARIANA SOUTO-MANNING,
& VIVIAN MARIA VASQUEZ, EDS.

Teaching Kindergarten: Learner-Centered
Classrooms for the 21st Century
JULIE DIAMOND, BETSY GROB, & FRETTA REITZES, EDS.

The New Early Childhood Professional:
A Step-by-Step Guide to Overcoming Goliath
VALORA WASHINGTON, BRENDA GADSON,
& KATHRYN L. AMEL

Teaching and Learning in a Diverse World, 4th Ed.
PATRICIA G. RAMSEY

In the Spirit of the Studio: Learning from the *Atelier*
of Reggio E·
LELLA GA

D1248010

To look for other titles in this series, visit www.tcpress.com

Early Childhood Education Series, *continued*

Leading Anti-Bias Early Childhood Programs:
A Guide for Change
LOUISE DERMAN-SPARKS, DEBBIE LEEKEENAN,
& JOHN NIMMO

Exploring Mathematics Through Play in the Early
Childhood Classroom
AMY NOELLE PARKS

Becoming Young Thinkers
JUDY HARRIS HELM

The Early Years Matter
MARILOU HYSON & HEATHER BIGGAR TOMLINSON

Thinking Critically About Environments for Young
Children
LISA P. KUH, ED.

Standing Up for Something Every Day
BEATRICE S. FENNIMORE

FirstSchool
SHARON RITCHIE & LAURA GUTMANN, EDS.

Early Childhood Education for a New Era
STACIE G. GOFFIN

Everyday Artists
DANA FRANTZ BENTLEY

Multicultural Teaching in the Early Childhood
Classroom
MARIANA SOUTO-MANNING

Inclusion in the Early Childhood Classroom
SUSAN L. RECCHIA & YOON-JOO LEE

Moral Classrooms, Moral Children, 2nd Ed.
RHETA DEVRIES & BETTY ZAN

Defending Childhood
BEVERLY FALK, ED.

Starting with Their Strengths
DEBORAH C. LICKEY & DENISE J. POWERS

The Play's the Thing
ELIZABETH JONES & GRETCHEN REYNOLDS

Twelve Best Practices for Early Childhood
Education
ANN LEWIN-BENHAM

Big Science for Growing Minds
JACQUELINE GRENNON BROOKS

What If All the Kids Are White? 2nd Ed.
LOUISE DERMAN-SPARKS & PATRICIA G. RAMSEY

Seen and Heard
ELLEN LYNN HALL & JENNIFER KOFKIN RUDKIN

Connecting Emergent Curriculum and Standards in
the Early Childhood Classroom
SYDNEY L. SCHWARTZ & SHERRY M. COPELAND

Infants and Toddlers at Work
ANN LEWIN-BENHAM

The View from the Little Chair in the Corner
CINDY RZASA BESS

Culture and Child Development in Early Childhood
Programs
CAROLLEE HOWES

Educating and Caring for Very Young Children,
2nd Ed.
DORIS BERGEN ET AL.

Beginning School
RICHARD M. CLIFFORD & GISELE M. CRAWFORD, EDS.

Emergent Curriculum in the Primary Classroom
CAROL ANNE WIEN, ED.

Enthusiastic and Engaged Learners
MARILOU HYSON

Powerful Children
ANN LEWIN-BENHAM

The Early Care and Education Teaching Workforce
at the Fulcrum
SHARON LYNN KAGAN ET AL.

Supervision in Early Childhood Education, 3rd Ed.
JOSEPH J. CARUSO WITH M. TEMPLE FAWCETT

Guiding Children's Behavior
EILEEN S. FLICKER & JANET ANDRON HOFFMAN

The War Play Dilemma, 2nd Ed.
DIANE E. LEVIN & NANCY CARLSSON-PAIGE

Possible Schools
ANN LEWIN-BENHAM

Everyday Goodbyes
NANCY BALABAN

Playing to Get Smart
ELIZABETH JONES & RENATTA M. COOPER

The Emotional Development of Young Children,
2nd Ed.
MARILOU HYSON

Young Children Continue to Reinvent Arithmetic—
2nd Grade, 2nd Ed.
CONSTANCE KAMII

Bringing Learning to Life
LOUISE BOYD CADWELL

A Matter of Trust
CAROLLEE HOWES & SHARON RITCHIE

Bambini
LELLA GANDINI & CAROLYN POPE EDWARDS, EDS.

Young Children Reinvent Arithmetic, 2nd Ed.
CONSTANCE KAMII

Bringing Reggio Emilia Home
LOUISE BOYD CADWELL

Emotionally Responsive Teaching

Expanding Trauma-Informed Practice With Young Children

Travis Wright

Foreword by Mary Benson McMullen

TEACHERS COLLEGE PRESS

TEACHERS COLLEGE | COLUMBIA UNIVERSITY
NEW YORK AND LONDON

Published by Teachers College Press,® 1234 Amsterdam Avenue, New York, NY 10027

Copyright © 2023 by Teachers College, Columbia University

Cover illustration by Bozhin Karaivanov / unsplash.

Chapter 4 contains excerpts from "On Jorge Becoming a Boy: A Counselor's Perspective," by Travis Wright, 2007, *Harvard Educational Review*, 77(2), pp. 164–186. https://doi.org/10.17763/haer.77.2.r230j143345x8750 Copyright © President and Fellows of Harvard College. Reprinted with permission.

Chapter 4 contains excerpts from "Learning to Laugh: A Portrait of Risk and Resilience in Early Childhood," by Travis Wright, 2010, *Harvard Educational Review*, 80(4), pp. 444–464. https://doi.org/10.17763/haer.80.4.w18726475585x5t2 Copyright © President and Fellows of Harvard College. Reprinted with permission.

Library of Congress Cataloging-in-Publication Data is available at loc.gov

ISBN 978-0-8077-6834-1 (paper)
ISBN 978-0-8077-6835-8 (hardcover)
ISBN 978-0-8077-8172-2 (ebook)

Printed on acid-free paper
Manufactured in the United States of America

Contents

Foreword   *Mary Benson McMullen*   ix

Acknowledgments and Dedication   xi

Introduction   1

1. **Teaching Children With Messy Lives**   7

    Developing a Shared Perspective   8

    Messy Lives as a Context for Development   11

    Trauma Is the Symptom, Not the Problem   14

    A Conceptual Framework for Thinking
        More Deeply   16

    Summary   21

2. **Essential Elements of an Emotionally Responsive
    Teaching Approach**   23

    Defining Emotionally Responsive Teaching   24

    The Essence of Emotionally Responsive Teaching   30

    Development and Emotionally Responsive
        Teaching   33

    The Aims of Emotionally Responsive Teaching   37

    The Emotionally Responsive Ethic   39

    Summary   40

3. **Teaching From Hope Versus Teaching From Fear**   **43**

   Self-Fulfilling Expectations   43

   Teaching in Treacherous Times   46

   We All Teach Our Own Story   57

   Summary   66

4. **Reframing Resilience for Children With Messy Lives**   **69**

   I Keep Me Safe   70

   Development Along Alternative Pathways   71

   A Developmental Pathways Approach   74

   Reframing Resilience   79

   Moving Forward   87

   Summary   88

5. **Redefining Trauma: The Embodied Experience of Threat**   **91**

   Sinking in the Pool   91

   The Embodied Experience of Threat   95

   The Stress Response System   100

   Differentiating Brief Stress, Adversity, Toxic Stress,
      and Trauma   107

   Summary   110

6. **Too Scared to Learn: The Impact of Fear on Development
   and Learning**   **111**

   A Shift in Worldview   112

   Adversity and Learning   118

   Summary   137

7. **Cultivating Emotionally Responsive Teaching**   **139**

   The Anchors of Emotionally Responsive Teaching   140

   Summary   168

Contents

8. **The Courage to Care**   **171**

    All Children Benefit From Emotionally Responsive Teaching   172

    Sustaining the Emotionally Responsive Teacher   176

    Summary   185

References   **187**

Index   **199**

About the Author   **207**

Foreword

"I am here to keep you safe."

Dr. Travis Wright's compassionate heart and soul are on full display as he relives and shares poignant moments from his vast and varied lived experiences in this, his brilliantly written first book. In it, he offers the reader real hope, inspiration, and practical advice about how to help *all* of our children move through and beyond perceived threats and betrayals that may otherwise leave them feeling overlooked, outcast, and afraid. Travis argues passionately and convincingly that to achieve this, the adults who parent, teach, and surround these children in homes, schools, and communities need to be emotionally responsive.

Travis provides a strong rationale for his theory of emotionally responsive teaching, one built upon a firm foundation of prior research and theories from education and psychology. He then applies his unique interpretive lens, one sharpened by over 2 decades as an early childhood educator, therapist, scholar, and more recently, as a parent. Throughout this work, one feels his deep conviction that we must help children who have lost trust in themselves and others to heal by helping them understand that they are seen, understood, and valued. But what makes this book special and so highly readable is how Travis's voice comes through as he weaves stories and anecdotes from his personal life, teaching, and counseling experiences throughout each chapter. His stories are at times heart-wrenching, and at other times uplifting and triumphant, but they are always revelatory, thought-provoking, and inspirational. He has created a powerful narrative that is both authentic and compelling, making us feel he is in the room with us as we read it, mentoring and guiding our efforts to be better, and more responsive with the young children in our own lives.

Central to understanding Travis's positioning regarding trauma-informed practice is his reframing of current discourse around "resilience" and "trauma." He compels us to dismantle and reconstruct our uses and understandings of these terms. He adds layers of nuance to notions of resilience, helping us to witness it in children exhibiting seemingly maladaptive behaviors. Such behavior, he argues, may be seen as strength—of resilience—in that it reveals children's strategies of emotional and physical self-protection. This reframing allows us to see these children as not "unsmart" or nonresilient, but as complex thinkers and problem solvers.

In addition, Travis's articulation of trauma and traumatic events forces us to scrutinize some currently held notions that offer "quick fixes" for teachers of young children. While recognizing the complex trauma young children may experience (e.g., abuse and neglect, violence in the home or community, poverty, racism, etc.), he teaches us that what matters most is a child's emotional and psychological response to that circumstance—how young children see and feel it. Thus, Travis's focus is not so much on the specific trauma but on how that thing or event is internalized as a threat. When a child perceives a threat, just as we all do when threatened, the psychological reflex to fight, flee, or freeze is activated. Thus, we need to look more deeply at any problematic behavior exhibited to consider what may have triggered the threat response.

Travis's reframing of the discourse around resilience and trauma calls for a paradigm shift in how we understand these terms and, more importantly, in how we help children. The currently popular practice of scoring children as more or less likely to be traumatized based upon the number of adverse childhood experiences is overly simplistic. Other than increasing awareness of challenges young children may face or be impacted by, this is rarely helpful. Worse, it can become yet another way to reduce children to a meaningless number, record it in their "permanent records," and move on.

Instead, we need to roll up our sleeves and be willing to problem-solve about how best to help individual children overcome and work through feelings resulting from mistrust of their environments, feelings of abandonment, and perceived betrayals by important adults in their lives. We need to be able to be an adult who reassures them and communicates, in all we say and do, as Travis says, "I am here to keep you safe."

—Mary Benson McMullen

Acknowledgments and Dedication

This book is dedicated to the family who gave me roots (Mom, Mamaw, Ginny, and Tracie) and the one who gives me wings (Matt, Ethan, Maren, and Olivia). *Emotionally Responsive Teaching* would never have been without the love, support, lessons, and laughter that each of you provide. It is from you that I have learned to see beauty in the struggles and found the courage to navigate the messy moments in my own life.

I would like to express my sincere gratitude to Dr. Nancy File, who believed in this work from the very beginning and encouraged me each step of the way. Nancy's thoughtful feedback and wisdom were invaluable in finding my way through a first book. I am also grateful to Sarah Jubar and Sarah Biondello, my editors at Teachers College Press, for your ongoing support and investment in this work. Many thanks, also, go to the production and marketing teams at TC Press for your efforts on my behalf.

The ideas in this book have been honed through the great fortune of working alongside many emotionally responsive educators. In particular, for the past 8 years, I have benefited greatly from ongoing conversations and collaboration with my colleagues Jani Koester, Shannon Stevens, and Jennifer Waldner in the Madison Metropolitan School District (MMSD) Transition Education Program. I am equally grateful to Mica Clark-Peterek and her colleagues in the City of San Antonio Department of Human Services/Head Start (SAHS) for their ongoing support and feedback. Thank you for creating opportunities to explore these ideas in practice and for your deep commitment to children, families, and teachers. I am forever indebted to the MMSD and SAHS educators and staff who participate in our professional learning communities, sharing their struggles, knowledge, and care for children and families. My insight and understanding are infinitely richer because of each of you.

Many thanks go to my colleagues in the field for your inspiration, research, and knowledge. Ideas do not form in isolation, and the opportunity to participate in conversations with each of you has surely influenced my understanding of emotionally responsive teaching. Particularly, I am grateful to my dear friends and colleagues Professors Lesley Bartlett, Rosemary Russ, and Simone Schweber, for always being willing to talk through a new idea, guiding me gently through the challenging moments, and, most especially, for reading drafts and providing feedback so generously. Drs. Jennifer Adair, Elizabeth Blair, Sharon Dannels, Maxine Freund, Nancy Kendall, Linda Lemasters, Mary McMullen, and Virginia Roach have supported me over the long haul, nurturing my commitment to children and families, seeing the best in me, and creating opportunities for me to grow. I am grateful for the ongoing support of my colleagues at the University of Wisconsin–Madison School of Education.

Graduate students are the unsung and underappreciated heroes of academia. Many thanks to those with whom I have had the great pleasure of working! There are far too many to mention, but I must acknowledge the particular contributions of Drs. Debra Bright-Harris, Jim Burns, Jocelyn Drakeford, Lorelei Emma, Kerrie Fanning, Marcia Jackson, JoElle Lastics, Chase Ochrach, Jeremy Shumpert, Michelle Stite, Amy Taubman, Patricia Venegas, Kristin Whyte, and Valaida Wise. Our conversations and your efforts on my behalf are surely reflected in this book.

The seed for the book was planted long ago by Ms. Ann Huckaby, my high school psychology teacher and mentor, who allowed me to experience firsthand the power of educators to change students' lives. I am but one of many whose lives are better because of Ms. Huckaby's emotional responsiveness.

To the children and families who have allowed me to walk with them through the challenges of their lives—thank you for trusting me to bear witness to your struggles and strength. You have allowed me to see the world more clearly, inspired me to work harder and smarter, and exposed more room in my heart than I knew existed. This book is from you, for you, and I hope that others will benefit from our shared journeys.

Emotionally Responsive Teaching

Introduction

There is much, much in all of us, but we do not know it. No one ever calls it out of us, unless we are lucky enough to know very intelligent, imaginative, sympathetic people who love us and have the magnanimity to encourage us, to believe in us, by listening, by praise, by appreciation, by laughing. . . . (Ueland, 1938, p. 148)

The children who most need our patience and support are often the most difficult to reach, their angry outbursts, tears, suspicious glances, and sometimes ambivalent attempts at learning and relating may feel overwhelming. Yet supporting these children in becoming more secure, connected, and competent is at the heart of what it means to be a teacher. This book is about just this—how to navigate the challenging terrain of connecting with a child who is deeply afraid, angry, and/or sad. Across 20 years of experience as an early childhood educator and school-based mental health counselor, I have come to understand that knowledge and strategies alone are not enough to support children who are struggling with injustice and other overwhelming life circumstances. Fostering such a connection also demands deep capacities for patience, generosity, perspective-taking, perseverance, and profound respect for the complexities that children with messy lives navigate. Perhaps most challenging of all, it often requires us to confront our own fears, vulnerabilities, and wounds. Framing this work as emotionally responsive teaching (ERT), in this book I seek to expand current conceptualizations of trauma-informed practice to encompass more broadly the relational demands of supporting children with challenging life circumstances. Those who seek to make a positive difference in the lives of these children must be supported in broadening our understanding and conceptualization of trauma and our role in children's lives, and in overcoming our own fears and insecurities. Such is my purpose in this book.

Increasingly, educators are interested in implementing trauma-informed practices—minimizing the impact of trauma on children's lives by reducing triggers and employing trauma-sensitive strategies (Lelli, 2021; Powell et al., 2020; Wright, 2013a). However, relatively little work has questioned what is meant by "trauma" or "trauma-informed approaches." Consequently, many use trauma as a synonym for whatever behaviors we may find challenging in our classrooms. For example, low motivation, high levels of conflict with others, learning challenges, attention deficits, and depression are frequently lumped together as symptoms of trauma, and while they certainly *could* be symptoms of trauma, they are not the only reason that children may exhibit such behaviors. Most trauma-informed models tend to prioritize compliance and self-regulation (Herrenkohl et al., 2019; Lelli, 2021; Steele & Malchiodi, 2011), failing to consider children's perspectives, the influence of context and circumstances on their behavioral and emotional responses, and the developmental processes underlying such adaptive behavior. This is a critical limitation as trauma is fundamentally a way of responding to overwhelming life circumstances that is individualistic, context-specific, and developmental (Wright, 2010, 2013a, 2013b). Traumatic experiences and exposure to chronic stress impact more than just behavior; they influence one's self-identity, perspective of others, cognitive development and learning, relationship to power and authority, academic engagement, and social–emotional growth.

In this book, I will reconceptualize the possibilities and challenges of educating young children with messy lives, such as those experiencing violence, chronic illness, maltreatment, inequity and injustice, and other forms of acute stress and adversity, and propose a model for emotionally responsive teaching. I will accomplish this by

1. arguing that predominant discussions of trauma fail to consider the ways that traumatic responses may facilitate both risk and resilience in children's lives;
2. describing the impact of challenging life circumstances on children's development;
3. articulating a framework for emotionally responsive teaching, which includes forming close personal relationships with children and their families, tending to cultural and social identities, respecting individual differences and abilities, developing pedagogical knowledge and instructional skills, trauma-informed approaches, understanding human development, and advocacy; and

4. providing readers with applied strategies for practicing emotionally responsive teaching in their classrooms.

Through discussion in each of these areas, I will also support readers in working to transform the systems of oppression that are being manifested through children's struggles in the classroom.

Conceptually, through this book, I seek to broaden and deepen the current discourse about trauma-informed practice. Most frameworks focused on trauma-informed practices seek to inform readers about the impact of trauma on children's mental health and behavior and provide strategies that might be used to minimize triggers and promote positive behavior. These frameworks are child focused and conceptualize the teacher as a benevolent facilitator, providing them with relatively high-level recommendations for helping children feel safe and empowered at school through regulation of the environment and teaching children about their emotions. This work is important and not at odds with my efforts to cast a broader understanding in the form of emotionally responsive teaching. However, by focusing primarily on the child's behavior and classroom structure, these models do not meaningfully consider healing from trauma as a relational process and neglect the central role that teachers, peers, and important others may play in supporting or further harming children navigating trauma and other forms of chronic stress.

The complex traumas experienced by children—such as chronic forms of abuse like maltreatment, neglect, community violence, deprivation, racism, and exposure to addiction—are typically enacted through relationships. In other words, it is people who hurt them. Often, it is people children love or who are responsible for keeping them safe who hurt them. These relational aspects of trauma undermine children's capacity to trust others, as well as their self-concept, view of the world, sense of safety, and orientation to relationships. For example, as opposed to building relationships based on trust and respect, such children might be oriented to avoidance of punishment, running from connection, perfectionism, anger, or shame and guilt. To overcome such deep-seated views of the self and others requires the opportunity for emotionally corrective experiences that allow the child to be seen, valued, and understood; for children who feel the need to hide, have been devalued, and are not clear about their own feelings and thoughts, this can be incredibly challenging. However, this is *the* work of healing. Figuring out how to see the best in these children when they are trying their hardest to convince us that they are "bad kids," or reaching out for connection as they run from us, is not easy, but it is what is required. In this book, we will step inside these relational challenges, and I will provide frameworks that guide readers through these idiosyncratic and sometimes overwhelming interactions.

ORGANIZATION OF THE BOOK

In Chapter 1, "Teaching Children With Messy Lives," I introduce the notion of messy lives and provide a rationale for emotionally responsive teaching. The term *messy* is meant to orient us to the circumstances being experienced by children, rather than our own reactions/diagnosis of how they should or might be impacted by them. My hope is that this term will further humanize children's life circumstances and help readers better empathize with them.

In Chapter 2, "Essential Elements of an Emotionally Responsive Teaching Approach," I define emotionally responsive teaching and present the essential elements of an emotionally responsive approach.

In Chapter 3, "Teaching From Hope Versus Teaching From Fear," I support readers in developing a child-centered perspective focused on understanding how children understand their own life circumstances. We will consider how our values and beliefs and social environment influence our actions toward and views of the children we teach. I will discuss the importance of ongoing self-reflection to ensure that our teaching practices are aligned with our students' needs.

In Chapter 4, "Reframing Resilience for Children With Messy Lives," I aim to help shift the way we think about ourselves to broaden our understanding of our students and their attitudes, beliefs, and behavior. I will encourage you to develop conceptions of resilience that are dynamic, ultimately recognizing that what might be a source of strength in one part of a child or family's life may be a source of risk in another. The goal of this chapter is to support readers in developing a child-centered perspective focused on understanding how children understand their own life circumstances so that we might be more empathetic and responsive to their perspectives.

In Chapter 5, "Redefining Trauma: The Embodied Experience of Threat," I present trauma as a physiological and psychological reflex to threat. Contrasting traumatic responses and willful behavior, I suggest why traditional behavior management practices may exacerbate the challenges of traumatized children.

In Chapter 6, "Too Scared to Learn: The Impact of Fear on Development and Learning," I take a nuanced look at the specific ways in which adversity and trauma may impact children's learning and development. I will share instructional strategies for addressing each of the learning and development domains potentially impacted by trauma and adversity.

In Chapter 7, "Cultivating Emotionally Responsive Teaching," I discuss the implications of "living out" an emotionally responsive approach and provide frameworks and strategies to guide implementation and evaluation of responsive practices.

In Chapter 8, "The Courage to Care," I will encourage you in cultivating the courage to care and discuss strategies for sustaining yourself while engaged in emotionally responsive teaching.

CHAPTER 1

Teaching Children With Messy Lives

Three years old, Trina is the holy terror of her preschool classroom. Biting, hitting, and spitting, she often refuses to listen to her teachers or respect her classmates. The principal feels so out of control that she has begun holding suspension hearings. However, Trina is a different child at home—quiet, nervous, and never venturing far from her mother's side. Often wetting her bed and crying out in her sleep, Trina is haunted by the nightly abuse she and her mother are forced to endure.

Gerald, only 6 years old, has already learned to be suspicious of authority figures. Though he did not witness the incident, he is aware that his favorite cousin was shot by police officers during a recent traffic stop. He has heard about George Floyd, Trayvon Martin, and Breonna Taylor. His mother told him that if he sees a police officer, he should stop what he is doing and stand still so that the officers might see his empty hands. He was chastised by his teacher for refusing to go near the police officer who visited their classroom during Community Helper week. Gerald is frustrated that he must cross his hands behind his back and avoid making eye contact with peers when his class moves through the hallway, asking his friend, "Is this a jail for kids?"

Eight-year-old Lyla used to love going to school. She danced through the hallways, drew pictures for her teachers, and enjoyed playing with friends. Now, after being in an automobile accident, she spends most days staring out the window, unable to complete her work or pay attention to her lessons. Though they fear she may be slipping from their reach, Lyla's teachers are afraid to push her too hard.

Ten-year-old Juan has difficulty making friends, connecting with his teachers, participating in activities, and paying attention. Though he was too young to remember the violence in his home country or the night that his family fled with him into the darkness, the fear surrounding those experiences still haunts him, making it difficult for him to reach out to new people. His inability to trust others is reinforced by his parents' reminders that his family will be deported if anyone discovers that they are not legally documented citizens of the United States. Though they rarely talk about their lives before coming to this country, Juan has heard enough to worry that his family would not likely survive if forced to return.

Though the details of each event are different, their impact is the same—Trina, Gerald, Lyla, and Juan are too afraid to learn. Haunted by painful memories, children such as these spend most of their days trapped in fear, reliving their worst experiences or running from terrifying events that they may not even remember. It is more difficult to convince them that the monsters under their beds are not real, that the bogeyman lives only in their imaginations, and that nothing bad is going to happen. In the mind of a child living in such a tumultuous world, mistrust is more protective than trust and fear is more powerful than hope. Sadly, when schools are unable to recognize and/or reach children, they cannot address their mission of enabling all children to learn. Understanding how adversity impacts children's development and learning is critical for providing them the support and understanding necessary for healing. The purpose of this book is to suggest a comprehensive approach for better responding to the emotional and learning needs of children navigating fear, anxiety, and other types of adversity.

DEVELOPING A SHARED PERSPECTIVE

To achieve this goal, we must change the paradigms that drive the fields of teaching and student support (e.g., counseling, social work, school psychology, and nursing), creating a unified approach that permits teachers and clinicians to work more collaboratively and that allows children to experience a more unified view of themselves when at school or receiving clinical support. A shared perspective would help teachers to think like counselors and counselors to understand the demands of teaching. At present, these two roles in a child's life are often viewed as being at odds with each other, with children potentially feeling torn between two important figures in their lives.

When working as a classroom teacher, I was often frustrated that the school counselor appeared to undermine my efforts in the classroom, seemingly ignoring behavioral infractions and allowing power struggles to go unchallenged. I perceived the counselor as being too aligned with the child and, sometimes, against me. It felt unfair that the counselor would know things about the child and her life that I was not told. In all honesty, I was also resentful that the counselor was able to enjoy the child one-on-one, outside the stress and chaos of the classroom, while I was expected to "keep the child in between the lines" in the midst of what felt like 20 other lanes of traffic.

In private moments of self-doubt, I feared that children liked the counselor more than me—running to them with glee, as if they were thrilled to escape my classroom and grateful to receive a reprieve from my presence. Truthfully, I did not understand their job and did not fully respect it. I viewed their work mainly as a break for and from the child. Though sometimes I saw differences in children's self-esteem and behavior as a result, rarely did the benefits seem overwhelming. Almost never did the counselor share what she was working on with the child, though occasionally she would "share the child's perspective of what I did" or give me a suggestion that felt misplaced or out of touch with the demands of the classroom.

As I began working in schools as a counselor, my perspective on this dynamic shifted. Through the counselor role, I began to see the classroom through the eyes of the child—one who may have been misunderstood, afraid, or pushed to the edges of the classroom. I heard how daily classroom practices and framings—data walls, "bad grades," "moving the clothespin," "low reading groups," "frowny faces"—shifted from "bad choices" to "I am bad" in the mind of the child. I began to see how children's lives outside of the classroom were impacting their experiences in school—though I was uncertain, given client confidentiality, how much I could share with the classroom teacher. Through time to talk with the child and efforts to connect and build relationships with families, I began to understand daily how stressors were impacting the child's sense of security, self-esteem, and academic performance. Outside the harried fray of the classroom—working with the child one-on-one, perhaps seeing her only once or twice per week for 30 minutes—I was able to be more generous and calm. Rarely in my day were children competing for my attention, and being present with them was my primary job. This was a far cry from what it felt like to be a teacher, where I often felt like I was in survival mode.

As a teacher, I was often focused on *how* a child should act and *how* a child should be performing. I would become frustrated when a child could not or would not do what I taught them or requested. My success and the child's progress were measured in terms of outcomes. As a counselor, my emphasis was often placed on *why* a child was responding in a certain way. I was much more concerned with process, meeting children where they were and helping them move forward incrementally. I celebrated the small victories—often with far too little awareness of how far the child might still need to travel. This was often much easier to do in the confines of the therapy suite, where the child had my full attention and scaffolding—with the same result being much more challenging to demonstrate in the overwhelming and resource-stretched classroom environment.

As a counselor, I was often focused on pointing out for the client how far he had come, while as a teacher, I felt constant pressure to focus on how far the child still needed to go. When these differences surfaced in conversations between the teacher and myself, they often manifested as the teacher expressing frustration that they had not seen the same change in the child and my becoming an advocate for the child, trying to convince the teacher of the child's ability. Reflecting back on how it felt to be on both sides of the conversation, I feel the sadness of my teacher self. It did not feel good to take the negative view of the child, to be the one arguing *against* the child. In truth, it felt yucky. On the other hand, when I recall my counselor self, I see how my advocacy could sometimes come off as strident or self-righteous. It felt good to be taking a stand for the child, but I recognize that I was defining my approach in contrast to the teacher. This, too, felt uncomfortable—especially as I know that their job is difficult and I have seen firsthand the havoc that their students are capable of wreaking. This stance forces me to admit that both the teacher and child often feel misunderstood and frustrated in such situations, with their good intentions often unseen or misinterpreted.

Over time, I have come to realize that when people are misunderstanding each other, or feeling at odds, they often feel exactly the same anger and resentment. Moving forward almost always requires untying this knot. Unfortunately, our impulse when feeling unheard or misunderstood is to either speak louder or stop speaking. In most all the schools I have worked in or visited over the past 20 years, I have witnessed this standoff between teachers and counselors—and frequently between teachers and administrators, counselors and administrators, teachers and parents, parents and administrators, and/or school leaders and central office staff. This is especially true in schools and communities that are under-resourced, under public scrutiny, and otherwise labeled as struggling or lagging behind. As days become harder and the work more challenging, just as we need each other most, we often feel most at odds. Perhaps this is the greatest injustice of injustice.

As a I look at this conflict among teachers, counselors, and children from a structural perspective—and from my own lived experience inhabiting each of these roles—I see that there are disciplinary perspectives that contribute to this standoff. Though teachers and counselors may be talking about the same child, their role in the child's life is often framed very differently. Teachers may be focused on learning, performance, and behavior, while counselors might be emphasizing adaptive coping, self-esteem, and self-regulation. These are not necessarily at odds with each other, but they are not necessarily aligned either.

Cultivating a shared perspective is critical to bridge the gap between teachers and counselors, the classroom and the therapy suite. And doing so is critical for the child, who is often left with the most difficult work of translating the demands of the classroom into their therapy or transitioning the skills developed in therapy to the classroom environment. As teachers and counselors become more aligned in purpose and efforts, they can provide greater integration and support for the child. Developing such a shared understanding and joined sense of purpose among teachers, counselors, and children is a primary contribution of the emotionally responsive teaching approach.

MESSY LIVES AS A CONTEXT FOR DEVELOPMENT

Throughout this book, I frequently use the term *messy* to refer to children's lives. Why? First, because life often *is* messy! This is no different for the lives of children. Far too often, adults conceptualize childhood as a time of relatively little complexity or complication. We often romanticize childhood as a time of play, imagination, and blissful lack of understanding. Even in times that are not as beautiful in this romanticized sense, we often assume that children are unaware of the challenges. However, this could not be further from the truth for many. Children frequently navigate complicated relationships, competing demands, heartbreak, disappointment, loss, confusion, and the full range of emotions that life might provoke. They experience global pandemics; contentious divorces and complicated custody arrangements; bullying and challenges developing supportive friendships; worries about a parent's mental health, addiction, physical struggles, or job loss; awareness of family financial stress; homelessness and high mobility; community violence; police brutality; polarized politicians; famine; war; immigration and migration; racism; heterosexism; xenophobia; weather emergencies; and many other kinds of general and daily strife. Children must endure their consequences, often with less power and agency and fewer resources with which to respond. In other words, children are often trapped in our lives—situations about which they have little responsibility or control, but with which they must contend. Yet, in my work as a counselor and teacher, I have observed that adults frequently underestimate the impact of their actions and decisions on the children around them. My hope is that the term messy will further humanize children's life circumstances and support readers in better empathizing with them.

Second, I use messy to unsettle the assumptions typically employed in discussions of trauma. Generally, trauma is discussed in terms of the characteristics of a particular event (e.g., witnessing violence or experiencing something scary), but trauma is a response, not an event. In supporting children and families, it is important to differentiate between traumatic *reactions*, which are evidenced by an autonomic physiological response (discussed in Chapter 4) and the challenging, confusing, chaotic, or complicated life circumstances that children sometimes navigate. In other words, not all challenging contexts lead children to develop traumatic stress responses. Further, sometimes young children develop traumatic responses to situations that may not seem overwhelming to adults. For example, overhearing a story on the news about war or a tragedy in another part of the world may trigger overwhelming fear and anxiety for children, who struggle to understand concepts like proximity, weather patterns, and politics. Though the same story may be upsetting for adults, it will likely be less overwhelming given that we have learned to cope with such negative news and developed cognitive skills to rationalize such potential threat. Likewise, children are often forced to endure challenging circumstances that they should not have to experience because they seem to be functioning "okay" or because the adults around them do not know how to go about supporting them. The term *messy* is meant to orient us to the circumstances being experienced by children, rather than our own reactions/diagnosis of how they should or might be impacted by them. In this book, we will consider together and separately how to support children demonstrating trauma and those navigating adverse circumstances.

Third, unlike the term *trauma*, which typically connotes the idea of an event, messy foregrounds that it is often the circumstances and/or social climate that affects children's perspectives and behaviors. Increasingly, we are learning that contexts infused with chronic despair, worry, and hopelessness—like living with a parent who is struggling with addiction, being bullied at school, or experiencing homelessness—facilitate the same cognitive, emotional, and behavioral responses as more acute events like being bitten by a dog or witnessing an automobile accident (Ford & Kidd, 1998; Herman, 1992; van der Kolk, 2000). It turns out that fear and hopelessness facilitate similar psychological and physiological responses (Kira, 2001; van der Kolk, 2000). Worrying about something happening—or doubting that difficult situations will ever change—seems to be as negative for our mental and physical health as actually experiencing the event itself.

Increasingly, we are learning that systemic inequities, like racism, poverty, gender-based discrimination, and homo/transphobia, facilitate traumatic responses in children; feeling afraid or less than, navigating stigma or the fear of rejection, can erode one's sense of safety and security. The slow burn of despair can be as corrosive as a moment of terror.

While chronic and acute stressors may cause similar physiological responses, they often manifest differently in children's understanding, behavior, and self-concept, and require corresponding differences in treatment and support. For example, children navigating chronic or contextual stressors, like ongoing parental conflict, hiding one's immigration status, or intense academic pressure, may have difficulty naming their fears, as what scares them is woven into the daily fabric of their lives. Children in circumstances such as these may be more likely to internalize these struggles, coming to view themselves as somehow deficient. Thus, the term *messy* is meant to remind us that even if children cannot tell us a story of what they are afraid of or what happened to them, they may well still be living in fear.

Supporting readers in broadening their understanding of trauma to include chronic stressors, like systematic injustice and disparity, is a fundamental goal of this book. My hope is that coming to understand the direct impacts of social disparity and stigma on children will empower and equip readers with the skills necessary to transform the systems of oppression that are being manifested through children's struggles in the classroom. I have learned that the "messes" most damaging to children are rarely of their own making—and require all of us to come clean.

Yet I do not mean to suggest that trauma is dictated solely by one's community or family demographics—and the term should not be conflated with one's social location or identity. We must not think that trauma is only experienced by children and families navigating poverty, racism, of other forms of disparity. While it is true that social stressors, like community violence, poverty, and racism, can increase the likelihood that one will experience some forms of trauma, terrible divorces, parents' mental health struggles, weather-related emergencies, and substance abuse are spread across demographic groups. It is important to embrace a "both/and" perspective in conceptualizing trauma, acknowledging the disparate effects of systematic stressors on children and their families and remembering that children and families everywhere may experience trauma and adversity. In the same way that we must avoid assuming that all children in some schools have trauma, we must not think that children in some schools have none.

TRAUMA IS THE SYMPTOM, NOT THE PROBLEM

Understanding the distinction and relationship between trauma and adversity is critical for educators and anyone else who is interested in supporting children and families. Adversity refers to the challenging circumstances of life. Trauma is a physiological and psychological response to adversity with implications for emotions, behavior, learning, physical health and well-being, self-understanding, and relationships (Perrotta, 2020; B. D. Perry, 2007; Terr, 2008). Essentially, trauma is the physical and psychological embodiment of the overwhelming circumstances around us, the conversion of fear and injustice in the world into intrapersonal suffering. Far too often, we forget that trauma is the *symptom* of adversity, and that the root causes of traumatic stress are those things that lead us to feel terrified, helpless, or hopeless. When we cast trauma as purely a psychological or behavioral problem, we shift the problem from what children are being forced to endure to how they act. Across 15 years spent working as a child trauma therapist, I have rarely, if ever, had a child referred to counseling because of what they may have experienced. Children are virtually always referred to counseling because of how they are behaving or performing academically. Framed less generously—children are usually referred for support because of how they make the people in their lives feel versus for what they are being forced to experience. In supporting children and families who are struggling, we must address both the adverse circumstances of their lives and how they are responding to them.

When we disconnect our understanding of how children are behaving or performing in our classrooms from the demands of their lives, we run the risk of pathologizing the child for adversity that is no fault of their own. As we will discuss in the following chapter, we may also inadvertently force children to choose between adaptations that keep them safe or connected in one part of their lives and those that might allow them to be more traditionally successful in school. For example, schools often demand that children submit to the authority of adults in the building without question, being compliant and submissive. However, it is not always safe for children to assume that every adult one meets will be acting with good intent. Especially for children growing up in the midst of violence, predators, or others who might hurt them, letting one's guard down and submitting to authority before knowing the adult is safe could be very risky. Yet for the child who has learned that skepticism is safer than automatically according respect to the adults in one's life, such behavior is often viewed as disrespectful or antisocial in the school environment.

As a result of this focus on behavior problems versus understanding children's behavior in context, increasingly, *trauma* and *trauma-informed* are becoming yet another set of terms, like *at risk*, that are used to categorize, disparage, and demoralize. Sometimes, these function as coded language for race, social class, or neighborhood context. Increasingly, in conversations with educators, colleagues are saying things like, "Well, that's trauma—I can't do anything about that," or "How could he not be traumatized given where he's from?," or "I bet every child in that school has trauma." This notion of trauma, as used in the broader discourse, is becoming a deficit frame, both for how children act and for who they are and where they live. This is, understandably, why many critical educators are beginning to bristle at the notion of trauma-informed instruction as the most recent variant of polite racism, with adherents of culturally responsive pedagogy sometimes critiquing trauma-informed perspectives as a deficit perspective for inadvertently linking race and social class with trauma. I share this concern.

In articulating my approach to emotionally responsive teaching, I seek to elevate the conversation about supporting children with messy lives beyond just behavior, mental health support, and classroom management to support teachers and other adults in viewing all children and their life circumstances in greater complexity and their own work and identities as teachers in greater nuance as well. By centering on the self-understanding and lived experiences of each child, the emotionally responsive teaching approach is fundamentally committed to helping the whole child be seen, valued, and understood—their traumatic experiences; racial, ethnic, cultural, and religious identities; and also their individual interests, strengths, perspectives, and beliefs.

This framework is meant to challenge readers to consider how both traumatic experiences and other aspects of identity might be supporting and undermining each other in particular contexts. For example, I have worked with many children who were viewed as being "tough" by their peers. In most cases, their tough behaviors were developed in response to environments where they felt scared or threatened, and were attempts to adopt the "language of violence" that had been used to intimidate them. The way toughness was viewed by the child and others was often reinforced by social, gendered, and cultural norms. While toughness became a force field of sorts for these children, intimidating others and making it less likely that they would have to worry about being bullied, such self-protective actions also threatened would-be friends and resulted in these "tough" children feeling more isolated and lonelier. As indicated in this example, emotionally responsive teaching is more concerned with how risk and resilience interact in a particular context, rather than with casting the way children think and act as either purely deficit or strength based. Rather, emotionally responsive teaching is meant to challenge us to consider deeply how we think about and represent the children and families with whom we work. We must be vigilant in resisting and disrupting simplistic, decontextualized, stereotypical, and oppressive perspectives.

It is in this spirit that I conceptualize emotionally responsive teaching primarily as an ethic—a guiding philosophy and moral commitment—for supporting children learning in the midst of challenging life moments. While in this book I will provide readers with knowledge and frameworks and suggest strategies to connect empathy, knowledge, and values to practice, please do not read the book purely as a "how to" guide. The information and strategies will rarely work if one's "heart" and view of the child are not aligned with them.

The essential element of an emotionally responsive approach is a deep commitment to care about children—how they are feeling, doing, and understanding themselves—despite how they make us feel. Thus, the fundamental transformation—or expansion—that must occur in the practitioner of an emotionally responsive approach is one of our own perspectives. To help the child imagine themselves differently, we must be able to see and understand them differently—and beyond what they might be doing in front of us or how they make us feel in the present. For children who are so fully convinced of their own badness or of the world's indifference, and who are masterful in convincing those around them just how bad they are or how scary the world is—this is no easy feat. But figuring out how to make the world safer for these children, allowing them to feel and be safer, and supporting them in seeing the best in themselves are the most important contributions that educators can make to society. To break cycles of abuse, greed, despair, judgment, and fear, we must foster conditions for healing and plant the seeds of hope. This is complicated work. It is the deep work of teaching and being human in community. It is the work that must be done to ensure that the promise of education—and our very future—has been achieved.

A CONCEPTUAL FRAMEWORK FOR THINKING MORE DEEPLY

Though the success of this book will ultimately be measured in the way it impacts practice, a major assumption underlying my approach is that in order to do better, we must think better. To this end, much of the book will focus on supporting you in thinking more deeply about what you are seeing in the lives of the children with whom you work and also understanding more explicitly what perspectives and experiences you are drawing on to interpret what you are seeing. My hope is that through reading this book you will learn to think about children, your relationship with them, and yourself in greater complexity. Ironically, in my own experience, as I have become better able to understand others and myself in more complexity, I tend to be able to feel more generous and to respond more constructively to their needs. To support you in deepening your understanding, I will provide several frameworks through the book to scaffold your thinking.

Already in this chapter, I have challenged you to begin thinking about children's (and our own) lives in context and to broaden your conceptualization of children's behavioral challenges as meaningful responses to deeper problems rather than simply being the problems in and of themselves. When thinking about trauma and behavior, we tend to conceptualize these issues as being psychological in nature—as intrapsychic phenomenon. In other words, when a child is struggling in our classrooms, we tend to use words like *self-esteem, behavior, performance,* or *mood* to make sense of what we are witnessing. Even if we might recognize that external factors are contributing to the child's difficulties, these ways of framing the child transform for us what the child is experiencing into how the child is acting, thinking, or feeling. Many times, we inadvertently take this a step further—viewing children's behavior and attitudes as indicative of who they are as opposed to how they are doing. When we decontextualize children's behavior and outlook from their social context and what they are experiencing in their lives, we shift the problem from being outside the child to, in many cases, being the child. In this way, we view the child as the embodiment of problems in their/the world, shifting our understanding of the problem from its cause to its symptom.

For example, for the past decade, much of my own work has been focused on children experiencing homelessness. Expectedly, navigating the loss of one's home and the related family and economic stress, not to mention experiencing the myriad other adverse events contributing to or resulting from a family's becoming homeless, is highly stressful and often traumatic for children. As a result, some homeless children develop mood and behavioral challenges and demonstrate difficulties in the school environment. However, despite educators understanding that homelessness is a major stressor in a child's life, I have never had a child referred to clinical support simply because of what they are enduring. Rather, children are almost always referred to counseling because of how they are acting. In other words, our understanding of the problem shifts from what the child is experiencing (homelessness) to how the child is acting (behavior). However, in my experience, educators—frequently stretched thin by monitoring how all of the children in the classroom are thinking and behaving—typically do not seek support for children until their behavior becomes overwhelming or out of control for the educator. Again, children are typically referred for support not because of how they are feeling but because of how they make us feel—when the child goes from having a problem to becoming a problem for us. Thus, in this example of homelessness, the social problem shifts from being outside the child, to being inside the child, to becoming the child.

Far too often, as in the previous example of children experiencing homelessness, the child comes to embody the social problem—and our perspective shifts from viewing the child as the victim of adversity to the child becoming the problem. In this shift, we stop focusing on homelessness as a social problem and begin viewing the child as having psychological and behavioral problems. Rather than telling the child that what they are being forced to endure isn't fair, we inadvertently communicate to the child that they are not measuring up, that we are frustrated by them, or that school is one more place that views him as defective or less deserving. Though I've never met a well-meaning educator in my life who would intentionally do this, I have met many who do so unintentionally—simply reinforcing the dominant narrative that we have been taught. The same is true for making sense of the actions of teachers and their teaching.

The Biopsychosocial Model

To resist these ways of thinking, we need to adopt frames that support us in viewing children and ourselves in greater complexity. The ways that we think about ourselves, others, and the world do not happen in a vacuum. The ways that we behave, relate, and understand ourselves are a product of how we feel (biological/physiological), how we perceive and understand (psychological) what is happening, and the social context (social) in which we are situated. In cultivating an emotionally responsive approach to teaching, we must be able to understand how the child's behavior, self-understanding, values, and resources are being influenced by and influencing each of these development systems: biological/physiological, psychological, relational, and social. The biopsychosocial model (Engel, 1981) is a helpful framework for conceptualizing the unique characteristics of each system as well as how they influence each other.

The general proposition of the biopsychosocial model is that biological, psychological (which includes thoughts, emotions, and behaviors), and social (e.g., socioeconomic, socioenvironmental, and cultural) factors all play a significant role in health, well-being, and social functioning (see Figure 1.1). Biological determinants include genetics, physical ability, brain chemistry, and cognitive functioning. Social determinants include social context and values, stressors and traumatic experiences, our family of origin and culture, and interpersonal relationships. Psychological determinants include our self-esteem and self-concept, how we interpret events as signifying something positive or negative about ourselves, and sense of self-efficacy. The biopsychosocial model posits that these factors interact with others in complex ways—influencing each other, too—to produce one's overall sense of self and view of the world. This in turn drives the way we act, think, and ultimately, what we do with our lives and how we relate to others.

Figure 1.1. The Biopsychosocial Model

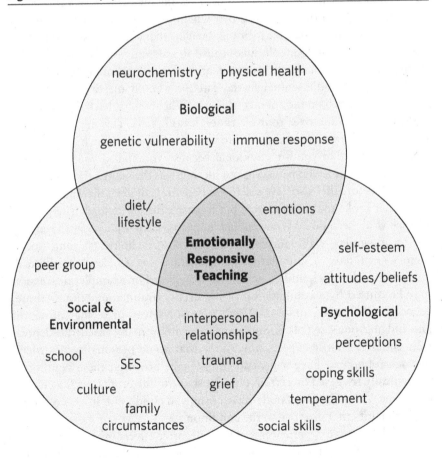

While this chart is meant to summarize how the biopsychosocial factors interact, in reality, the psychosocial model would be best represented as a complex web with many interactions across the different areas. Most important is to understand that these interactions are not static. As factors shift and change, as we encounter new experiences and perspectives, our mental health, behavior, and self-understanding also change.

According to the biopsychosocial model, mental health is the product of many forces occurring in different levels over time, which come to have a cumulative effect on the individual. These forces can be negative or positive. If the negative influences overwhelm the positive, then one might develop mental illness or a negative sense of well-being. Typically, such suffering is the cumulative effect of many negative forces or influences. It is unlikely that poor mental health or negative self-esteem would result from one specific incident, though there might be one incident or aspect of one's life that becomes a tipping point, overwhelming one's capacity to cope.

Negative experiences take their toll. Imagine that you had a stressful morning at home. One of your colleagues called in sick and you have to help pick up the slack at school, two of your students had an argument in the classroom, your principal asked if you might stay late for a family meeting, and you left your favorite lunch on the counter at home. When you sit back down at your desk, you spill water over your afternoon lesson plans. This might bring you to tears or make you feel that you hate your job. Someone watching this scene might perceive that you are emotional because you spilled your water. But while soiling your lesson plans was not ideal, it was the many other things that happened before that also gave rise to your reaction. Spilling the water was the straw that broke the camel's back, but it wasn't the entire load. The point is that we've all been there. When enough happens, it can tip us over the edge.

In a similar way, adversity—biological, psychological, and social factors—can have a cumulative effect, leading us to develop physical, emotional, relational, and/or academic struggles. For example, depression may be caused by a combination of life events (trauma, emotional abuse, economic challenges, or stigma) and a person's way of seeing the world and judging one's self. It is not one factor alone that caused the depression. Similarly, most experts now agree that some personality disorders, like schizophrenia, have a genetic component; however, these conditions are typically triggered by certain types of stressful life events, such a chaotic experiences and negative family relationships in childhood. It is a combination of factors that give rise to the condition.

While negative experiences can have negative effects on our well-being, the biopsychosocial model also suggests that positive influences—supportive teachers, a responsive school environment, developing positive peer relationships, receiving mental health treatment, eating healthy food, and sleeping more, for example—can lead to improved health and functioning. Thus, the biopsychosocial model is not just a way of understanding challenges to well-being. It also provides a framework for promoting positive functioning as well. This means that we should not view people who are struggling as different in some fundamental way; rather, they are navigating a different combination of factors.

Throughout this book, I will be paying attention to how the world influences the child, how the child influences the world, and how teachers, peers, and other close relationships may be reinforcing or reframing these interactions. As you continue reading, I encourage you to return to the biopsychosocial framework to think about how social contexts, interpersonal relationships, and scary events impact children, socially, psychologically, and physiologically. Likewise, as teachers, children's responses to their lives in your classroom frequently impact how safe and stressed you feel in your body, at your job, and as a person in the world. Teachers can change the way the world sees the child and how children think about themselves in a world that doesn't always see the best in them. As you try to better understand the relationships among the self, others, and society, as well as thinking, feeling, and acting, I encourage you to draw on the biopsychosocial model to support your thinking.

SUMMARY

In this chapter, I have defined the term *messy lives* and provided a rationale for emotionally responsive teaching. I use the term *messy* to unsettle the stereotyped knowledge that readers may bring to discussions of trauma. Likewise, children's responses to various life circumstances vary along a continuum of adversity—with some children struggling to cope with events that may not seem quite so overwhelming to adults and other children coping relatively well with circumstances that some of us might find too intense. The term *messy* is meant to orient us to the circumstances being experienced by children, rather than our own reactions/diagnosis of how they should or might be impacted by them. My hope is that this term will further humanize children's life circumstances and help you better empathize with them. I have also presented the biopsychosocial model as a framework for conceptualizing the intersectionality of context, identity, and physical development in traumatic response and recovery.

CHAPTER 2

Essential Elements of an Emotionally Responsive Teaching Approach

Most generally, through this book, I suggest the importance of developing perspectives of children and families that are complicated and complex. Recognizing that life is often messy, our ways of understanding children and their behavior may sometimes require us to develop messy, or less simplistic, ways of understanding them as well. We must challenge ourselves to resist and disrupt simplistic, decontextualized, stereotypical, and oppressive perspectives of children and families—to seek out and build on their resilience. By presenting teaching and learning as reciprocal and relational acts that require teachers to listen and speak and that demand children be allowed to do the same, I will make a case for the central role that teachers might play in the lives of children, helping them to feel safe in a world that is sometimes scary, teaching them to hope, and supporting them in learning.

I hope that being encouraged to embrace complexity and to avoid oversimplification of children's behavior might feel liberating, especially in a teaching environment that often seeks to reduce something as complicated as learning and behavior to standards, strategies, and outcomes. However, in practice—especially in a teaching environment that prescribes rubrics, scripted curricula, and formalized assessments—I can imagine that leaning into such complexity might feel overwhelming. I get it! However, don't let fear or anxiety stop you from trying. For the remainder of this book, I will do my best to help you feel more comfortable translating these ideas into practice. In this chapter, I will define emotionally responsive teaching and present the essential elements of an emotionally responsive approach. In subsequent chapters, I will discuss the implications for "living out" an emotionally responsive approach and provide frameworks and strategies to guide implementation and evaluation of responsive practices. In the final chapter, I will support you in sustaining the courage to care and discuss the importance of ongoing reflective practice in sustaining your emotionally responsive approach to teaching.

DEFINING EMOTIONALLY RESPONSIVE TEACHING

Emotionally responsive teaching (ERT) is a holistic educational paradigm focused on creating reciprocal relationships and restorative learning experiences that equip children and teachers with the knowledge, skills, values, and resources necessary to develop a positive identity, pursue meaningful work, support enriching relationships with others, and sustain an ethical impulse. My ERT paradigm is guided by an emotionally responsive ethic (ERE) explicitly focused on humanizing the school environment, searching for goodness, understanding how teachers and children are understanding the world and themselves, and co-constructing the teaching and learning process so that children and teachers may feel seen, heard, and valued. In other words, through ERT, I seek to integrate ways of thinking about children and ourselves, ways of being with children and ourselves, and ways of supporting children and ourselves in teaching, learning, and growing.

My framework for ERT incorporates research and understanding from the fields of education, developmental psychology, and counseling, including my own research, clinical insights, and wisdom gleaned from 20 years spent working directly with children, families, and teachers as a classroom teacher, counselor, researcher, Head Start administrator, and teacher educator. I, and my notion of ERT, have been influenced greatly by the work of Michael Nakkula and Sharon Ravitch (Nakkula & Ravitch, 1998), Robert Selman (Selman, 1975; Selman et al., 1997), and Catharine Ayoub and Kurt Fischer (Ayoub & Fischer, 2006; Ayoub & Rappolt-Schlichtmann, 2007; Fischer et al., 1997). Gloria Ladson-Billings's (Ladson-Billings, 2014, 2021) work on culturally responsive pedagogy and Ann Masten's (Masten, 2014, 2021; Masten et al., 2021) efforts to understand children's resilience are also reflected in my thinking. My understanding of the search for goodness in the lives of children, families, and teachers is shaped by Sara Lawrence-Lightfoot's (Lawrence-Lightfoot, 1983, 1997) work in the area of schooling and portraiture. Vivian Paley (Paley, 1986, 1991, 2001, 2005) will forever be my role model in listening carefully to children, paying attention to their experiences, and how they make sense of each other, themselves, and us.

I wish to acknowledge that I am not the first or only person to use the term *emotionally responsive* in conceptualizing my approach to schooling. Lesley Koplow (1996, 2002) and her colleagues at Bank Street College, for whom I have a great deal of respect and whose work I admire greatly, have made important contributions to the field of early childhood education through their work to cultivate "emotionally responsive practice." Similar to ERT, Koplow (2021) recognizes the importance of supporting teachers in deepening their understanding of themselves, trauma, and child development in order to better respond to the emotional needs of children. A primary goal of emotionally responsive practice is to foster teachers' empathic understanding of children by supporting them in confronting their own traumatic experiences. Koplow's work is complementary to ERT in that it acknowledges the importance of relationships and creating a classroom environment that is sensitive to the emotional needs of children experiencing pain or worry in their lives.

However, ERT is significantly different than emotionally responsive practice in focusing more holistically on how children, teachers, and families develop knowledge, skills, values, and resources, particularly in the context of adversity. The central focus of ERT is supporting educators in becoming attuned and responding affirmatively to the unique emotional lives and identities of the children and families with whom we work. Given that trauma and adversity fundamentally shape how one understands the world and oneself, it is necessary to develop a deep understanding of trauma and trauma-informed practices in order to connect with and understand who children and families navigating adversity are trying to become.

Understanding the impact of trauma and incorporating trauma-sensitive strategies is an important aspect of ERT, but rather than being the lens through which we conceptualize the role of adversity, it is one of several lenses that we draw on to understand our students, families, and ourselves. ERT also expands previous work on emotionally responsive practices to integrate the psychological and developmental processes underlying children's responses to trauma with their academic and cognitive consequences. ERT is novel in integrating clinical and developmental frames to elucidate how trauma and adversity impact learning and to inform teaching and instructional practices.

Responsiveness

The responsiveness of ERT is not just to the trauma experienced by children and families, but rather to their emotional, academic, and identity needs more broadly. Emotional responsiveness is the fertile ground in which the seeds of learning must be planted. Instruction, ongoing support, a safe and affirming environment and similar resources are used to cultivate learning and the child's well-being and to fertilize our relationship and grow their positive self-concept and abilities. Mastery in the form of learning outcomes, positive peer relationships, an optimistic outlook, and plans for the future are the fruits of our labors. We do not reap such a harvest simply because we demand it. Only through tending to the seeds that we have planted—providing lots of love, light, and protection—will they grow. Like gardening, success in teaching is achieved through the "everyday-ness" of it, adjusting our care based on the conditions afforded by each day, providing extra nutrients in periods of draught, pulling weeds that threaten the roots, and some days just taking a look to make sure that everything is growing ok.

There are no shortcuts in teaching. The only way to help children learn, grow, and develop a positive sense of self is through experiencing what it feels like to be loved, seen, valued, and understood. Similarly, children will not think of themselves as smart or having potential simply because we tell them so. We must allow them to experience these things and internalize them for themselves. However, if we don't tell children that they are capable nor allow them to experience what it is like to succeed, they may not even give themselves a chance to try. Particularly for children navigating messy lives, attempting to learn in environments that are sometimes chaotic or unsafe, it can be challenging to see the best in themselves—so buffeted are they by the waves around them. Even Olympians would swim more slowly in the choppy seas than in the calm environment of the swimming pool. And even there, attempting to swim a lap during a hot summer all-swim would seem a futile act. There is reason that we remove all obstacles and attempt to standardize conditions when expecting that swimmers might achieve a world record.

ERT is about understanding that children who may not be swimming the fastest time nor performing at their best do not lack the capacity to swim. Continuing with this metaphor to illustrate emotionally responsive teaching, ERT is:

- noticing the child's comfort level in the water;
- helping them to relax and invest in becoming a swimmer;
- teaching the basics (safety, an overview of the strokes, how to function in a team, the rules of the game);
- accepting them for the stroke they prefer to swim;
- teaching them to swim because it is good for them and they like it, even if they never compete or are unlikely to win a race;
- encouraging them without condition as they practice;
- pushing them to swim lap after lap to build skill and endurance;
- making them get out of bed and practice on days they aren't in the mood and insisting they take a day to rest when they aren't taking enough care of themselves;
- providing nonjudgmental corrections and constant encouragement;

- challenging them to push themselves as they begin to feel the power in their arms and legs and the strength in the lungs;
- cheering for them as they compete and consoling them in defeat;
- celebrating their victories while teaching them to win and lose gracefully;
- letting them decide if they would like to keep swimming, perhaps on a new team or in a new place;
- reminding them of the lessons they have learned and underscoring our belief in them; and
- letting them know that we will hold them in our hearts even when we are not there to support them directly.

If we have done our job well, they will remember what we have done for them and how we have done it, and they will teach their own and other children to swim, investing their resources and their time in ensuring that all children benefit from the opportunity. Such is the way of emotionally responsive teaching.

Obviously, swimming is not the only metaphor that may be used to illustrate what it means to engage with children in a way that is emotionally responsive. However, as you will discover later in the book, it is a powerful one for me personally, given my daughter Olivia's accident. But ERT is not just about what happens when children get into the water, or the classroom. As pointed out throughout this book, ERT recognizes that children may have unequal access to opportunity and require therapeutic support to nurture their healing and to be able to engage the learning process. Consequently, advocacy, engaging families, ensuring access to therapeutic, and other types of support are all critical to support children navigating challenging lives.

An ERT approach calls us to balance our view of children as learners with the understanding that they are people, with complex lives, hopes, dreams, fears, and stressors. The same is true for their families, who should matter to us not just because they are the parents of the children with whom we work, but because they are important people in and of themselves. Consequently, rather than focusing on children's learning because it is our job, emotionally responsive educators focus on supporting children's learning because they care about them and know that learning will build their self-esteem, allow them to communicate and relate with others more productively, and foster more opportunities for them in their futures.

In my own teaching life and in my research with other teachers, I have found that when we commit to students because we care about them, this often manifests through increased investment in our instructional practices, improving the quality of classroom environments, building stronger relationships with families, and advocating more effectively. In contrast, when I have seen schools and teachers focus primarily on what and how teachers teach, neglecting the values underlying their commitment to teaching, teachers are more likely to express disappointment and frustration in children and themselves and become more frustrated and disillusioned by the teaching process. In such spaces, teachers become "strategies" and children "outcomes," and school becomes one more place where success breeds anxiety and privilege, and those who struggle become frustrated and frustrating.

A broader possibility of the ERT approach is creating a unified perspective that allows teachers and clinicians to work more collaboratively and that allows children to experience a more unified view of themselves when at school or receiving clinical support. A shared perspective would allow teachers to draw on the knowledge of counseling and counselors to better prepare children to be successful in school and other parts of their lives. At present, these two important supports in a child's life are often misaligned and disconnected, and sometimes viewed as being at odds with each other. Especially for children living fractured lives, such lack of integration may result in less effective support at best or more confusion at worst.

From my own lived experience inhabiting each of these roles, I have come to appreciate that though teachers and counselors may be talking about the same child, their role in the child's life is often framed very differently. Teachers may be focused on learning, performance, and behavior; counselors might be emphasizing adaptive coping, self-esteem, and self-regulation. These are not necessarily at odds with each other, but they are not necessarily aligned either. Finding a shared perspective and vocabulary is critical to bridging the gap between teachers and counselors, the classroom and the therapy suite, and most importantly for the child.

As it stands now, the child is often left with the most difficult work of translating the demands of the classroom into their therapy or transitioning the skills developed in therapy to the classroom environment. As teachers and counselors become more aligned in purpose and efforts, this will lead to much greater integration for the child and the support the child is receiving. Developing such a shared understanding and joined sense of purpose among teachers, counselors, and children is a primary contribution of the emotionally responsive teaching approach. In the spirit of creating a shared understanding for those committed to working within an emotionally responsive approach, in the following section I will discuss each element of the definition for ERT to better illuminate the assumptions and commitment underlying the paradigm.

A Paradigm or Ethic—or Both?

A paradigm is a way of looking at something, an organizing perspective for one's actions and beliefs. I have chosen to call ERT a paradigm because it is meant to be an organizing perspective for:

1. thinking about how educators and student support professionals might engage their work in schools;
2. approaching teaching and learning in our classroom;
3. providing support to children, families, and ourselves;
4. incorporating principles and values into our teaching lives.

Given these elements, paradigm seems like an appropriate term for the scale and scope of what emotionally responsive teaching is seeking to accomplish. Yet the term *paradigm* does not wholly capture the "spirit" of how I understand and experience emotionally responsive teaching.

For me, teaching is not just something that one does; it is also an expression of who one is, a way of being in the world. To better capture this essence of an emotionally responsive approach, I also consider ERT an *ethic*. An ethic is a guiding philosophy and moral commitment. In reading this book, I hope that you have "felt" the commitment, passion, worry, joy, and so many other emotions that are present in my teaching life. For me, teaching is very much an embodied experience—it makes me laugh, cry, feel frustrated, tired, happy, connected, isolated, and elicits in me "all the feels." To connect with children in their joy, and especially in their struggles, we must feel their emotions, and more importantly, they must feel ours. Standing with children in the midst of their struggles—supporting them in facing challenges that we did not create and that we may find overwhelming—is very much a moral commitment. Doing so when we are not sure what to do or how to do it is a leap of faith. In these ways, ERT is very much an ethic, a guiding philosophy about who children are and why they matter and a moral commitment to stand with them as they navigate the messiness of their lives. But it is more than just commitments and values—it includes frameworks, strategies, and approaches.

For these reasons, I conceptualize ERT as both a paradigm and an ethic, encompassing how we think, what we do, and why we do it. The term *paradigm* is meant to capture our thinking and principles—and is the head of ERT. The term *ethic* is meant to capture our feelings and values and is the heart of ERT. And there we have it—emotionally responsive teaching is meant to speak to both our head and hearts.

Though I present ERT and ERE here as distinct components, in practice they are meant to be fully integrated, with each influencing and being influenced by the other. As practitioners of emotionally responsive teaching, this will be evidenced by aligning the ways we think about and act with children in our classrooms. For the sake of simplicity, I have chosen to refer to the overall framework as emotionally responsive teaching; however, it is important to remember that this term is meant to include both the paradigm (ERT) and the ethic (ERE).

THE ESSENCE OF EMOTIONALLY RESPONSIVE TEACHING

Holistic

ERT is holistic both in recognizing the biological, psychological, and social determinants of learning and development and in its emphases on creating learning experiences and environments that are generous, restorative, trauma sensitive, culturally responsive, and that seek to transform the systems of oppression that are manifested through children's struggles in the classroom. In other words, ERT is concerned with more than children's learning; it is focused on their development and well-being and the social structures and relationships that influence who they (and we) get to be in schools.

ERT is meant to elevate the conversation about supporting children with messy lives beyond just behavior, mental health support, and classroom management to support teachers and other adults in viewing these children and their life circumstances in greater complexity and their own work and identities as teachers in greater nuance as well. I recognize that I have focused a great deal on the commitment required by teachers and support professionals to engage in emotionally responsive teaching. Yet, to sustain this work, it is important to be responsive to our own emotional and physical needs as well. In Chapters 7 and 8, I will share strategies for sustaining ourselves in the midst of teaching responsively and suggest strategies for setting appropriate boundaries and caring for ourselves.

The ERT commitment to holism is evidenced in helping all of the child be seen, valued, and understood—their traumatic experiences, racial, ethnic, cultural, and religious identities, but also their individual interests, strengths, perspectives, and beliefs. ERT recognizes culture as fundamental to the way individuals understand themselves and the world and integrates culturally responsive pedagogy (CRP) (Ladson-Billings, 2014) as a lens to inform our understanding and conceptualization of children's identities. However, from the ERT perspective, cultural perspectives are essential but not sufficient to understand who the child is and is becoming. Rather than being *the* lens through which we see the child, CRP becomes *a* lens in emotionally responsive teaching. "Who is this child and family, who are they trying to become, and what support do they need to get there?" are the organizing questions in the ERT approach. We would then consider, "How does culture influence the way this child and family understand themselves and impact their ability to actualize the vision that they have for themselves," as an essential consideration in actualizing the broader vision the child and family hold for their lives. But we would also consider the child and family through the other lenses, identities, social locations, and values that they identify as being important to them.

Similarly, the ERT approach begins with the assumption that meaningful learning experiences are situated in a society, community, school, and classroom—and that actions at each level influence what is happening at every level. In order to support children's learning, actions must be taken at each level, being coordinated and aligned to provide an integrated context in which children might develop. However, the ERT approach prioritizes the particular influence of the teacher, as they are the ones with the most direct relationship with the child and who most directly reflect how society is viewing the child.

Relationships and Reciprocal Transformation

The belief that everyone has something to teach and that everyone has something to learn is an organizing value for ERT. Traditional models of teaching place the teacher over the child, with the teacher being the holder of knowledge and the child being the recipient. In such a framing, knowledge is taught "at" the child rather than being constructed "with" the child. In contrast, in ERT, learning is viewed as a process of developing a shared understanding of both the content and each other. Implicit in this view is the belief that knowledge is created through and within relationships. Reciprocal transformation, or how each person (both adult and young person, mentored and mentor, teacher and student) is transformed in a relationship, is a central consideration in ERT. In ERT, critical reflection is used to examine more thoughtfully how children, families, and we as educators are transformed through our shared interactions and experiences. Fundamentally, ERT celebrates that teaching is not just about how we change children and families, but also is an opportunity for them to change us as well.

Restorative Experiences

The praxis of emotionally responsive teaching involves creating learning experiences, lessons, relationships, and explorations that allow children to view themselves as capable and competent. Practitioners of ERT must be able to view the child simultaneously as capable and competent and wounded and afraid—as one who is capable of healing and one who is hurt.

In order to use trust as guides in their journeys, children and their families must understand that the destination we imagine for them is one of justice, strength, and well-being. It would be dangerous to follow anyone who assumes that we will not survive or who is hell-bent on guiding us to our destruction. Consequently, we must hold for our students a vision for themselves that is strong, smart, and healthy while being able to see clearly what is required for them to get there.

I use the term *restorative* to connote the idea of returning to our strength—as opposed to seeking out something we do not yet possess. ERT begins with the assumption that children do not enter the world broken, and though their spirits may be bruised, they may be healed and return to a place of wholeness. Frequently, children navigating messy life circumstances are viewed from a deficit perspective, often being seen as a product of what they do not have or for what they are not yet. But, from an ERT perspective, this is not the case. We seek to honor the fact that children enter the world possessed with the capacity for knowledge, connection, and joy. Our job as educators is to liberate and expand these capacities.

Likewise, those who have been hurt and then learned to heal may well be the strongest among us and certainly the most capable of guiding others in their own healing journeys. As teachers, I believe we are strongest when we have examined our own pain, understand it, and draw on it to see how resilient and capable we are. When we use our wounds to see how strong we are rather than how weak, we are less afraid of being vulnerable—and are more willing to sit with the challenges of others as well. Teaching children who have been hurt—seeing the best in them—is also an opportunity to catch a glimpse of our best selves as generous, patient, and caring. These moments remind us of who we are—they restore us—rather than helping us see who we might become. The same occurs when we support children in overcoming challenges and seeing who they really are. ERT is about restoring our view of ourselves as capable and competent.

Restorative is also meant to suggest that the teaching endeavor should be organized around the needs of the child rather than demanding that children organize themselves around the demands of the classroom. This is to say that we should teach with an understanding that children in our classrooms have been wounded and that rather than teaching around these hurts, we should teach in a way that heals them. When classrooms do not make allowances for the needs of the learner, they tend to reinforce the negative messages the learner has internalized about themselves. For example, children who feel left behind usually have this perception reinforced in classes that do not help them catch up. In "learning-centered classrooms," where teaching is organized primarily around standards and what children "should" be able to do, children who struggle are often reminded of how far they fall short. Data walls, high-stakes assessments, and student-ranking sheets offer frequent reminders that they are not as good.

In contrast, in ERT classrooms, children are encouraged to see themselves as capable and confident—provided with learning experiences that draw on their strengths and knowledge. Such classrooms are organized around "islands of competence"—where teachers are committed to identifying children's strengths and ensure opportunities for them to feel a sense of mastery and capability. This sometimes requires teachers to move more slowly, to improvise, or to return to previous lessons in order to support children in building a sense of mastery. Such an approach is not only necessary to teach students who struggle to engage and learn in the short term, but over the long haul, this is the only way to build their mastery and self-esteem. Consequently, a restorative approach to teaching restores children's positive sense of self and promotes their self-efficacy.

DEVELOPMENT AND EMOTIONALLY RESPONSIVE TEACHING

The ERT paradigm is developmental in that it assumes that individuals change and grow over time. However, rather than viewing development as simply the process of maturation, ERT is built on the notion that development occurs in context and is shaped by experiences and through relationships. Emotionally responsive teaching recognizes that individual, interpersonal, community, and social development are intertwined, with these elements mutually influencing each other over the life span. Consistent with a biopsychosocial perspective, ERT also assumes that one's individual life trajectory is shaped not only by one's social context, but also through one's biological and psychological development as well. Consequently, in ERT, it is important to understand one's perspective before deciding what support is needed and how best to provide support. We should be curious about how one's life has unfolded and how one tells their own story, listening for the experiences, identities, values, and relationships with which one identifies most closely and/or reluctantly.

Asserting that development occurs in context also means that how we act, how others view us, what we know, and what we can do, for example, may also vary based on the environment we are in. For example, I am often surprised when parents of children who are shy in school share with me that their child is never quiet at home. Likewise, I once happened on one of my students selling candy on a street corner. I marveled at his confidence in approaching passersby and his ease in handling money and making change, particularly as this child often faded into the background of our classroom and struggled to compute basic math problems inside our math lessons. Indeed, most of us act differently—and maybe even speak, think, or view ourselves and others differently—in different parts of our lives. What I might say to my best friend may be different than what I would choose to share with a colleague, and how I interact with my husband in private is different than how we might choose to communicate in more public settings.

In ERT, rather than simply conceptualizing how children act as evidence of their character—or assuming that how we see the child is definitive of who the child is or might become—we recognize that different environments and relationships demand and allow children to act and view themselves differently. For example, while in the classroom it may benefit a child to engage academically or to be perceived as studious; on the playground, in one's family, or in others places in one's life, this value may not be shared. Children may be taunted or bullied for engaging academically, with "book smarts" being viewed at odds with "street smarts." In my own family, some important relatives viewed education as a threat to our way of life and my connection with them, and I was encouraged not to take school so seriously. In the classroom, we might view a child who is disengaged as "not curious" or "not smart," but it may just be that the child has not yet had an opportunity to explore or be celebrated for these virtues, or that such engagement might threaten values or important relationships in other parts of the child's life.

Rather than viewing a lack of knowledge or engagement as deterministic or defining of who the child is, an ERT perspective would indicate that the contexts in which the child is developing lack alignment or congruity with regard to educational perspectives. ERT does not assume that just because children may struggle with something in the home or school environment that they may be struggling similarly in the other. In the ERT approach, it is important to pay attention to what children are able to do and how they may think within and across the various parts of their lives and support them in building on and transferring knowledge and skills across domains. In supporting this child, we would both aim to negotiate better alignment across the various parts of their life and help them differentiate the ways they act based on the environment, providing support for and honoring the knowledge, skills, values, and resources necessary to navigate each. For example, what might be considered rude in one environment could be perceived as acceptable in another. Helping children learn to shift their behavior based on the demands of different environments is often essential for their well-being.

When a child's home and school share similar values, perspectives, languages, and cultures, they are often viewed as being "smart," "competent," "skillful," "engaged," and as exhibiting "good behavior" in the classroom. However, when children's lives outside of school do not align as seamlessly with the classroom environment, they are often viewed as "failing," "falling behind," "disengaged," "disrespectful," and as having "behavior problems." Yet the same things that get the child "in trouble" at school may be prized or necessary in other parts of their life. Fighting, for example, may cause lots of problems at school, but may be the currency of power and respect on the playground. Or, while teachers may demand our compliance, some children have learned that it is not safe to do everything that some adults insist they do. When we allow ourselves to view these children as growing across multiple contexts, building knowledge, skills, values, and relationships in each, our perspective may shift from viewing them as developmentally delayed to possessing developmental complexity. From my perspective, the developmental challenge for children growing in the midst of messy lives is not the absence of growth, complexity, or potential—but rather the challenges of too many competing demands and too few resources.

From this perspective, children with messy lives are being spread too thin developmentally. Rather than allowing them the space to hone their abilities in fewer, more aligned developmental domains, we ask them to figure out how to act differently in too many domains with too little support. In ERT, we recognize that different environments and relationships may provide differing amounts of support and resources, all of which influence who and how the child is and how they might be able to present themselves. Thus, rather than asserting who a child is, in ERT we ask, "Who is this child allowed to be and supported in becoming in a particular environment?" In an emotionally responsive teaching approach, we would not assert that a child lacks resilience or grit, as if these are innate characteristics, with children either having them or not. Rather, we would ask, "How is this child being resilient in this or that part of his life," or, "How has this child been supported (or not) in demonstrating or investing in persistence and determination? How have these attitudes benefited or caused risk for them across varied parts of their life?"

Across the fields of psychology, education, and counseling, it seems that every 5 to 10 years we coalesce around a shiny new term to reinforce the notion that a particular character trait or psychological capacity is the primary driver of one's life trajectory. Historically, this has been framed in the negative, with words like character defects, at-risk, and developmentally delayed being used to describe the absence of positive development. More recently, with the advent of positive psychological perspectives, we have shifted to more affirmative framings, such that notions of resilience, grit, and mindfulness have been invoked most recently to suggest that children possessed with more of these qualities function more adaptively. While I appreciate this focus on identifying children's positive capacities, potentially enhancing their strengths, I am troubled by the implication that it is simply one's character, disposition, or psychological capacity that determines one's trajectory. For children who have been forced to endure messy life circumstances or other types of adversity and injustice, who have been put down, shut out, or told to shut up, it seems unfair to suggest that if they only had a little more determination or "grit," their lives would be better.

Likewise, while mindfulness is a helpful skill set—and possessing the capacity to ground oneself and remain in the present is certainly beneficial for children navigating challenging lives—it is not enough to support children in coping with their lives. We must actively work to change the conditions, opportunities, and encouragements that children experience. By shifting our focus from how children have been treated to how they are coping with such treatment, we risk abdicating our social responsibility for what we have allowed to be done or not done to and for them. In other words, if we frame the problem as being children's behavior, attitude, or character, we fail to hold ourselves accountable for the injustice, trauma, deprivation, and minimization they have been forced to endure. In ERT, we view behavior and negative outlook as the manifestations of adversity rather than being the cause of them or the challenges of children in our classrooms. While it is important to support the child in coping with their pain and the injustices they have endured, we must not confuse this with solving the underlying problems that caused them to hurt in the first place.

THE AIMS OF EMOTIONALLY RESPONSIVE TEACHING

In a paradigm focused on teaching children in school, you may be surprised that I did not include academic achievement and learning as primary aims of an ERT approach. Indeed, as an educational paradigm, academic success and formal learning are important priorities in ERT. However, in this paradigm, academic success and learning are shifted from the primary outcomes of the teaching endeavor to important strategies for supporting children's overall self-concept and well-being. Central to an emotionally responsive approach is the organizing belief that children matter more for who they are than how they perform. Similarly, while learning is an important consideration in children's lives, it is not the only one, and for children fighting for their survival, it may not be their most essential need in the present moment.

ERT is about creating the conditions, opportunities, and relationships that inspire and allow children to learn—teaching them because we care for them—rather than organizing our attitudes and beliefs about children around how they are learning. One of the most profound lessons I have learned in my teaching life is that children will try because we think they can do something long before they think they can do it themselves. The abilities to establish a trusting, positive relationship with a child and to mirror back to them a positive view of themselves are the anchors on which all learning, relating, and self-esteem are grounded.

Teaching children with the "big picture" in mind is central to the emotionally responsive approach. Though letter recognition, content knowledge, and math concepts may provide the context for our interactions with children, these are not the be-all and end-all of our work with them. Our broader commitment is to ensure that they are empowered and equipped with the skills, dispositions, and competencies to make choices about the direction of their lives, be healthy and well, and build a network of meaningful connections. Certainly, children will not be able to pursue such pathways without academic knowledge and skills, and it is our job to ensure that they receive the educational instruction necessary to develop them.

Academic skills and formal knowledge are essential for a bright future in today's world, but they are not sufficient. We have all witnessed bright, accomplished, well-educated people fall apart, do bad things, hurt other people, and fail in public and private ways. Richard Nixon managed to become president of the United States, but lost it all because he struggled to trust others and lied. At the pinnacle of his career, actor Will Smith humiliated himself by being unable to manage his anger onstage at the Oscar awards ceremony, and possibly painful triggers from his past.

At the moment in which I am writing this, ego and self-interest are fomenting wars, moral crisis, a global pandemic, corrupting our political institutions, and inflicting immeasurable injury to the environment. These problems have arisen not because we lack knowledge, but because self-interest, greed, a lack of common values and shared purpose, and leaders who benefit from our fractures would rather divide us than pull us together. To change course, we must prepare our children to engage each other and the world differently. As teachers of young children, we are not only developing the child in front of us, but shaping the world they will create and the generations that will be impacted by their actions.

The following specific aims are meant to support emotionally responsive educators in focusing on the big picture in our work. Here I will define them. In subsequent chapters, I will provide suggestions for ways they might be supported in our classrooms.

- **Positive Identity** is characterized by one's ability to feel a sense of worth about who one is and who one is becoming. Positive identity means that we like who we are. Ultimately, positive identity is about how one feels about oneself—as opposed to how others view us. In the ERT paradigm, the ultimate goal of our efforts is to lay the foundation for children to grow into adults who feel good about themselves.
- **Meaningful Work** is one's sense that how she or he contributes to the world is important, impactful, and appreciated by others. Ideally, such efforts would be intrinsically meaningful to the individual—filling one with a sense of purpose, industry, and fulfillment—and also valued externally, in the form of appreciation and self-sustaining financial compensation.
- **Enriching Relationships** are connections with other people that provide us with a sense of belonging, enjoyment, and support. Some characteristics of enriching relationships are respect, intimacy and sharing, reciprocity, interdependence, communication, effective conflict resolution, emotional support, shared experiences, and joy.
- **Ethical Impulse** is defined by both one's sense that it is important to be a "good person" and the willingness to contribute to the social good. Individuals with a strong ethical impulse recognize the needs of others and are willing to do what they might to help, balancing the needs of the group with their own needs and interests. An ethical impulse helps us recognize that our actions have consequences for others and that our decisions and actions should be undertaken with an awareness of how others will be impacted by them.

Ultimately, we want to prepare our students to leave the world a little better than they found it, to find fulfillment in the way that they spend their time, to love, and to allow themselves to be loved. As previously discussed, these capacities are not purely intellectual—they are embodied, internalized ways of being in the world. It is not enough to say that we wish these things for children—in order to build the capacities essential for navigating the world in these ways, children must experience them!

THE EMOTIONALLY RESPONSIVE ETHIC

The emotionally responsive ethic (ERE) is how we facilitate the emotional, ethical, and embodied experiences that allow children to heal and/or grow and internalize the aims of the ERT approach. Next, I will define some of the core ethical commitments and dispositions that characterize the ERE and are essential in cultivating ERT.

- **Humanizing the School Environment** is a commitment to value children, their parents, colleagues, and ourselves as people with full lives, emotions, rights, priorities, and capacity for joy. When we humanize the school environment, we make it more humane, more suitable for growth and development. In humanizing spaces, we experience empathy, kindness, positive regard, and we feel as if we matter.
- **Searching for Goodness** is an explicit commitment to seek out what is best in children, their families, our colleagues, and ourselves. Rather than focusing on children's deficits and needs, we are guided by their resources and strengths, looking for, building on, and magnifying what is best in them. When we search for goodness in others, they see their best qualities reflected back—they know what we like about them and that we believe in them. This is not to say that we are unaware of the areas for growth, the messy parts of one's life and the frayed edges of one's abilities; it is that we do not view them as definitive or even defining of who one is and might become. When searching for goodness in others, they trust that our efforts to support them are in the spirit of growth and support versus a fear of their failure.
- **Understanding** is the commitment to learn both what others think and why they think it. ERE recognizes that teaching and learning are not just about the facts or skills that we acquire, but what they mean to us and how they will fit (or not) into our lives.

- **Co-Constructing Teaching and Learning** is the recognition that teaching and learning are reciprocal acts, the mutual transfer of knowledge and understanding, and shared investment. ERE celebrates that we all have something to teach and to learn, including in our teaching lives with students. Though ERT is both a relational and a reciprocal approach, this is not to imply that the needs and perspectives of teachers and children are shared equally.

  In other words, while we spend a great deal of time thinking about who our child is becoming, we should not expect them to be equally invested in our personal life or trajectory. While we do want them to care about us, and it is appropriate and important to share information about ourselves that help students feel connected to us, everything that we share with them is in the spirit of their growth and development. The teaching and learning relationship is one-sided, and its main purpose is to support the child and their family in learning and growing—and ERT is fundamentally centered on the child and who they are trying to become.

- **Seen, Heard, and Valued** are the embodied experiences necessary for developing reciprocal relationships, a sense of connection, and a positive self-identity. Feeling seen is the experience of being recognized for who we are, of being responded to in a way that truthfully reflects our experience back at us. Feeling heard is the experience of being listened to and understood. Valued is the experience of feeling important and appreciated, as if we matter. In the ERE, this commitment is shared by and extended to teachers, children, and their families—and these embodied experiences are the best indicators that ERE is being cultivated.

SUMMARY

In this chapter, I have provided a framework for emotionally responsive teaching. Though each of these elements are important components of cultivating an emotionally responsive teaching practice, they are not the only elements. Each of us brings our own wisdom, perspective, experiences, and "ways" to our teaching life, and ERT is meant to allow us to express this authentically in our praxis.

This section is not meant to be read definitively as a checklist or how-to, but rather as a guide for your reflection on becoming more emotionally responsive in your work with children, families, colleagues, and with yourself. My hope is that you might return to the elements discussed in this chapter time and again as reflection points for your practice and understanding. In this same spirt, I will offer suggestions and inspirations for implementing the various aspects of emotionally responsive teaching in the following chapters.

CHAPTER 3

Teaching From Hope Versus Teaching From Fear

Central to cultivating an emotionally responsive perspective is understanding that our own experiences and belief systems, including our values and biases, influence our teaching practices. It is essential to recognize that our individual beliefs do not exist in isolation; rather, they are intertwined with broader belief structures such as our cultural background, family history, and social location, and are reinforced by our social environment, including media coverage, political engines, and religious systems. Moreover, beliefs tend to self-perpetuate; researchers have shown that most of us are apt to use whatever cognitive tricks are necessary to turn even disconfirming evidence into support for existing beliefs. Thus, if we take as given that questioning or overturning our existing beliefs are needed to reach all students, research (Nakkula & Ravitch, 1998; Wright et al., 2019) suggests that it is going to be no easy task.

In this chapter, we will examine the ways we understand ourselves—how our implicit and explicit values and beliefs influence our actions, the impact of our social environment on our self-understanding and views of the children we teach, and the importance of ongoing self-reflection to ensure that our teaching practices are aligned with our students' needs. In the following chapter, we will draw on this shift in the way we think about ourselves to broaden our understanding of our students and their attitudes, beliefs, and behavior.

SELF-FULFILLING EXPECTATIONS

Previous findings (Fang, 1996; Kim, 2013; Rist, 2000), including my own research (Wright, 2007, 2010; Wright et al., 2019), reveal that teachers often hold deficit perspectives of children navigating challenging life circumstances like homelessness, poverty, and/or community violence, anticipating that such children will misbehave, be unmotivated, or have trouble focusing. Such beliefs directly influence how we design our classroom environments, structure learning opportunities, and perceive and respond to students and their families. Our belief systems serve as the lenses through which we make sense of the knowledge and experiences we encounter in our classrooms. Given the power of our expectations to shape how we view and educate our students, becoming cognizant of our belief systems and implicit biases is critical in monitoring how they may be influencing how we teach, perceive, and influence our students.

Our expectations for student academic performance, behavior, and learning potential have been shown to bear strongly on children's chances for success in our classrooms. Because teachers' expectations can function as self-fulfilling prophecies, we may afford fewer enriching opportunities for learning and express less warmth and encouragement to students we perceive as low-achieving, our habits in turn impeding students' chances at school success. Research (Valencia, 1997) has shown that teachers tend to believe that students who fail in school do so because of internal deficits or deficiencies, rather than as a function of an inequitable system or powerfully challenging personal circumstances. Such deficit thinking is particularly common among teachers who work with students who differ from them in racial, ethnic, gender, and social class backgrounds.

In the fields of counseling and psychology, we refer to these types of effects as *reactivity*. Reactivity is a psychological phenomenon that occurs when someone changes the way they behave or think because of how another person perceives them or makes them feel. Two particular types of reactivity that are relevant to classrooms are the Pygmalion effect and the Golem effect. In the Pygmalion effect (Chang, 2011; Szumski & Karwowski, 2019), students change their behavior based on what they perceive their teachers expect from them. If a teacher maintains high expectations for students, they will perform better than if the teacher held low expectations for them. Similarly, the Golem effect (Nurmohamed, 2020; Rowe & O'Brien, 2002) happens when teachers have low expectations for their students, fostering in them a tendency to work less diligently and demonstrate worse performance.

As teachers, we are also subject to these same types of reactions. It has been demonstrated (Rausch et al., 2016; Redding, 2019) that when teachers perceive students like them or are more attentive to their instruction, they tend to grade them higher even if their work isn't better than that of students who paid less attention or seemed more critical. Similarly, we tend to identify more positively and feel more comfortable when interacting with people who share our values, beliefs, and cultural practice or who we perceive as being less challenging to us. However, the reverse is true for students who challenge us or who we may perceive as being different than us.

For example, in my work with LBGT children and adolescents, I have often witnessed the queer-identified student being blamed or punished for their "disruptive" reactions to episodes of bullying versus the children who are harassing them being held to account. On several occasions, when I have been videotaping in the classroom at the time of the events, I have been able to process the incidents with the classroom teachers—who insist they would never intentionally discriminate against a child. Because I have known many of these teachers personally for a period of years, I believe them! However, as a result of our trusting relationships, teachers have courageously reviewed the films to process their reflexive responses. In doing so, they have often recognized that perhaps they do feel less comfortable with the bullied student. One teacher even described "[w]alking on eggshells sometimes, worrying that [she] will say the wrong thing." Upon deeper reflection, she realized that this discomfort often played out in her interactions with the student in unintentional ways, such as assigning the student to participate in reading groups led by the co-teacher, being less likely to call on the child in class, or interacting less informally with the child.

It is important to recognize that despite our stated values and intentions, all of us harbor unexamined biases that influence our actions in ways that we might not be aware of. Accepting this about ourselves and giving ourselves permission to examine our actions—being open to finding things in them that may not make us proud—is the first step in transforming our instructional practices.

This is particularly true when working with children navigating messy life circumstances. As we will discuss in greater depth in later chapters, children with messy lives often present as sullen and suspicious, just as would most of us when navigating tough times. The challenges in their lives may distract their focus from the lesson at hand, make them less chatty and moodier, and lead them to present as shy, withdrawn, or critical. As a result of stress, disappointment, exhaustion, and discrimination, these children often come to expect little from the world and sometimes less from themselves. When a child tries hard to push us away or to convince us that they are bad or worthless, sometimes—in our own frustration and feelings of failing them—it is easy to become convinced that they are right. As I said in the introduction, the children who most need our love and support are often the most difficult to like—and frequently the most challenging to relate with. But we must not lose sight of who the child might become and what they deserve.

If nothing else, holding on to what is possible for the child—planting the seeds of hope and possibility—is the single most important thing that we can do to begin developing in them a foundation for self-esteem and agency. Working to differentiate what we expect of children and how we teach them from how they make us feel is the first and most fundamental step in cultivating an emotionally responsive approach to teaching.

TEACHING IN TREACHEROUS TIMES

Now more than ever, being able to turn inward while finding and holding onto our best selves is critical and challenging. Yet inward is not the only place that we should look to understand how social forces may be shaping the way we feel about ourselves as teachers and about the students we are seeking to support. Schools are on the front lines of society's struggles, the places where social forces, community values, and individual needs intersect. Teachers are often forced to navigate social challenges that society is far from resolving and bridging differences that wedge people apart in virtually every other part of the world. Though our politics are increasingly at odds and political leaders cannot seem to agree on most anything, teachers are expected to keep peace in their classrooms and facilitate an environment where each child has the necessary support to reach their full potential. This is the great promise of the American educational system, of turning to each other and creating an equitable society. Schools are society's best opportunity for people to convene across difference, share in experience and knowledge, and grow together through open dialog. Yet whenever politicians and parents feel out of control, when society and social institutions become frayed, schools become yet another battlefield, and teachers are drafted as soldiers in the culture war. Unfortunately, we are now teaching in such times.

This is not to mention the impact of natural disasters and public health crises. The COVID-19 pandemic has taught all of us not to take school—or physical proximity—for granted. Teachers, children, and their families must worry about their physical health while ensuring that children are healthy and educated, and all the while society cannot reach consensus about how to do either. As I write this book, we are at war over both critical race theory and wearing masks in the classroom. The consequences for each are profound with regard to how children come to feel safe and valued in our classrooms, yet even this does not seem capable of bringing us together in the present moment.

Though upheaval and unrest are not unfamiliar challenges, what feels different in this present moment is that teachers are no longer uniformly viewed as pillars of the community and are often met with skepticism themselves. The mistrust for each other that has been fomented at the social level has become projected onto teachers and teaching. At the same time that teachers are called on to right social inequity and to make the world a better place for our children, teachers and schools are often accused of being one of the reasons for the downfall. Though it is true that many of the turns in the American educational system have been for the worse, reinforcing inequity and narrow views of knowledge, it is also true that most still enter teaching because they are deeply committed to being part of the solution and making schools better for children and society. However, from the societal perspective, the line between failing schools and failing teachers is increasingly blurred.

Such ambivalence has resulted in a crazy-making policy climate—with many contradictory views of teachers and teaching. For example, at the same time that states are creating more accountability structures for teachers and providing more oversight of teachers and teacher education programs, they are also making it easier for individuals to become certified as teachers, in some cases creating certification tracks for individuals who have never taken an education course. Likewise, as classrooms and learner needs are becoming more diverse, teachers are being forced to implement increasingly standardized approaches to learning with even more regulation about what may (and may not be) said in the classroom. With all of these contradictions, many teachers report feeling stressed and overwhelmed while simultaneously feeling overly scrutinized (Berryhill et al., 2009; Collie et al., 2017; Eslinger, 2014; Gonzalez et al., 2017).

Such a treacherous climate is hugely problematic for the self-reflection and vulnerability needed for emotionally responsive teaching. When we are forced to justify how good we are amidst ever-changing metrics and the stakes for appearing vulnerable are high, admitting that we might need support or identifying areas for further growth and development become more threatening and less possible. It is virtually impossible to keep our guard up and let it down simultaneously!

Echoing and reinforcing this dynamic, teacher professional development and evaluation are more often discussed through the language of performance and accountability rather than focusing on empowerment and support. With outcomes and data tracking driving teacher rating systems, child-level performance is often the difference between being viewed as a "good" or "bad," "effective" or "ineffective" teacher. In these systems, teachers are evaluated based on how children perform on standardized indicators of learning, which are taught through standardized curriculum offerings. In such models, teachers are evaluated based on how well they get children to comply with these standardized expectations. Teachers who teach successful children are viewed as good teachers, and are often rewarded financially or otherwise as a result. In contrast, teachers who teach children who struggle to meet expectations are viewed as less effective or bad teachers.

In such a high-stakes environment, teachers are incentivized to teach children who are most likely to meet expectations and to view children who struggle as barriers to the teachers' success. Sadly, this often results in the children who need the most understanding and support from teachers being viewed with trepidation, anxiety, and ambivalence. To be fair, such accountability standards are meant to ensure that all children receive high-quality instruction. However, as implemented presently, my experience is that the current accountability focus creates a culture where children are valued more for how they perform than for who they are. Further, it allows children's needs to be viewed as disruptions rather than opportunities for support. When teacher success is pitted against children's needs, the classroom becomes one more competitive environment where children who struggle the most are likely to benefit the least—and the stakes for admitting that we as teachers might have room to grow are too high.

Some might suggest the way around this tension is to merely lower the standards children who are struggling at school must achieve. However, I have already shown that such an approach will do nothing but lower students' views of themselves and their capabilities. Rather, I wish to argue that we should provide different levels of support for them—and their teachers. This framing honors equity—some people need different levels of support to achieve at the same level—rather than an equality frame, which endeavors to provide everyone exactly the same amount. Unless we as teachers realize that we are embedded in this culture, we inadvertently play these dynamics out on the children we teach.

Social Inequity and Schooling

For almost a decade I lived and worked in Washington, DC, first as a 6th-grade public school teacher, then as a university professor, and finally as deputy chief for Early Childhood Education for Washington, DC Public Schools. These roles allowed me the opportunity to participate in schools as both an insider and outsider, helping me to appreciate the system-level challenges facing a large urban school district while also holding onto the view that many children and families in the district were not receiving the education that they deserved. During my time as a professor at the George Washington University and as an active member of the DC early childhood education community, I was frequently invited to conduct professional development trainings for educators and implemented research and service projects in public and charter schools across the city. In these spaces, teachers viewed me as an outsider and seemed to be more comfortable sharing their critical perspectives with me in a way that they may have felt less comfortable doing so later, when I became school administrator. However, working as a district-level administrator allowed me to become familiar with many more schools across the city and the differences among them. Taken together, these opportunities allowed me to witness firsthand how their social environment influences how teachers think about themselves, their jobs, and the children and families with whom they work.

Perhaps there was no better place than Washington, DC, to witness firsthand how differences in socioeconomic status, race, and other forms of difference manifested in how classrooms were structured and children perceived. In sharing the following demographic data, I aim to provide evidence of systemic differences. In the subsequent section, I will consider how these demographic and economic differences manifest in children's learning experiences and environments.

Though relatively small in land mass—the entire city compromises only 68 square miles, meaning that its two farthest points are less than 10 miles apart—Washington, DC, has a population of 700,000 people, making it the 21st-largest city in the United States. In this relatively small physical space exists the largest income inequality of any city or town in the nation. This means that some of the wealthiest and most poverty-stricken neighborhoods in the United States are separated by only a few miles. Thus, though DC residents may live in close proximity to each other, how they live might as well be worlds apart—a dynamic that has changed far too little in the 20 years since I first began my connection with Washington, DC.

In 2016, the year for which the most current data is available (Naveed, 2017), DC households in the top 20% of income level had 29 times more income than the bottom 20%. The bottom fifth of DC households had just 2% of total DC income in 2016, while the top fifth had a staggering 56%. These economic differences manifested primarily along lines of race. For example, during 2016, the average income for White DC residents was greater than $120,000 annually, while Latinx residents averaged just over $60,000 and Black residents earned just under $40,000 on average—which was actually a decrease from the year before. Though current data for DC is presently unavailable for comparison, several recent reports indicate that income and racial disparity have only worsened in the district and across the nation—now at the highest level in the United States since the Great Depression. A 2021 report (Busette & Elizondo, 2022) from the Brookings Institution indicates that income inequality has increased over the past 40 years, largely as a result of increasing average income among the top 20% of earners. In other words, the wealthiest Americans are getting richer while lower income Americans are staying poor.

Such income disparity also equates to disparity in educational and other opportunities. Structurally, this happens in part through the both the housing economy and the way schools are typically funded in the United States. Put simply, wealthy people tend to live among other wealthy people, and neighborhoods are largely segregated by the income of their residents. This segregation is reinforced through schooling because children typically attend neighborhood schools in the United States and because schools are largely funded through property taxes. Even in school districts where children are given the opportunity to choose where to attend school, transportation challenges, convenience, stigma, and other barriers often reduce the likelihood that children might be able to choose a school other than the one closest to their homes.

From a practical standpoint, in Washington, DC, this means the children living in homes with the lowest incomes tend to attend schools in southeast or northeast DC—Wards 7 and 8. In Ward 7 and Ward 8, for the years 2014–2018, the average household incomes were $60,615 and $53,417 respectively. In contrast, most of the economic wealth of the city is located in northwest DC or near the U.S. Capitol area—in Wards 2 or 3, with average household incomes of $152, 985 and $195,279 respectively, during the same period. In 2019, Black-identified individuals made up 92.4% of the population in Ward 7 and 89.2% of the population in Ward 8, while White individuals were the largest percentage of the population in Ward 2 (65.4%) and Ward 3 (70.9%). These trends in economic and racial segregation are mirrored in the quality of schools children attend. For example, during the 2018–2019 academic year, 89% of DC public schools in Ward 2 and 100% in Ward 3 received the highest ratings of quality (a score of 4 or 5) by the DC State Office of the Superintendent (OSSE). In contrast, only 19% of schools in Ward 7 and 11% in Ward 8 received the same rating.

Certainly, these statistics are powerful, but how do these stark differences manifest themselves—and become reinforced—on a daily basis in our classrooms? What do such economic, racial, and quality differences mean in practice? Drawing on my own experiences working in Washington, DC, in the following section I will document how differences at the social and community level impact the way teachers view and instruct children and the ways children are allowed to learn and think about themselves. Specifically, I will document the difference between teaching children from a place of hope and teaching children from a place of fear.

A Broken Promise

In 1999, during my first year teaching 6th grade, I taught at one of the lowest-ranked and most economically challenged schools in the district. Nine hundred and ninety-six students in grades pre-K through 6th attended this elementary school. All but 11 identified as Black or African American. The remaining students identified as Latino(a). Of the 49 staff members, only three identified as White, with all the rest identifying as Black/African American. There were four males in the building, and I was the only one who self-identified as White. Virtually every student in the building received free lunch benefits.

From my classroom, one could see the dome of the U.S. Capitol Building, the seat of power for the wealthiest nation in the world and a professed beacon for democracy and justice. Yet, though the building was only 15 blocks from my classroom, almost none of my 12-year-old students had ever taken the bus downtown to see it. For them, the promises of that building—of our democracy—seemed too far out of reach. In my classroom of 20 students, 15 read at the 2nd-grade reading level or below. Only three of my students could read at the 4th-grade or above level. There are many other statistics that I could provide to detail just how challenged were the students—and how they had been failed so many times—but suffice it to say, the great promise of America had already been broken for them.

Rather than thinking of these statistics as a classic tale of the achievement gap, I want to be clear: These students were not failures. We—the American public school system—had failed them. I still remember every child in that class, how difficult it was for many of them to trust me, and how hard they worked for me once they did. I can still see Michael's face when he mastered multiplication, Sahara's smile when she delivered her first speech, and the sound of Ricardo's "I did it, Mr. Wright" when he made his first "A" on a spelling test.

As I was being oriented to my new teaching position, I was provided scripted content, forms that I should use to document how my instruction aligned with learning standards and basic expectations, and required to post a data wall ranking my children from top to bottom based on their scores on the weekly learning assessments. We were told that this was to support administrators in monitoring the progress of teachers and to help focus our attention on student performance, but it also served to create a hierarchy in our classroom that pitted students against each other and publicly shamed many students who already doubted their capacity to be successful. Over time, this data wall also came to pit students against teachers—and embodied our own sense of struggle.

In fact, there seemed to be so little trust in us that the district mandated that the school implement a highly structured reading recovery intervention—and eventually one for math and standardized testing preparation as well. Virtually the whole day became filled with standardized content and instruction. It seemed as if the intention of the intervention was to make teaching "teacher proof" and learning "student proof." For each day of the week, teachers were provided with a scripted lesson plan for the 90-minute reading block and were evaluated both on student progress and the fidelity with which we implemented the model. Each teacher was provided a kitchen timer that we were to set before each component of the reading unit. We were required to teach with our doors open, and a monitor walked the hallway listening for buzzers. If our buzzer was more than a minute or two out of synch with the others, the monitor would stick her head in the classroom to find out why we had stalled. If a student failed to understand the concept, we were instructed to keep moving forward so as not to penalize the others. The assumption was that material was covered multiple times and that students would eventually master the concept once they had encountered it often enough.

While as a novice teacher, I actually appreciated the structure and content provided by the program, I did not find it empowering, and over time I became troubled by the fact that the approach seemed to be "at" children and teachers instead of through and by them. Increasingly, it felt like students were being asked to respond to the questions of others as opposed to being invited to clarify or follow their own questions and interests. Reading was something one did, a task, versus students coming to view themselves as readers, an identity. In short, I felt like I was training students rather than educating them.

As I began to feel increasingly overwhelmed by these concerns and the level of need in my classroom—and became immersed in the social anxiety that our school was failing and our students falling ever farther behind— I reached out to my principal for support. Without an aide, the support of a special educator, or enough skill to balance the complex needs of my students, I spent hours each day spinning my wheels and each night planning for what felt like little benefit to my students. Sensing my distress, I was instructed by my principal to pick the student in each performance bracket—below back, basic, and advanced—closest to "moving" to the next-highest one and focus all of my teaching efforts on these three children. It was explained that I only needed to move three children one level to meet my "target" and contribute to the schools required benchmark for the year. I was told explicitly that my success for the year would be measured by the learning progress of these three children, and these were the students that I was asked about during my regular performance conferences with building administrators. When I asked what I should do to support the others, I was told, "Keep them busy. If you can't move your three, you probably won't be here next year to help the others anyway."

Though there are many things tragically disturbing and ethically wrong with this approach, it does help communicate the siege mentality that pervaded the school. At each level, students, teachers, and administrators were all struggling to survive. Like a battlefield, cases were triaged, and those that had the greatest likelihood of survival were prioritized. But these were children, and the decisions we were making each day would potentially impact their prospects and well-being for the rest of their lives. Of all of the challenges I have faced in my life, navigating this treachery remains the most painful. To stay was to participate and to leave was to abandon. Though I was trying my best, I knew in my heart that I was not able to do enough. Each morning as I drove to school, at a stop sign 2 blocks from the building, I would suddenly become nauseous, most days opening my door to vomit just moments before arriving at the school. I often wondered if my students were having the same reaction and cannot imagine that they were not.

So out of control did everyone feel—had things become—that the principal required that we spend time each day during the first 12 weeks of the school year practicing how to walk quietly in the hallway, in single-file lines with our hands to ourselves. Time and again I heard adults in the building—and inside the community, outside the community, on television—say that "inner city children were destined for a life of crime, for prison, for addiction unless we could get them under control." I began to believe that instead of being afraid *for* our students, society was afraid *of* them.

When students stepped out of line or the noise level for a particular class distinguished itself in the building, students were forced to spend their recess period standing in straight lines on the playground, surrounded by the sounds of other children though unable to look at or join them. Recently while watching documentary footage that included a prison lockdown, I flashed back to scenes of students in our school standing "on line," so similar was the image. As the year progressed, we were often required to reengage in such drills in an effort to regain order in the building.

Time and again, in urban school after urban school, I have watched teachers and administrators lording over lines of Black and Brown children demanding that they walk in silence through the hallways, eyes on the head in front of them and hands behind their backs. When I think about how this practice prepares students for success in the world outside of school, the only place where I can imagine that such lessons would be beneficial is in prison. Silence, discipline, and control are the organizing values in these spaces. In contrast, in schools where teachers worried more about where their students would attend college than if they would graduate from high school, I have observed that students are permitted to walk more casually through the hallway. In several high-end preschools, I have heard teachers invite students to think about their favorite animal and to imagine and mimic their gait on the way through the hallway—one more opportunity to imagine, express, and create. No one worried about these students being disruptive, rather it was expected that they would be seen and heard.

Time and again I heard teachers in the building warn students that if they misbehaved, they would end up in jail. Though we typically used this to indicate that what we were asking them to do was to help them have a brighter future—in retrospect, I think we had already created what must have felt like a prison for them. In fact, several times each week police officers were called to respond to incidents within the building. Though most often it would be the principal who would call for help in breaking up a particularly violent fight, escorting an angry parent from the building, or pressing charges against an angry student who "keyed" a staff member's car, I can recall several times watching colleagues use their cell phones from inside their class to call 911 directly to report a student for an angry outburst. On one such occasion, I watched a particularly small 4th-grade boy, Bernard, being dragged up the stairs by two police officers in full view of most of the intermediate-level student body. Though we were the ones who warned students that stepping out of line would mean "time for the crime," teachers were frequently the ones calling the police on them. If we could not see the best in them—or create the conditions for their success in school or help them feel safe—what messages were they internalizing about the world, the system, and themselves?

Submitting to Authority

In this school, and in many of the schools I have visited, the implicit and explicit message was that learning required submission and that knowledge was something that might only be imparted once the child and teacher yielded to the authority of the school. In such an environment, I watched some children and teachers eventually comply, simply doing what we asked, how we asked, when we asked, but with little curiosity or passion. We rarely invited them to ask questions or to demonstrate agency in their learning or in our teaching. Most often we focused on rote memorization or teaching to achievement tests.

While some did accommodate the demands of the school, far more either came to believe the negative expectations that were communicated of them or they became resistant to the seemingly negative view the school held for them by ultimately acting out and "disrespecting" the school. Perhaps these students were the most psychologically healthy—refusing to accept the negative view that was being presented of them. However, the price for their resistance was high as these were often the students most like to be expelled, suspended, or viewed most suspiciously. One can only try to escape—or be pushed away so many times—before one stops trying or showing up at all. Perhaps it is no surprise that in 2020, Washington, DC, had the lowest high school graduate rate (68.5%) in the nation (Dewitt, 2020). Yet children are not the only ones to drop out in such challenging environments.

When I look back on my time teaching in Washington, DC, I felt powerless and naïve. I knew in my gut that what was happening was not right, but I also did not know how to change it. Even when I raised concerns to colleagues or supervisors, they were dismissed. Lacking confidence in my ability to be an effective teacher in the environment and feeling overwhelmed myself, I retreated to my classroom and did my best to facilitate a different experience for my students. During this year, I realized that I did not yet have the skills to teach students whom school had failed for so long. I also had the sense that systemic changes were necessary in order for meaningful change to ever be achieved. For both of these reasons, I made the painful decision to leave the school after that first year, returning to graduate school to hone my skills and understanding. I still feel conflicted about this decision as I have since learned that stability of relationships and teaching experience improve the effectiveness of instruction. But I have also learned that my hunch was right, that social forces, social policies, and social disparity were all shaping my efforts and my students' experiences in our classroom.

Regardless, these are still the students whose faces I carry with me when I think about what school should be and the stories that inform my scholarship and advocacy. I will forever be haunted by one mother's comment following our 6th-grade graduation ceremony. After learning that I would not be returning the following year, she asked, "Tell me, Mr. Wright, why do all the good teachers leave?" Though I explained that I was not yet a good enough teacher and was leaving to become more skilled in order to provide her children with the best teacher possible, she remained incredulous. I have often reflected on this moment—wondering what she meant by good and leaving, did she feel like she had the choice to leave as well or did she feel stuck with whatever option she was given. How did my decision to leave shape her view of herself, her children's educational prospects, and other teachers who looked like me? Wanting desperately to let her and the other children and families in my classroom know that I remained committed to them, despite my decision to leave—and struggling to say goodbye myself—I shared my phone number with each person at the ceremony and invited them to call me anytime that I might be of help or support. Though more than 20 years have now passed since that day, I have yet to change my phone number—as a constant reminder of both these children and my commitment to them.

Despite, and partially because of, my decision to leave teaching to become better, I remain troubled that the students who most need experienced, highly skilled teachers are often the least likely to have them (Lai et al., 2021; Rivera Rodas, 2019). Research (Christian-Brandt et al., 2020; Kwon et al., 2021) consistently demonstrates that veteran teachers are more likely to seek out and remain in higher-achieving or less-challenging schooling environments. New teachers, on the other hand, are more likely to be hired into lower-performing and more economically disadvantaged schools (Bettini & Park, 2021; Bruno et al., 2020). With overwhelming need and less opportunity to develop one's teaching craft through exposure to effective models and mentors, many passionate novice teachers are not given the support necessary to transform their potential into skill as these schools are more likely to have higher rates of teacher turnover and teachers who are rated as being less effective than peers in higher-performing schools. Over the years I have often spoken with exceptional teacher colleagues who eventually made the decision to leave schools struggling to provide adequate instruction and support to children—in part to seek out a position that would be less taxing and where they might receive more support and resources—but mainly because they were tired of being perceived as a "bad teacher." Again, our perceptions of teachers, students, and their potential are inextricably linked with where they live, how they look, and our preconceived notions about both.

Clearly, these examples are egregious and unacceptable. Unfortunately, I do not think they are isolated. Time and again, across my career, in ways both subtle and more dramatic, I have witnessed children being silenced and shamed by the teachers who are supposed to see the best in them. While visiting schools in Ohio, Minnesota, Texas, Wisconsin, Massachusetts, Tennessee, and many other states across the nation, I have watched similar episodes unfold—witnessing children being locked out of classrooms, hearing children threatened and called names, listening to teachers and children who feel worried about their safety in school, and consoling teachers' tears because they want things to be better in their school and feel powerless to change anything. In some cases, when a child's needs might be particularly challenging or profound because of years of neglect and oppression by our schools, the only thing that teachers feel they can do to get additional support for the child or to feel safer and saner themselves is to work to have the child removed from their classroom. Typically, this is accomplished through having the child identified as requiring special education, which requires a diagnosis and label that will likely follow the child throughout their educational career. Or to be expelled from the classroom. Rates of both special education identification and expulsion have increased over the past decades (Diament, 2022; Giordano et al., 2022). The same is true for even the youngest learners, with researchers having documented ever-increasing rates of expulsion and suspension for preschool students (National Center on Early Childhood Health and Wellness, n.d.)! Do we feel so hopeless and helpless—so under-supported and overwhelmed—that we are ready to give up on 4-year-olds?

WE ALL TEACH OUR OWN STORY

Though I disagree with the damaging strategies and abusive interactions that I have often witnessed in schools—and carry deep regret about the times in my teaching career when I was not the best version of myself—it is important to recognize that these actions did not occur in a vacuum and that the teachers who committed them may have been well-intentioned. I have also come to appreciate that while some practices may clearly be inappropriate or damaging, there are probably others that mean something different to children when practiced by teachers inside their cultural milieu. While a tone of "toughness" in school may have been outside of my experience and uncomfortable for me, it may not have meant the same to my students and colleagues. As a gay White man with a strong southern accent, certainly an outsider to the cultural context in which I was teaching, I cannot fully understand or appreciate how our students might have been making sense of my colleagues and their actions; And I am certain that the same behaviors from me would have meant something very different to them and inside the community.

Though I wish to honor and recognize our different locations and experiences, there must also be the space to question and critique each other's practices and our own. With the perspective of hindsight and many more years of experience, I can now appreciate that there is a difference between "tough love" and being too harsh in our classrooms, one being experienced as high expectations and supportive and the other harmful and hurtful. Walking with many children as a counselor, bearing witness to their schooling experiences and supporting them as they make sense of them, has taught me that learning outcomes do not always justify the approach. Losing far too many students to violence underscores that teaching children to fall in line may feel like a matter of life or death, and sadly this may be true. The ongoing tragedy and violence of school shootings and police brutality certainly underscore the sense of urgency. Yet when we teach from our open wounds, those whose scabs have yet to fall away, we often risk exposing our students to the same pain. But when we have learned to heal, teaching from our own wounds can provide a pathway for others to do the same—imparting the wisdom that allowed us to return to a place of strength.

Teaching From Hope Versus Teaching From Fear

In the same way that our biases and personal experiences influence our teaching practices, so do our hopes and fears for our students. As we come to care about students about whom we also harbor bias, this often presents as fear of and for them. We do not walk around thinking, "I have bias about my students and have concerns about their prospects and potential." It is more likely that we think, "I worry about my kiddos and hope they can do okay." For example, if we are biased to believe that children living in low-income communities attending urban schools are likely to fail in school, when we begin teaching a child with this social location, we will likely feel worried or anxious about their academic performance. Rather than organizing our instructional program around positive expectations for the child, it is as likely that we might become more focused on preventing the child from failing. Though this difference may seem subtle, in my experience, classrooms organized around success and those designed to prevent failure look and feel incredibly different. This example illustrates how our biases may be manifested as fear and anxiety in our teaching practices, displacing our hopes and good intentions.

When teaching students for whom we are afraid—or whom we might actually fear—our good intentions do not always translate into teaching that is good enough. In our efforts to help them avoid pitfalls and tragedy, we inadvertently re-create the very situations we hope they will avoid. For example, during my time in Washington, DC, we were so afraid that our students might go to jail that we unintentionally created an educational prison. Fearing their failure on the tests that would be used to compare them (and us) with others, we taught them rote memorization and discrete facts. In the process, we did not foster in them a love of learning or critical thinking. We are often so afraid that our students will fail that we stop preparing them to succeed. Sadly, unless we prepare our students to dwell in the worlds we dream for them, they will have no choice but to inhabit the lives we fear.

The challenge is that we are often unaware that we are teaching from a place of fear. In all the years that I have been involved in education, I have never met an educator who went to work every day because they hate children, yet I have often witnessed seemingly well-intentioned people do or say things that are damaging to their students. I, too, have struggled at times to align my values with my actions, particularly when I am feeling frustrated with or concerned about the child with whom I am working. I have found this seeming contradiction one of the most perplexing challenges of my career. However, through back-to-back conversations that occurred during professional development trainings with pre-K teachers representing both underperforming and overachieving schools, I think I may have just found a way to better understand this seeming paradox.

Prior to each training, I had the opportunity to observe the teachers at work in their classrooms. One of the things that stood out for me during the observations is that teachers in each of the affluent schools had chosen to incorporate lofts into the design of the classrooms. In these rooms, I noticed that students could climb to the upper zone, cozy up with a book out of the teacher's view, or use the apparatus as the basis for pretend play—becoming a castle, pirate ship, or burning building in need of assistance from firefighters. More generally, these classrooms were more likely to organize learning around interactive centers, to integrate the day through thematic plots, and to resist direct instruction. In these spaces, there were virtually no rows and desks, and I observed very little utilization of technology, like touch screens or tablets. Children spent a great deal of time talking with each other, experimenting with materials, and solving problems that teachers had orchestrated for them. Frankly, though the classrooms were happy and stimulating, they often looked "broken in," meaning they did not appear filled with things that were shiny and new. Conversations in the classroom typically centered around questions—with teachers asking children to expand on their work or children asking teachers for more information to help them move forward in their explorations.

In contrast, the classrooms with students from the most economically strapped families were often filled with technology. Sitting mainly in rows of desks, students spent much of their time wearing headphones and interacting with tablets, though I saw them spend much less time interacting with each other. Teachers used smart screens and spent much of their time coordinating technology—assisting students with log-in information, passing out headsets, or monitoring progress. Almost every 15 minutes, students were being asked to stop what they were doing, watch some type of instructional video—usually including a song or dance—and then return to their screens or work independently. A few times per day, teachers would call students on the carpet—reminding them to sit on their assigned square—for a large group lesson. They would then be released to their seats to spend more time working independently or quietly with their neighbors while their teacher convened small group lessons in another part of the room. Interestingly, never did I see a loft in these early learning classrooms.

A few days following these classroom observations, I reconvened with the teachers during a professional development training that I facilitated. As an opening activity, I shared my observations and invited teachers to ask questions or make comments. As part of these conversations, I asked teachers to share their decision-making processes for incorporating a loft into their classrooms. In those classrooms with lofts, teachers appreciated that lofts allowed students to explore—even to hide—in the classroom. Teachers appreciated that lofts allowed students to develop a sense of agency through exploration and self-control by learning to keep themselves safe on the apparatus. When these teachers mentioned safety, I asked if they ever worried that students might hurt themselves. Uniformly, they acknowledged the inherent risk of such a structure but indicated that accidents could happen anywhere. They were more focused on how the students might benefit versus how they might be hurt. One teacher even commented, "We all have to learn to keep ourselves safe, to be in charge of our bodies. It seems to me that if someone is going to fall, doing so from a height of 5 feet under the supervision of a teacher who is there to help you would be the best possible way to learn how to pick yourself up again."

In contrast, in those classrooms without lofts, I asked teachers to explain their decisions. Without exception, their first response was related to safety, expressing concerns that the children might hurt themselves or each other. One teacher shared additional concerns about violating school district policy, which required that children always be in plain sight of their classroom teacher. Another indicated that she worried that her children would fling themselves off and break an arm. One participant laughed and responded, "I feel like my students are barely under control anyway. There is no way I'm going to invite them to jump and climb inside the classroom. No way!" In these classrooms, it seemed that self-control was something that needed to be earned versus taught, and the children were not trusted to keep themselves safe. Similarly, the teachers were much more concerned about avoiding chaos or getting in trouble themselves, for violating policy or causing too much commotion in their school building.

Later in the morning, also as part of the training, I invited participants to list their hopes for their students. Across attendees, the list of hopes was typically the same, regardless of the student population with whom the teachers worked. One might imagine the types of things teachers wished for their students: college education, meaningful work, happy lives, joy, economic stability, good health, and so on. Following the discussion of their hopes, I would ask teachers to discuss their fears for their students. Here the lists diverged. In the wealthier parts of town, the lists were frequently short, with teachers indicating they feared that their students would not get into a good college, would become involved with drug and alcohol abuse, or would not be successful. In the less-affluent parts of the city, the lists were expansive. Here teachers feared students dying, going to prison, not being able to read, teen pregnancy, abuse, gang involvement, drug or alcohol abuse, not graduating from high school, or being killed by one of various random acts of violence. Teachers expressed concerns about getting in trouble, losing their jobs, being hurt at school, or not being able to prevent something awful happening to a child or knowing that they might not have been able to prevent their student from growing up to hurt someone else. To end the discussion, I would ask teachers to think about their instructional practices and then consider, "Are you teaching from your hopes or your fears?" Usually there was silence.

Time and again, through these and similar conversations, I came to realize that virtually all teachers—regardless of where we teach or whom we teach—share similar hopes for our students. The difference in how we teach is often found in our fears. What I noticed is that in schools where teachers fear less, they teach more reflexively from their hopes—preparing students for the lives they dreamed for them. In contrast, when we are overwhelmed by anxiety, fear, or worry for our students, our actions and interactions become more based in these fears. Though this may seem like an obvious insight, I have found it both profound and uncommon.

As teachers, particularly in challenging circumstances, we have to remain connected to our hopes for students. We convince ourselves to keep going because we want the best for our students. These hopes are what others ask us about and what administrators, colleagues, and society draw on to motivate us. Yet virtually no one asks us about our fears or frustrations in a deep way—and rarely do we give ourselves permission to confront them. Of course, we complain and criticize, but this is not what I mean. Venting and complaining are not the same as interrogating our inner selves, giving ourselves permission to acknowledge our fears and vulnerabilities and examining how our life stories may be influencing the lives that we are allowing our students to inhabit.

Critical Reflection as an Essential Practice

Identifying, critically reflecting on, and changing in response to one's biases and fears are the pathway for transformation, shifting our teaching from a place of fear to a place of hope. For me, critical reflection occurs when we can: (1) understand how our actions and perceptions of our students are rooted in our own life stories and our understanding of the world; and (2) understand how our students make sense of us and our actions through their own experiences and understandings of the world. When we can begin to see ourselves from the perspectives of our students and understand how they see themselves and the world, we are then equipped to expand and/or challenge the ways they think about themselves, their place in the world, and others.

Nakkula and Ravitch (1998) posit that our prejudices come to light most clearly when confronting our misunderstandings of others and our feelings of being misunderstood by them. Consequently, identifying and resolving misunderstandings and misperceptions of oneself and the other are viewed as essential to arriving at a place of authenticity, trust, and shared understanding. For Nakkula and Ravitch, the very purpose of education—of being human—is the relational process of negotiating a shared understanding of each other and the world.

In explaining their understanding of this process, Nakkula and Ravitch (1998) describe:

> When misunderstanding occurs, it creates the opportunity for our worldview, which is generally held firm and taken for granted, to become shaken, knocked off center in a manner that requires a re-centering or, perhaps more

accurately, a revising. If there is a genuine attempt to understand incidents of misunderstanding—that is, to attempt painstakingly to see the various contributions to it—a revised view of the perspectives of both self and others is almost certainly required. (p. 89)

Their framework holds that by engaging in a recursive process of self-exploration, dialogue, and critical reflection, teachers can become more generous in their interpretations of the children with whom they work—and of themselves.

As a starting point for this process, each of us should be aware of where we come from and what we are bringing with us into our lives as teachers. We should also, over time, work to understand how our students and colleagues would answer these same questions for themselves. As we encounter difficult moments in our classrooms—or notice reactions to situations that may be getting in the way of our reaching a student or feeling hopeful in ourselves—we should remind ourselves to consider:

- What is this student bringing up for me?
- How did this moment feel like something I have felt earlier in my life?

As we reflect on each day in our teaching life, and especially the difficult moments, we might begin by asking ourselves:

- When did I feel most uncomfortable or afraid?
- When during the day did I feel the most like the person I want to be?
- When did I feel the most disconnected from myself and/or my values?

In thinking critically about our instructional practices, we might ask:

- How did this moment or educational activity reflect my hopes for the students I teach?
- How did it reflect my fears?

In planning for our upcoming interactions, we might think about:

- How might I communicate my hopes for my students today or through this activity?
- What fears might I be communicating or reinforcing?

As you become more comfortable having these conversations with yourself, I hope that you might engage with your students around such questions. At the very least, I hope you will ask them:

- What do you think that I hope for you?
- Why do you think this?
- How do I show you?

Similarly, be sure to discuss:

- What do you think I fear for you?
- Why do you think this?
- How do I show you?

Drawing on this shared conversation as a model, you might then create opportunities for students to think about these questions for themselves and within themselves:

- What are my hopes?
- What are my fears?
- Where did I learn them—who taught them to me?
- How do I demonstrate these fears in my life?
- How do I demonstrate hope?

Over time, sharing these conversations with each other will allow you to see yourself as a product of your life and through the eyes of your students. Similarly, your students will be able to better understand how their experiences influence them and the way they perceive and respond to learning opportunities and you. Through this process of developing a shared understanding, you will also develop trust and care for yourselves and each other—and more awareness and curiosity for both of you and the world. This is the heart of learning and relating and perhaps the most important dispositions that we can nurture in ourselves and instill in our students.

I do not mean to imply that this process will always be easy or comfortable, nor that it should be. Nurturing and care in the way that I am presenting them are not simply about finding comfortable spaces in which to relate—sometimes they require us to roll up our sleeves and dig into the hard work of working through things together. If we do not acknowledge the barriers that our students face, they will not accept our empathy and concern for them as authentic. If we cannot be viewed by them as interested and capable of caring about the challenges of their lives, they will not trust us to support them. Rather than blindly encouraging students to see beyond their circumstances, we should support them in thinking critically about ways to face them head-on.

We should not avoid critical discourse with students about the details of their lives. Talking with students about their lives, engaging them in critical discourse about the challenges they face, communicates to them our belief in their power to overcome. More than just care and concern, such meaningful support empowers students to view themselves as having agency in the lives and empowers them to face their challenges more courageously. In contrast, when we ignore the details of our students' lives, our silence may be interpreted as discomfort or a lack of confidence in their ability.

Shifting the Paradigm

Sadly, Washington, DC, is not unique in its disparity or torment. Though I drew on my experiences in the district to illustrate how disparity manifests itself in the lives of children and teachers, it is important to keep in mind that these examples are not meant to impugn only our nation's capital—though I hope they might stir greater action on behalf of the children and families living there. I use them to underscore the experiences of children and teachers everywhere that such inequity exists. Also, please understand that these are not just big city problems, though they may play out differently in smaller communities. For example, in the rural community in which I grew up and presently live, these dynamics tend to play out within the classroom as opposed to across classrooms or schools. This resonates with my own experiences as a child. A precocious learner but from a home headed by a young single mother, my questions were often perceived as "talking too much" or as disruptive. However, friends from more affluent or socially connected families were often praised for the same behavior. Though they were routed to the talented and gifted program, I was sent outside to bang erasers. It wasn't until the 4th grade when a new teacher from outside our small community identified me as a child with strengths and referred me to the program herself, shifting even the way I understood myself and changing the way others perceived me for the rest of my educational career.

As a case study, our nation's capital demonstrates that family demographics, neighborhood characteristics, educational opportunity, and school performance are inextricably linked. However, while there is much consensus on the relationship among these factors, there is less agreement on how they influence each other and why such disparities exist. As I have listened to these debates over many years, it seems that some believe that poverty reflects intrinsic differences in people's ability and motivation, while others view historical and structural disparities as the root cause of these differences. Though an enormous body of empirical data and the lived experiences of many suggest that it is overwhelmingly the latter, there still exists sufficient commitment to the former attitude for it to often present itself in policy and political debates. Even for those who do not subscribe to such deficit perspectives, these notions have been used for so long and so extensively that they are deeply embedded in our culture, institutions, and our bones. Unless we are ever vigilant about acting on such implicit (and explicit) biases, and even sometimes when we are, we are likely to inadvertently reinforce them. Similarly, despite our efforts, many of these structural barriers are so pervasive that we are embedded in them—like the way neighborhoods are structured, where our child attends school, and the way society reappropriates wealth and opportunities. However, as we become more aware of these structural inequities, we can become more critical of them and mindful about the way we are potentially reinforcing them in our classrooms.

Though sweeping policy changes and structural responses are largely outside the scope of this book, it is important to understand that choosing to view the children in our classrooms differently—and supporting colleagues, the families with whom we work, and others in your community in doing so as well—is an important step in changing the discourse and practices around education in this country. When we think differently, we act differently, and we can also reframe the questions others may ask us in a way that is more responsive to what we know about and see in the lives of our children.

SUMMARY

Part of the important work of developing an emotionally responsive perspective lies in understanding how our belief systems, including values and prejudices, influence our teaching practices and the ways we interact with children and families. In this chapter, we explored how individual beliefs are intertwined with broader belief structures, which are propagated by media coverage, political engines, and religious systems. Research (Kim, 2013; Wright, Nankin, Boonstra, and Blair, 2019) has shown that teachers often hold deficit perspectives of children navigating challenging life circumstances like homelessness, poverty, and/or community violence, anticipating that such children will misbehave, be unmotivated, or have trouble focusing. Such beliefs directly influence how we design classroom environments, structure learning opportunities, and perceive and respond to students and their families. Thus, while questioning, and sometimes overturning, existing beliefs is critical if we are to reach all students, it is no easy task.

Identifying, critically reflecting on, and changing in response to one's biases are pathways for such transformation. In this chapter, we focused on the importance of critically reflecting on our attitudes, beliefs, and approaches to supporting children who have experienced trauma. I provided readers with a framework for examining their perspectives and deepening their understanding. By engaging in a recursive process of self-exploration, dialogue, and critical reflection, we can become more generous in our interpretations of the children with whom we work. Such critical reflection enhances our capacities to create emotionally responsive and culturally relevant learning environments that support children navigating life challenges.

CHAPTER 4

Reframing Resilience for Children With Messy Lives

Through my work with children and families with messy lives, I have observed that what might be a source of strength in one part of a child or family's life may be a source of risk in another. Similarly, what might be protective for one child may be detrimental for others. In considering the implications of these observations through the lens of child development and the practice of education, I have begun to question whether current frameworks and approaches adequately account for such complex development.

A fundamental difference between my emotionally responsive approach and other perspectives in the field is this emphasis: Rather than asking if children's attitudes and behavior are adaptive, we should be asking how and in what environments are their attitudes and beliefs adaptive and maladaptive. Such an approach also has implications for the way we perceive children's strengths, allowing us to rethink our perception of their resilience. Rather than asking if children are resilient—conceptualizing resilience as a character trait—a more appropriate framing would consider how children are demonstrating resilience in a particular context.

The purpose of this chapter is to articulate such a child-centered perspective on development, focused on how children understand their own life circumstances and the ways they behave. The goal of this chapter is to support you in developing a more complicated perspective on children's behavior and development, prioritizing how children understand their own life circumstances and the ways they behave. I also wish to illustrate that how we think about children has important implications for what we expect of them and how we interact with and teach them.

In the first part of this chapter, I will present the notion of developmental pathways as a framework for better conceptualizing the complexity of children's development, particularly those navigating trauma and adversity. In the second half of this chapter, I will draw on my research on the concept of resilience to better illustrate that how we think informs what we expect of children and how we interact with them.

I KEEP ME SAFE

I met James while working as a mental health counselor at East City Elementary, a public charter school adjacent to a large urban housing development. Five years old, James had been referred to counseling for refusing to follow classroom instructions; hitting his teacher, Mr. Elias; and frequently running away from the classroom. During our initial conversation about James, Mr. Elias, a 20-year veteran of public schools, described James as "the most disrespectful little kid I have ever seen!"

Before interacting with James, I conducted an observation in his classroom to get a better sense of his behaviors and what might be triggering them. I noted that James seemed fully engaged when playing with his classmates and that they seemed to respond positively to him. However, it was striking that he never allowed his back to be turned to the teacher. A subtle dance, James was always turning to make sure that he could keep an eye on Mr. Elias. Though slightly more tolerant of Ms. Dawson, the assistant teacher in the classroom, James also seemed very guarded around her. Given his seeming trepidation about adults, I decided to build a connection with James inside his classroom before asking him to spend time alone with me in the play therapy suite. I also hoped that watching his classmates interact with me could help further his trust and provide a model for prosocial engagement.

For almost 2 months, I spent a few hours each week playing with James and the other children in his classroom, occasionally even joining the class on the playground. I went out of my way to acknowledge James anytime we happened to cross paths. Though he was initially reluctant to interact with me, James became slightly more relaxed as other children in his classroom began to engage with me more comfortably. Soon, I thought that James would be ready to transition from the classroom to the therapy suite so that we might begin focusing on his counseling more directly. To allow James the opportunity to prepare himself for the transition, I began to remind him at the end of each classroom visit how many days remained before we would begin working together in the therapeutic playroom. Though James would sometimes reciprocate my goodbye, he never commented on my intention for us to transition to the playroom. I assumed that his lack of acknowledgment meant acceptance of the plan.

On the morning of the first anticipated playroom visit, I walked to the door of James's classroom, presented him with the "magic key" (a therapeutic technique that is meant to provide a transitional object for the child and to provide them a sense of control in transitioning from the classroom to the less familiar setting of the playroom), and asked if he would like to lead us to the therapy suite. He simply took the key, threw it across the room, and said, "I ain't going nowhere with you."

Attempting a therapeutic response, I replied, "It can be scary to visit a new place. I will do everything possible to make sure you are safe."

James took a swing at my knees and said, "Leave me the f*** alone."

Though shocked, I asked James calmy, "Can you tell me why you would like to stay here?"

He said, "I don't know you. Mommy says I can't talk to no strange people. They want to kill little kids."

"Some people do hurt children, but I promise that I will not. I want to help you feel safe," I replied.

Putting his hands on his hips, James looked at me and said, "I keep me safe."

Needless to say, we did not go to the playroom that day.

Without going further into the painful history underscoring James's insistence on keeping himself safe, even this brief interaction makes sense in the context in which it emerged—a neighborhood with a high concentration of sexual offenders living in close proximity to children whose parents often work long hours to make ends meet. His vigilance was heightened by James's mother, given her own experience as a childhood sexual abuse survivor. Though maladaptive in the classroom environment, where positive relationships with teachers and respectful behavior are generally assumed a precondition for learning, James's mistrust of adults is highly protective in his world outside of school where his basic survival and safety needs are threatened.

In other words, how James has learned to navigate a scary part of his life is at odds with what he must do to be successful at school.

DEVELOPMENT ALONG ALTERNATIVE PATHWAYS

Far too often, children such as James are forced to choose between attitudes and behaviors that help them survive difficult circumstances and dispositions that will help them be more successful at school—a conundrum with potentially life-threatening and long-term consequences. For example, if

James begins to assume goodwill from every adult he meets in his neighborhood, he might experience increased risk for abuse in that context. Likewise, if James is unable to develop positive relationships with teachers and continues to feel unsafe at school, he might be less successful academically and less inclined to engage school-based opportunities. Sadly, both abuse and academic failure would have potentially life-altering and long-term consequences for James.

The type of development that occurs in messy, chaotic, extreme, complicated, or otherwise atypical circumstances cannot be "normative." Given that development occurs in response to the demands of one's environment, if one's environment is extreme then one's behavior will likely be extreme or outside the norm as well. Historically, when a child's development does not progress along normative or "typical" trajectories, the child is said to be developmentally delayed. However, I think a more veracious way to frame our understanding of the child would be to say that they are developing along an alternative pathway or trajectory. Rather than framing the child as being deficient or delayed, it would be more accurate to examine how the knowledge, skills, and values that the child is developing are aligned with the developmental demands of each context they are being asked to navigate. In others words, rather than asking if the child is developing normatively, perhaps we should shift our focus on how the child is developing and how the skills, attitudes, and beliefs they are developing in one context are aligned with the demands of the other contexts in which they are growing.

Likewise, given the sheer number of children experiencing trauma and adversity, it is fair to wonder if there is such a thing as a "normative" development. The idea of the "typically" developing child seems out of touch with the realities of the lives of many of today's children and families. For example, in my own work (Wright, Taub, Fetter, & Shumpert, 2017) examining the impact of poverty and homelessness on children's development, I have found that children from middle-class families, low-income families, and families experiencing homelessness develop along three very distinct trajectories within the school environment. In virtually every school-based domain that I examined—for example, reading and math performance, behavioral infractions, and attendance rates—children in low-income families performed one standard deviation lower than children from middle-income families, and children experiencing homelessness performed two standard deviations lower than children from middle-income families and one standard deviation lower than low-income families. This finding was stable across outcome measures, meaning that regardless of the type of difference I examined, on average, children's development varied consistently as a function of their family's socioeconomic and housing status. This finding underscores the role that one's social environment plays on one's performance in school and the types of developmental outcomes that are privileged in schools.

Typically, the worlds of education and educational policy take a psychological view of behavior, preferring to think about attitudes and actions as originating within the child and comparing demonstrated behavior to normative developmental expectations. Though we understand that behavior happens in context, we often discuss how children are behaving independently of it. For example, when we assess a child's behavior by indicating that they are acting out in our classroom—using terms like "misbehaving," "hyperactive," "sullen," or "disengaged"—rarely do we contextualize this behavior by indicating that our lesson may not have gone as planned, that the child's family is in the midst of a divorce, that we used a harsh voice when chiding the child the day before, that we were reviewing material the child had mastered, or that something had happened at home. Even when we can understand that these conditions may have been contributing to the child's behavior, the language that we use to describe what is happening almost always locates the challenge *within* the child versus between the child and the environment. For example, we might say he is lagging behind, underperforming, or acting out. Though we will occasionally think about accommodation strategies—shifting some aspect of the environment or our expectations—such an approach is, in my experience, less common and often occurs only once the child's development has been labeled as fundamentally delayed or atypical, such as in the case of learning or behavioral special education diagnosis.

Increasingly, we think about children's behavior and performance from a basic brain-based perspective—examining the relationship among brains, bodies, and behaviors. As a result, educators and counselors tend to focus on behavior problems and developing strategies to manage children's emotions and behavior. In contrast, the emotionally responsive approach emphasizes understanding why children are responding in the ways that they are, clarifying the demands of the environments in which children are being asked to adapt, and supporting children in developing the skills and understanding necessary to navigate the complexity of the competing demands of the environments in which they live and learn.

This is not to say that brains, bodies, and behaviors don't matter—they do! But we should always be mindful that the ways our bodies respond, our brains think, and our behaviors are enacted in the world are being informed by culture, relationships, who we think we are, and what we think of others. Rather than "changing behaviors," an emotionally responsive approach would be more concerned with helping children understand the expectations of a particular environment and developing knowledge, skills, and attitudes that will allow them to navigate the demands of the environment more adaptively. Implicitly, this means that an emotionally responsive educator does not view behavior as "bad"; rather, it is misaligned with the demands and expectations of the environment. Or as I would explain this to a child in my classroom, "This way of doing things may work for you out there, but it isn't going to work as well for you in here. Let's find another way to handle your business at school."

A DEVELOPMENTAL PATHWAYS APPROACH

As a framework for conceptualizing both the complexity of development and the ways in which development is often fragmented or divergent, I have found the developmental pathways approach (Fischer et al., 1997) helpful. Rather than thinking about development as a ladder, moving from one stage to the next, or a linear process, with one developmental milestone progressing to the next in an orderly fashion, Fischer et al. conceptualize development as a web with different skills developing in different domains at different speeds at different times. For example, many of us have different vocabularies that we use to communicate with others. We often use different vocabularies in different environments and may speak differently to the same person in different environments or may speak similarly to the same person in different environments, depending on our language skills, the relationship with the person, the expectations of the environment, how we value being perceived in the environment, and whether we perceive the conversation that we are having in the environment as public or private. Deciding which word to use, with which person, in what environment is complicated! I appreciate that the developmental pathways framework provides language and a conceptual model for discussing development in a way that accounts for such messiness.

Consequently, the developmental pathways framework recognizes that development is a process that is naturally fractionated, meaning different parts of us develop at different rates and in different ways. In returning to the metaphor of the web, skills, emotions, knowledge, and awareness of context, for example, are discrete strands of development. However, these strands often intersect, influencing each other and becoming integrated or separated, like the connection points on a web. In other words, what we can do, who is asking us, and how we are feeling about it—along with much knowledge and many other skills—all come together in a moment when we "behave" or "understand." Sometimes this happens such that the various strands reinforce each other, becoming integrated, and other times they do not, splitting or becoming disintegrated.

Thus, rather than thinking about development as an outcome, from a developmental pathways perspective, development is a process of organizing and coordinating different "strands," or domains of development, in levels of increasing complexity over time. When the way that we think about ourselves and our abilities aligns with the demands of a particular environment, we might call this an integrated developmental pathway. When these things are not aligned, we call this a nonintegrated developmental pathway.

Returning to James as an example, it might be said that the skills—vigilance, running away, and mistrust for adults—that James developed to protect himself in the community context were misaligned, or did not allow him to develop along an integrated pathway, in his classroom. Rather than thinking about James's behavior as "bad" in the classroom environment, we would think about it as maladaptive, meaning that James was struggling to integrate his current understanding and skills for self-protection and self-efficacy with the demands of school.

To support James in developing a more integrated developmental pathway, it would be important to help him differentiate Mr. Elias and other men who might help him from those who might hurt him, for example. Once this has been achieved, it would be important to help James understand that protecting himself in the school environment might be accomplished through building a positive relationship with his teacher and allowing himself to engage the curriculum less defensively. This would allow James to further differentiate how safe he might feel in school from how safe he feels outside of school. Over time, this might support James in distinguishing from vulnerability in a negative sense—*the feeling that someone might hurt me*—and vulnerability in a positive sense—*if I let my guard down and accept that I don't know everything, I can learn new things.* As James learns to trust himself and others more, while also being able to acknowledge his vulnerability both at school and in the world, James will arrive at a more integrated understanding of himself and a differentiated understanding of the world. In other words, how James views himself across contexts—at school and in his neighborhood—will be more integrated, such that he will trust himself to cope better with both environments, allowing him to feel more stable within himself. However, his view of each environment will become more differentiated, recognizing that what is required to be safe is different at school and in his neighborhood.

In order to navigate the demands of these two very different environments—school and his neighborhood—James must develop complex understandings of himself and each environment and the necessary skills and dispositions for each. It would be difficult for anyone to deny that such an achievement would require developmental complexity and a great deal of cognitive, emotional, and physical energy. All of this would be required above and beyond James's investment in his learning and academic performance and would likely draw on his reserves for such traditional academic expectations. Thus, if we only looked at James's grades or performance on standardized achievement tests, where his performance might appear average or below, we would be missing the broader understanding of his demonstrated developmental complexity and his developmental potential.

After all, each of us only possesses a finite amount of time, energy, resources, and capacity. When children grow up in environments that are well aligned with the demands and expectations of their schools, these resources may be invested primarily in their learning and prosocial development. However, when children must invest their resources in navigating the demands of challenging and/or competing environments, this draws on the reserves available to focus on learning and other types of growth. Thus, children's academic and other educational outcomes are not always the best indicators of their developmental complexity, which is likely a much better proxy for their overall potential.

Similarly, as teachers, when we do not work to align the demands of children's lives inside and outside of school—or to support them in bridging the gaps between these environments—we undermine the resources they have available to invest in their learning. For children with messy lives, whose resources are already taxed, this may be the difference in being able to engage the curriculum some or not at all. Unfortunately, in most cases, academic achievement is still the proxy most often utilized to make claims about children's potential.

Developmental Complexity Versus Developmental Outcomes

I recognize that outcomes, achievement, and performance matter, particularly in the way that schooling and achievement are structured presently. And there are some outcomes, like being able to read (Suldo & Shaffer,

2008), making friends (Lu et al., 2021), and feeling comfortable taking positive risks (Marcionetti & Rossier, 2021) that are intrinsically important for a child's well-being and overall quality of life. But in a high-stakes environment like the one in which we are teaching presently, an emphasis on outcomes may misrepresent the developmental complexity of the child, particularly for those navigating messy lives. For example, when I was in graduate school, I was involved in a research team that sought to understand the combined impact of trauma and poverty on children's development. As part of our investigations, we conducted a study (Ayoub et al., 2006) of children in families living in urban poverty to document cognitive differences between children who had experienced trauma and those who had not. As a first step in the study, we asked children to tell us a "nice" story. We then analyzed each story to determine the level of cognitive complexity evidenced. Typically, non-traumatized children would tell rich stories about positive events being enjoyed by friends and family. They often went something like this:

> It was the best day ever when people were nice to me. In the morning I woke up and realized it was my birthday. My mom and dad sang to me first thing, which made me very happy. I went to school and my friends were very nice to me. My teacher had a small present for me. After school, my best friends and family went for pizza and I got a present. It was the best day ever.

In contrast, children who had experienced trauma, especially those who lived in the context of chronic stress and adversity, often told much simpler stories, like, "My mom and I walked to the store to get chips, but my brother ate most of them without asking me." As one might expect, when examining nice stories for evidence of cognitive complexity, we found that children who had experienced lots of nice things had more complex understandings of nice. Initially, our conclusion, just as in most studies (Lewis et al., 2021) was to find that children who had experienced trauma tended to have less cognitive complexity than children who had not been traumatized. This well-intentioned conclusion conformed with our assumption, and underlying ethical commitment, that trauma is bad for children. As advocates for children, we hoped this finding might be used to create more support for children navigating challenging life circumstances.

The only problem was that for those of us on the research team who worked with children growing up in such circumstances, this finding did not represent our understanding and experience of the children with whom we worked. Though it was true that some of the children did not perform as well academically or relate to others as prosocially, we never interpreted this to mean that they weren't "as smart" or cognitively complex as non-traumatized children. In fact, given what these children had to deal with on a daily basis—often just to get to school in one piece—our suspicion was they might have developed even more complex views of themselves and the world. The challenge was how were we to prove it?

After much deliberation, the research team decided to return to the same children and invite them to tell us a different kind of story, a "mean" story. As we expected, when children who lived in the midst of adversity were asked to talk about mean things, they related stories that were incredibly rich. For example, one child related:

> I was lying in bed trying to go to sleep when I heard people screaming. I was afraid. All of a sudden, mom ran into the room, grabbed me out of bed, and hid me in the closet. She seemed so scared and told me to be quiet. Right after, dad ran into the room and tried to hid under my bed. Right then the cops ran into my room too. They grabbed daddy and drug him out the door. I was so mad and sad and scared.

In contrast, when we asked the non-traumatized children to share a mean story, their stories were often much less complex. For example, one child actually stated, "My brother stole my chips and I was mad at him for being mean." Perhaps surprisingly, when we compared the cognitive complexity of the mean stories for children who had been traumatized with the nice stories for children who had not, we found that up until a certain age, children with messy lives actually scored higher on our measure of cognitive complexity when we looked at their most complex story, not caring whether it was nice or mean. However, we did find that beyond a certain age or with increased levels of trauma, children's stories began to decrease in complexity when compared with non-traumatized fears (Ayoub et al., 2006). One way that we interpreted this was as a threshold effect—up until a certain level, trauma may actually support our thinking in becoming more complex. However, when life circumstances become overwhelming, we seem to shut down and our view of the world becomes less complex. This finding deeply resonated with my own perceptions and experience.

One way of thinking about these findings is that children who have experienced trauma and those who have not may be "smart" in different ways, one being an expert in navigating a world that is not scary and one knowing how to face a world that can be terrifying. The skills and attitudes required to navigate each type of world are fundamentally different; it would be like growing up in different cultures and speaking different languages. In a world that feels safe, children might look for shared interests, appreciate opportunities to share, and seek opportunities for connection. In contrast, in a world that is scary, one might run constantly from danger, fight to defend oneself, and seek refuge and a safe place to rest.

Given that our classrooms tend to assume safety and respect, children from scary worlds often struggle to speak the language or understand the rituals. When they are silent—or when they show us what they know and it does not make sense—we assume that they may lack knowledge, skill, or intelligence. Rather, it is just that they are attempting to communicate in a language in which they are not fluent. Unfortunately, we often confuse such silence or "miscommunication" as an indication of children's potential. As we have discussed previously, when we begin to doubt children, they often begin to doubt themselves. Perhaps the most damning consequence of such underestimation is lowered expectations. As discussed in the previous chapter, our expectations inform how we think about children, their prospects, and how we teach and interact with them. When we view children as failing, we often do not provide them the resources necessary to thrive.

REFRAMING RESILIENCE

In the previous section, I have suggested that shifting the way we understand children's development will allow us to develop a more complex view of their potential, especially for children navigating the demands of multiple environments or challenging lives. For the past 20 years (Wright, 2007, 2010, 2013a, 2013b), I have sought to support this attitudinal shift by focusing on children's resilience in addition to, or as a part of, the way we understand their potential and achievement. By focusing on resilience, my hope is that it would orient people to the ways in which children are demonstrating strength versus simply documenting all their adversity and its negative consequences. However, in coming to pay more attention to how this term, *resilience*, was actually being used in conversations about children, I came to appreciate that we cannot just change our language—we must change our understanding in order to achieve the paradigm shift required to become more emotionally responsive.

Such reflections are timely as, increasingly, researchers, policymakers, and practitioners are interested in promoting resilience, focusing on positive development as opposed to minimizing risk. However, relatively little work has questioned what is meant by the term *resilience*. The prevailing definition, better than expected outcomes in the midst of adversity (Masten et al., 1990), provides little operational guidance. Consequently, many use resilience as a synonym for whatever adaptive outcome one may be privileging: academic achievement (Burton, 2020), positive peer interactions (Furrer et al., 2014), or self-regulation (Annalakshmi, 2019), for example. In this paradigm, resilience is typically viewed as an *outcome* rather than as an ongoing process of positively responding to one's changing environment. As a result, these outcome-oriented perspectives fail to consider how the social context may be influencing both the way children are behaving and how we are making sense of their behavior. This is a critical limitation as what counts as resilience is fundamentally context specific and an ongoing process of development.

Drawing on critical perspectives, here I contemplate the advantages and limitations of current discussions of resilience through presentation of two case examples emerging from my ongoing research efforts, the first focused on the demands of respect in the preschool classroom, the second exploring the risk and resilience associated with various preschool masculinities, and the third focused on the behaviors of maltreated children in the preschool classroom. In the context of this book, I pay particular attention to how discussions of resilience may be reflecting stereotypical notions of race, class, and gender. As well, given their relative powerlessness in the debate, I am also mindful of the ways in which policy and applied interventions implicitly conceptualize children and childhood, and the implications of particular actions on young children and their development. In doing so, I wish to argue that static notions of risk and resilience factors fail to consider the ways that various influences may facilitate both risk and resilience in children's lives. To conclude, I will discuss the implications of such a perspective for educational practice and developmental theory.

Resilience as a Reframing of "At Risk"

The present focus on resilience emerged, in part, as a response to the language of "at risk" that permeated the world of research, practice, and policy for much of the last 2 decades. This conceptualization has been critiqued for framing children and families as lacking the cultural and moral resources for success and being in need of compensatory assistance from the dominant society (Sleeter, 1995). As such, the at-risk discourse has been argued to be implicitly racist, classist, sexist, and ableist (Lubeck & Garrett, 1990). In response, Swadener & Lubeck (1995) advanced the notion of "children and families at promise" as a way to orient to the possibilities of children and families rather than to their deficits.

The language of resilience emerged, in part, as a response to these and similar critiques. However, though its intent may have been to orient toward promise, it is frequently used in concert with notions of risk to further classify and demoralize individuals. For example, the language of risk and resilience, or risk and protective factors (i.e., Eklund et al., 2013), suggests that one is either at risk *or* resilient, with those not conforming to dominant expectations of success being further diminished. Typically, resilience is constructed as a constituent element of identity—one is either resilient or not. Thus, resilience (or the lack of) becomes yet another label bestowed on the individual by the dominant society.

Again, the prevailing definition of resilience is "better than expected outcomes in the midst of adversity" (Masten et al., 1990). Such ambiguous framing begs the questions: Whose expectations are being privileged? And on whom are such expectations being placed? Given social inequity, power, and privilege, it is most certainly the values and priorities of the dominant society that are imposed. And it is those sitting at the margins who are imposed on. Thus, it might be argued that the dominant discourse of resilience, much like the one informing the notion of "at risk," are implicitly racist, classist, sexist, heterosexist, and ableist. In this way, the language of resilience has oriented us to the importance of "promise," but has done little to deconstruct the privileging of dominant notions of success and classification systems, which reify deficit perspectives.

As an antidote to these critiques, it is important to develop conceptions of resilience that are dynamic, allowing multiple perspectives of and from the individual to emerge. Following, I will present two case studies (Wright, 2007, 2010) to represent and clarify the contextual nature and the dynamic developmental processes underlying resilience.

A "Good Boy": The Risk of Early Loss. One month short of 3 years old, Jorge was well on his way to becoming a little boy. He was said to be "the mirror image of his father," with short wavy brown hair, dark brown eyes, and a light beige complexion that reflected his Latino heritage. Besides his father's physical appearance, Jorge also shared his nickname, "Macho."

I had known Jorge since he was 16 months old, the first child I met while working as a counselor at his child-care center. While uncommon for children to participate in therapy at such a young age, Jorge's center was the site of a university research project aimed at fostering the positive development of children and families living in poverty. Originally, Jorge was referred to therapy mainly as a preventative measure, his family's socioeconomic status and father's sporadic involvement in his life making Jorge particularly vulnerable to future challenges. However, in recent months, therapy had helped Jorge with the unexpected departure of his father and the Department of Social Services' removal of Swahim, Jorge's 6-year-old half-brother, from the home due to a contentious custody dispute between Jorge's mother and the boy's father. Given the impact of these events on Jorge's mother, she had become overworked and depressed, sometimes struggling to maintain a consistent routine for Jorge and his 5-year-old sister, Shanille.

I was assigned to work with Jorge by an insightful clinical director who believed "The little guy could benefit from a male presence in his life." For well over 2 years, Jorge and I spent close to 10 hours a week together, in his classroom, on the playground, and in his weekly therapy sessions. Recognizing our special connection, several teachers at Jorge's day care center often jokingly referred to him as my "son." Despite my corrections, Jorge even called me "daddy" for the first 6 months of our time together. I heard Jorge's first sentence, held his hand as he learned to hop on one foot, and supported him through his father's and brother's departures from his life. My relationship with Jorge has been the most profound learning experience of my educational career.

Becoming part of Jorge's life challenged me to confront parts of my own. Though our experiences and communities were different in many ways, I did see much of myself in Jorge. I know what it is like to live in a home filled with both good times and worry. I was raised by a hardworking, single mother in an under-resourced southern community; I have also felt unsafe. My own father walking out on us when I was still a boy allowed me to connect with Jorge's experiences of loss, not necessarily understanding them, but certainly being able to empathize.

In thinking about the kind of man I wanted to support Jorge in becoming and my explicit charge from the day care's clinical director, I was challenged to think about the kind of man I hoped to be. Attempts to reconcile the values of my childhood with those of my current life as a gay graduate student at an Ivy League institution allowed me to recognize that communities and cultures often have conflicting notions of what it means to be a good man—and that failure to conform to these standards may be painful. Yet I also wondered what is lost in conformity? Given that many men in this society struggle to sustain close relationships, experience intimacy, and express emotions, it seemed that being a good man also comes at a cost.

In cultures where men are expected to stand on their own, not cry, and be a tough guy from a very young age, around 3 years old in most Western societies, men simply do not have permission or the skills to feel close and vulnerable. Coming to see my journey as one shared by Jorge, and all men, forced me to question the kind of partner, father, and friend I would work to become. I was also led to consider, as a child psychologist, what kind of boys and men would I support my clients in becoming? Years spent reflecting on these questions (Wright, 2007) now lead me to wonder how was Jorge impacted when his behavior and emotional needs contradicted the norms of his day care environment?

My relationship with Jorge underscored for me that becoming a boy— becoming a man—is a difficult journey. Separating from care and relationships is a critical but painful achievement necessary to becoming the strong independent man so celebrated by society's dominant culture. My relationship with Jorge straddled the time in his life when the challenges of becoming less dependent on caregivers are most acute. Our connection allowed me to empathize with the pain Jorge experienced in moments of conflict between his needs and the social/cultural demands of the world around him.

More particularly, this experience highlighted for me the risk and resilience of various masculinities. For example, Jorge's uncles enjoyed the fact that he frequently fought with other children, got in trouble at school, and maintained a tough exterior. They said that he was a "good boy." However, in the classroom, this behavior placed him at risk of academic failure, poor peer relationships, and greatly limited his educational prospects. As his therapist, I struggled to determine what type of resilience I should be promoting. What might allow him to be successful in school could have estranged him, or worse, from his family and community. However, not preparing him to be successful in the school environment had equally damning consequences. In other words, resilience at school may have placed him at increased risk in other parts of his life, or vice versa. Similarly, he was not viewed as a resilient child at school, even though his behaviors were very adaptive for the environment in which they developed.

For children like Jorge, who experience such early loss, the demands of this socialization process are particularly insidious. In the midst of coming to terms with the fact that many in his early life walked away from him, Jorge was forced to confront another world that was pushing him away. When he cried, he was told that he should not. When he asked for connection, it was sometimes withheld. He was taught that to be caring is to be a girl—at the same time, learning that to be a girl is a really bad thing. Much larger than him, the roots of these responses were held in the values of this little boy's world, culture, social class, and location—all forces that are very difficult to circumvent. As a result, depending on the context and who was assessing him, Jorge was labeled as both resilient and not.

Having worked with Jorge for such a long period of time, in different domains, while also building relationships with other people important to him, allowed me to realize that what happened to Jorge in one part of his life had direct implications for how he responded in another. Recognizing that Jorge was telling me his story through his behavioral and emotional responses helped me to better understand his actions and understandings inside the classroom. Taking a holistic perspective on his life was central to the effectiveness of my work with him.

While this is not a new or innovative understanding—most of us know that what goes into children is what comes out of them—it has been my experience that it is often not one that is implemented in our work with children, particularly those who are very young. Many times, it seems, people use children's life experiences against them, to justify why it would be challenging to foster their development. However, through my work with Jorge and other small children, I have found that in developing a deep understanding of children's life experiences, we might engage them in their behavior more fully, reframing and refocusing understandings to become more positively adaptive.

Reframing Risk as Resilience. Sixteen-month-old Goddess had never learned to laugh. It is unclear if she never experienced laughter or if she had simply given up on it. With a very dark complexion and distant eyes, Goddess most often arrived at school bundled in her dingy pink coat, covered with the smell of cigarette smoke. Spending most days sitting silently in the corner of her toddler classroom, she did not smile, play, or ask her teachers to hug, console, or sit with her. Though taller than most of her 16–20-month-old classmates, five rowdy boys and two equally energetic girls, Goddess sought none of the same attention. She did not run around the room, ask the teacher to "Help me, please," cry, throw, pinch, hit, laugh, dance, sing, or annoy. She simply sat. Oftentimes Goddess's gaze was fixed, staring blankly out the window. Other times, she clearly gazed within, her blank expression signaling that, though physically present, her thoughts had carried her to another place.

I met Goddess when working as a counselor in her classroom. Goddess's school was recognized as a therapeutic preschool by the state's

Department of Social Services, with approximately one-third of the children attending living in state custody or living under the supervised custody of their families due to substantiated claims of abuse or neglect. Initially assigned to the school by the court system, Goddess was born into the protective custody of the state, her mother giving birth to her while incarcerated on drug charges.

Goddess and I spent close to 10 hours a week together, in her classroom, on the playground, and in weekly play therapy sessions. Though initially assigned to her for 1 academic year, I volunteered as clinical staff for more than 4 years in order to further my support of Goddess and several other children. I heard Goddess's first laugh, rubbed her back as she struggled through naptime nightmares, and supported her through family struggles.

Goddess provides a poignant example of the consequences of negative experiences in early childhood. Learning about life through the perspective of a mother struggling with depression and addiction, Goddess never expressed the typical emotions of childhood, nor had the manifestation of them ever served to meet her needs. Barely more than a year old, she already questioned the world's ability and desire to respond. Goddess rarely enjoyed the moments of pleasure necessary to develop positive reactions, like laughter. As well, growing up in a world that often failed to respond to her cries, she also never fully developed her tears. Internalizing the world as a place of assault, Goddess had already started her retreat.

Unfortunately, the necessary barriers she created to protect herself also began to isolate her from opportunities to develop new knowledge, skills, and expectations. Looking inward, Goddess failed to learn many of the skills necessary to communicate to the outward world, as well as to generate positive responses from it. Though none of us at the school intentionally overlooked Goddess, her lack of affect did not efficiently draw us to her at first—only confirming her perceptions of her place in the world.

Though Goddess should not be expected to advocate for herself at such a young age, it was to her detriment that she did none of the things of "typical" children to draw adults to her. Across my experiences as an educator, through the pre-K through university levels, I have observed that the children most difficult to like almost always receive the worst treatment from peers and adults. In a highly competitive environment, like the classroom, Goddess, and those who have never honed their skills eliciting positive responses, are labeled as behavior problems or lost in the shuffle.

Perhaps this is the most insidious consequence of maltreatment—if one is poorly "loved," it is difficult for one to know how to be lovable. As well, if one is raised by a depressed or absent caregiver, never seeing a smile, one does not know how to manufacture or recognize laughter. Unfortunately, for many maltreated children who never come to expect much from the world, this attitude is often an important determinant of their future life outcomes.

Goddess's silence, however, can also be understood as a resilient act of self-preservation inside the environment to which she was responding. While in the classroom her silence did not serve her well, it was an efficient response to experiences of maltreatment in other environments. If a caregiver is absent in her response, crying does not serve to have one's needs met. Similarly, if one is uncertain of one's next meal, learning not to cry is a very efficient way to conserve energy for survival. For those children at risk of physical abuse, it makes much sense to become as invisible as possible.

Though initially my emotional response was to feel sorry for Goddess, I soon came to respect her strength. While no child should have to experience such maltreatment, Goddess did endure. Rather than a sign of brokenness, changing my perspective on her silence allowed me to recognize in her someone who was fighting to live. Through this reframing, I could begin to imagine her laughter. Rather than trying to "save" or change Goddess, I eventually came to understand my role as supporting her own inherent strengths. As I began to see more clearly these possibilities in Goddess, she and those around her began to see them more clearly as well. In the same way that expectations may be the most damning consequence of risk, perhaps they are also the greatest hopes for resilience.

Through my work with children like James, Jorge, and Goddess, I have observed that as they become more trusting, they frequently become more outwardly focused, less temperamental, and share more positive affect. Soon, they begin to receive more positive attention from teachers and peers, building additional social–emotional skills through interactions with them. Similarly, as teachers begin to see these children in a different light, I have noticed that they often begin to find more enjoyment in engaging with them, experiencing a greater sense of efficacy and gaining energy from their students' affection. It is the mutual transformation that occurs between children with messy lives and the important relationships in their lives that inspire and sustain a support network for them—greatly improving their future prospects.

MOVING FORWARD

The way educators, counselors, and parents understand children's behavioral responses has important consequences for children's identity development, academic success, and attitudes about schooling. As such, it is important to develop pedagogies, dispositions, and classroom environments that honor the complex skills children developed to navigate their messy lives. Rather than locating the injustices of their world as internal to these children—viewing them as having behavioral problems or as not resilient—we should recognize the ways that their actions are logical and meaningful in the context of a world that may be turned upside down or that may be functioning according to a different set of values.

For example, perhaps rather than demanding respect and "good behavior" as a precondition to learning, classrooms should be structured to provide greater autonomy to children and thus space for respect and interdependence to emerge. Moving from educational narratives that *assume* respect to framing the work of teachers as needing to *earn* it, we may create space for more positive and less oppositional images of children to emerge. Perhaps this will allow teachers more flexibility in seeing the adaptive capacities of their students. Additionally, this shift would support them in being more creative in figuring out how to support students in either building on these adaptations that are serving them well in the nonschool environment or better developing their capacity to differentiate social contexts and appropriate skill sets.

Surviving Versus Thriving

When young people navigating difficult life circumstances attempt to manage their complex emotions, they are frequently dismissed as "crying out for attention," or their silence is interpreted as defiance, and they may be labeled "at risk" or "disrespectful." Behaviors like keeping their guard up or not trusting adults that keep them safe in the scary parts of their lives are branded as "problems." Ever more frequently, the children most in need of a safe place to learn and grow are expelled from our classrooms for causing too much trouble or having too many learning needs. Perhaps we are afraid that the chaos surrounding their challenging lives will be too complicating for our own? Or, more generously, maybe we fear that it is too late for our efforts to make a difference, or that the effort required for doing so would demand more than we are capable of providing?

When children are forced to choose between adaptations (beliefs, skills, and values) that keep them safe and/or connected to those whom they love or are dependent on and things that potentially challenge or move them away from those adaptations, they will always choose the former. In other words, in the short term, survival is the issue, even if survival choices jeopardize skill development and future opportunities. Consequently, schools must not compete. Rather than devaluing what children bring with them into our classrooms, we should find a way to at least honor and acknowledge individual sources of strength in some part of their lives. For example, we might say to the child who is invested in presenting as physically tough, "I can tell that you do a good job of making others afraid to pick on you when you are playing in the park, but you do not have to do that in our classroom. I am here to keep you safe." Failure to do so induces shame and inferiority at worst, and pushes children further and further away from embracing schools as safe and emotionally protective spaces at best. A child may not be or have all that we wish for them, but what they do have is the world to them, and in it is the fertile ground of hope. For as the children discussed in this piece suggest, they will be resilient regardless—change always happens. It is in which context they will be allowed to develop that is fundamentally at stake.

SUMMARY

In this chapter, I argue that static notions of risk and resilience factors fail to consider the ways that various influences may facilitate both risk and resilience in children's lives. I encouraged you to develop conceptions of resilience that are dynamic, ultimately recognizing that what might be a source of strength in one part of a child or family's life may be a source of risk in another. Similarly, across individuals, what might be protective for some may be destructive for others. Drawing on the examples of Jorge and Goddess, I illustrated that it is important to recognize that children with messy lives often navigate competing value systems and expectations. Rather than forcing them to choose one or the other, we should endeavor to support such children in developing more sophisticated strategies and supports for navigating these complicated circumstances.

A fundamental difference between this book and others in the field is this emphasis that children's hardwired traumatic responses must be understood both in the context of the environment in which they may be maladaptive and in the context in which they might be protective. Typically, psychological research takes a clinical view of traumatic responses—preferring to understand from a basic perspective how brains, bodies, and behavior adapt to trauma. Educational researchers tend to focus on behavior problems related to trauma, and developing strategies to manage children's emotions and behavior. My framework for emotionally responsive teaching is focused on understanding why children are responding the way that they are, clarifying the demands of the environment in which children are being asked to adapt, and supporting children in developing the skills and understanding necessary to navigate the complexity of the competing demands of the environments in which they live and learn.

CHAPTER 5

Redefining Trauma

The Embodied Experience of Threat

In previous chapters, I have focused primarily on the importance of shifting the way we understand ourselves, the children with whom we work, and their families in crafting an emotionally responsive teaching approach. In this chapter, we will focus instead on broadening our understanding of how messy lives influence the way children and families understand themselves, schooling, and us. The purpose of this chapter is to define adversity, stress, and trauma, and detail the impact of messy life circumstances on children's development and schooling. I will differentiate between challenging life experiences and traumatic responses, casting the stress response as a physiological and psychological reflex to threat as opposed to challenging behavior or behavior problems. We will take a nuanced look at the specific ways in which adversity and trauma, more specifically, may impact children's learning and development.

I begin by sharing a personal experience, examining the impact of a traumatic event on my child, my family, and myself. My intention is to provide an example that you might draw on to illuminate the concepts and potential impacts of trauma that will be discussed subsequently in the chapter. I also hope that you might be reminded of the possibility of healing and growth that can result in the aftermath of traumatic experiences. Sometimes the experiences that scare us the most help us see more fully how strong we are as well.

SINKING IN THE POOL

When she was 3 years old, my daughter had a near drowning accident. One second, she was laughing and the next she was silent. After jumping in the shallow end of the pool one last time with her sister—against our order for them to remain out of the water and begin drying off to leave (which is also why they were no longer wearing their protective life jackets)—Olivia playfully taunted us to jump in and get her. My husband and I watched as she accidentally took one step farther into the deeper part of the pool, bouncing away from her sister's splashes. Recognizing that she was likely in too deep, I proactively jumped into the water to retrieve her. We did not even realize at first that she was struggling, so quiet was the unexpected gulp that caused her lungs to seize with a water-filled breath. It was not until I passed Olivia to Matt on the edge of the pool that we realized that she was not breathing. Matt began patting her on the back as I instinctively ran into the hotel lobby to ask the attendant to call 911. Right behind me, Matt ran screaming into the hotel lobby with our little girl, who had already turned blue. I began mouth-to-mouth resuscitation, and realizing that she no longer had a pulse, soon transitioned to CPR as well. Three minutes later, when I heard the sirens enter the parking lot, she vomited the water that she had inhaled. Just as the paramedics kneeled beside us, Olivia gasped for her first breath.

After a scary 24 hours in the hospital and a battery of tests, the doctors finally shared that there were no signs of permanent physical damage, explaining that it might take much longer to identify any cognitive or neurological effects—though they provided some hope that the likelihood of such negative outcomes had been minimized because we were able to take such swift action. Yet the emotional bruises were far from healing—both Olivia's and our own. While words are not enough to describe our gratitude that our daughter had survived, it was not relief that I most experienced following the event. For weeks and months afterward, I was haunted by the fragility of Olivia's life and my family's. I could not shake the thought that I was just a breath and a few minutes from both losing my child and having what is most important to me in the world shattered. While I was grateful that I somehow managed to perform CPR successfully, the experience did not help me feel stronger or more confident. Rather, I felt lucky that it worked. So overwhelming was the experience that I often recollected it from outside of my body, as if I was watching it rather than having lived it. For a while after the event, I found myself thinking that maybe Olivia had not survived—and that I had simply stepped through the looking glass into an alternate reality to bear the grief. So real was my fear that I would lose her, it began to feel easier to believe that I had.

I was consumed by images, recollections, of Olivia's face, Matt's screams, the sound of the ambulance, and the cold feel of her skin. Though I was physically sitting in work meetings, teaching classes, or spending time with the family, it was just as likely that my mind had wandered to the pool, the hospital, or images of Matt and me sitting silently in our house—30 years in the future—gripped by the torturous sounds of silence, our relationship built on the shared experience of loss and grief rather than the joy and love that had previously brought us together. These images and recollections typically floated in and floated out, like a stream that was constantly flowing through my thoughts. However, sometimes, they presented themselves out of nowhere, catching me off guard and filling me with panic.

Months after the accident, I was driving the girls home after stopping by our favorite snow cone stand for a treat. When I glanced into the rearview mirror, I caught a glimpse of Olivia's blue lips—turned that way by her favorite flavor, Blue Raspberry. Though she was happily eating her slushy in the back seat, I could only see the image of her following the accident, lying on the ground, unresponsive. Immediately, I was crippled with the exact same feelings that I had endured that day. Before I could even think about it, I pulled onto the side of the road and ran around the car to check on Olivia—who looked at me like I had gone crazy. I managed to pull it together enough to reassure the girls that everything was okay, but I had to take a minute outside of the car and out of their views to get myself together before climbing behind the wheel. Thankfully, we were close to home, and I didn't have to hold it in for long. As soon as we pulled into the driveway, I sent the girls inside, seized the steering wheel for dear life, and cried unconsolably. And these are just some of my reactions.

Everyone in our family was impacted by the experience, and most especially Olivia. For the couple of months after the event, she seemed simply as if the wind had gone out of her sails. Our once confident and outgoing little girl became quieter and seemingly more fragile. She had difficulty falling asleep and found it more difficult to separate from us—and we had more trouble being away from her, too. I found myself waking in the middle of the night to check on her, touching her chest to make sure she was breathing. She, too, was more likely to wake with nightmares—crawling into our bed to fall back asleep.

The traumatic effects of the accident presented most dramatically in Olivia's outlook about herself and the world. Each night during dinner, we take turns sharing our high point and low point during the day. Regardless of how good the day had been or the special activities in which she had participated, for over 2 years Olivia responded that she had no high point. Her low point was always, "Sinking in the pool." Despite our best efforts to help her feel distance from the event, to have opportunities for healing and to experience her strength, the defining moment of her life up to that point—that she seemingly relived day after day—was the moment that she made a mistake and almost died. This sense, that something bad was going to happen, permeated every part of her worldview. As her birthday approached, she assumed that she was going to be disappointed. When trying something new, she doubted her ability to do it. The sense that she was out of control started to morph, manifesting itself in all sorts of ways. The previously well-attached and trusting child began to worry that we would forget her or that something would happen to us while we were apart. When I made an offhanded remark about getting old, she became concerned that I was going to die and leave her. Eventually, she just got tired of being worried—and frustration and anger became her baseline. She would lash out at her sister, stomp her foot when she did not get her way, and tried to control her environment and those around her.

For the rest of the summer after the accident, none of us had any appetite for swimming, and we organized our social outgoings to avoid any water-related gathering, though previously trips to the lake, tubing down the river, or going to the pool were family favorites. Over time, we realized that we were reinforcing Olivia's fear—and our own—that we should be afraid of the water, that maybe it, she, and we weren't safe. Eventually, we decided that it would be important for Olivia to reenter the water, to see how strong she could be and to regain her sense of control. We decided that enrolling her in swimming lessons would provide a structured experience for building her confidence and competence. Knowing that she was a stronger swimmer would also help us relearn to relax and have more trust in Olivia's ability to take care of herself—and that a lifeguard was literally within an arm's reach would help us manage our own anxiety in the process.

Facing fear was hard for all of us. Olivia clung to the side of the pool and her instructor for the first couple of weeks in swimming. I paced the edge of the pool on pins and needles for the entirety of the lesson. But over time, we both learned to relax. As Olivia began to trust herself in the pool, she started to feel more confident in other parts of her life as well. Yet even now—7 years after the accident—when Olivia feels like she's "drowning," the feelings of insecurity, panic, and fear of disappointment can quickly rise to the surface.

Living with her vulnerability is something that Olivia—and we—will have to carry with us for our lives. As she confronts new challenges, when those old scars begin to ache, she will have to stare down her fear that something bad might happen. And it will be impossible for her, or us, to deny that could be true. However, because of her work and healing, and also because of her pain and the near tragedy that she endured, Olivia has also come to understand just how strong she is. In addition to being the little girl that didn't know how to swim, who lost control, and who almost drowned—she is now the girl that faced her fears, who learned, who survived, who swims!

Olivia came to this understanding herself, sharing with me during a conversation I was having with her 4 years after the accident. One night as were chatting after dinner, Olivia asked me about my own fears, wanting to know if I was scared of anything now and when I was a child. I answered honesty, sharing some things that scare me, before turning to her and asking, "When have you been most afraid?"

She responded right away, "When I sank in the pool."

"That was scary for all of us," I said.

"Yeah, I used to think about it all the time. But I don't think about it so much anymore," she answered.

"I'm glad," I replied. "What do you think helped you stop?"

"My mermaid," she answered matter-of-factly, referring to the doll that my sister had sent to her almost immediately after the accident. It had become one of her most prized possessions and led to a deep love for all things mermaid for a few years during Olivia's early childhood years. Only in retrospect were we able to realize what a powerful symbol this had to be for her.

"How did Mermaid help?" I wondered aloud.

"I am Mermaid too. I did not just sink in the pool. I learned to swim. And dads helped me," Olivia explained. "I don't worry much anymore. I am going to be okay. And dads will always help me."

On hearing Olivia's explanation, I felt a tension in my chest release—one to which I had become so accustomed that I had forgotten that I once lived without it. Knowing that she was okay helped me feel better, too. All I could say in the moment was, "That's right, varmint. You are strong and you can always count on us."

Olivia caught the tear roll down my cheek and said, "Jeez, Daddy T. You don't have to cry about me sinking anymore. I'm okay." And she is.

Though I would never choose for Olivia, or our family, to have endured such a tragedy, there has been some beauty in the struggle. In confronting how vulnerable she is and how capricious life might be, Olivia also had an opportunity to tap into her courage and come face-to-face with her strength. While she continues to live with the knowledge that life can sometimes spiral out of control, she also trusts her ability to navigate such difficulties. Accepting that sometimes things veer off course, despite our best efforts, has allowed Olivia to relax some of her need for control and perfectionism. Because she has faced so many of her own feelings—and felt the weight of others' worry for her—she is incredibly attuned to others' feelings and is confident in expressing her concern for them. More than once, I've heard Olivia say to others, "I'm sorry you are sad. It will be okay." When I think about how deep and real this lesson is for her and how hard she worked to earn this wisdom, it helps me understand why folks seem to find extra comfort in what we affectionately call "Livy love."

THE EMBODIED EXPERIENCE OF THREAT

Olivia's story is a powerful reminder that the impact of terrifying moments extends well beyond the physical consequences of the event and also the individual. Though the event lasted minutes, its consequences rippled through

Olivia's life—and those touched by it—for years. Not infrequently, my mind still drifts back to thoughts of the experience. Sometimes it is because something else scares me—one of the girls getting hurt on the soccer field or being jolted by their screams of laughter while swimming in a lake. Other times, the thoughts creep in during moments of pride or when I am counting the blessings of my life, when suddenly I remember that I almost lost her. It is these effects of coping with the knowledge that we are vulnerable and can be hurt—hypervigilance, fearing another loss, and anxiety and worry, for example—that define trauma.

The term *trauma* is most often used incorrectly, as a generic way to describe children's difficult life circumstances or their challenging behaviors. However, as we will discuss subsequently in this chapter, trauma is not the circumstances of one's life, it is the *response* to life challenges. And not all adversity is traumatizing. Finally, it is not accurate to conflate trauma, which is a reflexive response, with willful behavior. Developing a more nuanced and accurate vocabulary for representing the experiences of children—as well as their behaviors and emotional responses—is essential if we are to respond to their needs in a more nuanced way as well.

Increasingly, the notion of trauma is being used synonymously with poverty, racism, or other forms of disparity. This is particularly the case for well-intentioned educators attempting to describe the behaviors of children with messy lives or from minoritized backgrounds. For example, one might say, "He is growing up in trauma" or "She has had trauma." Unfortunately, such incorrect usage of the term reinforces a deficit perspective of families with these social locations and implies that such identities are inherently damaging. While I do appreciate the effort to acknowledge that how children are behaving in our classrooms may be in response to what they are experiencing, it is problematic to equate who they are—their identities—with what may have happened to them as a result. For example, being gay is not traumatic, though being exposed to homophobic bullying or being rejected by one's family or friends may certainly lead to toxic stress or trauma. Similarly, not all children who live in poverty are traumatized, though economic strain and the slow burn of despair may certainly lead one to feel helpless or hopeless.

In my own work, I am moving away from trauma as a language for framing my perspective and moving toward the notion of threat, recognizing that the fundamental experience of messy life circumstances is that of feeling threatened. This feeling that we might be challenged, unsafe, destabilized, or insecure is the physical manifestation of adversity in our bodies. The internalized sense that we are not okay and that bad things might happen to us is the essence of stress and is the organized experience of our adaptive coping.

Words like *trauma, behavior problems, psychological diagnoses,* or *social inequities* often capture the consequences of feeling afraid—but to truly empathize, validate, and understand the child who is struggling, it is essential that we recognize in a deep way that they feel threatened—uncertain, unsafe, and perhaps already hurt—in their bodies and in the world. It is this sacred truth that we must hold in our minds and our hearts to be effective in taking the child's perspective and being emotionally responsive to their needs.

I have found that conceptualizing the child as threatened or afraid, as opposed to traumatized, has allowed me to better orient to the child's experience of their life. To connect with the child who is standing in this deep place of threat, allow yourself to imagine what you might do if your world was a scary, unpredictable, or punishing place. How would you adapt? How would you feel if the one who makes it most scary is supposed to be the one to protect you? When I think about the child through the label of traumatized, I find myself also thinking about the child through the language of "symptoms," "behaviors," and "problems."

In other words, the language of trauma and stress positions me to "look at" the child. However, when I hold the child in my mind as feeling afraid or threatened, I find myself oriented to how they are feeling and perceiving themselves and the world. This framing positions me to "stand alongside" the child—empathizing with what the world feels like for them and looking at their world through their eyes. When I think about the child through their emotional experience, caring about how they feel, I find it much easier to extend empathy and generosity to them and respond to their actual needs. Given that this is the goal of an emotionally responsive approach, I will often use the terms *threatened* or *afraid* as synonyms for *stress* and *trauma* for the remainder of this book. In the following section, I will detail how the body responds to perceived threats and the impact of feeling threatened on children's physiological, cognitive, and social development.

Understanding the Impact of Threat: A World Turned Upside Down

Though toxic stress and trauma may impact each child differently, there are a number of symptoms common to children (see Table 5.1) living in the context of threat. Vivid memories that are recalled repeatedly, repetitive behaviors, trauma-specific fears, and negative attitudes about life and people in general are the four most consistent signs of childhood trauma (De Bellis & Van Dillen, 2005). As well, highly stressed children are likely to frighten

Table 5.1. Signs and Symptoms of Traumatic Stress

Children Ages 0–2 Years	Children Ages 3–8 Years
• Act withdrawn • Demand attention through both positive and negative behaviors • Demonstrate poor verbal skills • Display excessive temper tantrums • Exhibit aggressive behaviors • Exhibit memory problems • Exhibit regressive behaviors • Experience nightmares or sleep difficulties • Fear adults who remind them of the traumatic event • Have a poor appetite, low weight and/or digestive problems • Have poor sleep habits • Scream or cry excessively • Show irritability, sadness and anxiety • Startle easily • Challenges with coordination and balance • Sensorimotor development challenges • Increased medical problems	• Act out in social situations • Impulsivity • Act withdrawn • Excessive compliance • Demand attention through both positive and negative behaviors • Display excessive temper • Be anxious and fearful and avoidant • Be unable to trust others or make friends • Be verbally abusive • Believe they are to blame for the traumatic experience • Develop learning disabilities • Exhibit aggressive behaviors • Experience nightmares or sleep difficulties • Experience stomachaches and headaches • Fear adults who remind them of the traumatic event • Fear being separated from parent/caregiver • Have difficulties focusing or learning in school • Have poor sleep habits • Imitate the abusive/traumatic event • Lack self-confidence • Show irritability, sadness and anxiety • Show poor skill development • Startle easily • Wet the bed or self after being toilet trained or exhibit other regressive behaviors • Increased medical problems • Somatization (stomachaches and other complaints about pain)

easily, experience anxiety in unfamiliar situations, and be clingy, difficult to soothe, aggressive, and/or impulsive (van der Kolk, 2005). They may also experience trouble sleeping, anxiety when trying to fall asleep, nightmares and/or bedwetting, lose recently acquired developmental skills, and regress to more immature functioning and behaviors (Blank, 2007). Unfortunately, there is no peace of mind for the child living in a state of such hypervigilance and far less energy for learning, thinking, and growing. However, being aware of these common symptoms may help identify children experiencing toxic stress and trauma and inform how one might support them and their family.

Threat and Children's Development

Feeling threatened affects how children see themselves and shapes what they expect from other people and the world around them. Particularly in the midst of traumatic circumstances, children's sense of security and safety may be undermined, replaced instead by anxiety, anger, or fear (Swann & Bosson, 2010). Especially when a parent is the source of threat, their unpredictable and abusive behavior may lead the child to develop relationships characterized by fear and insecurity and to have difficulty forming personal attachments (Fearon et al., 2010). If a child thinks that the world is out to get them or that their guardians are unable to keep them safe, growing up becomes very scary.

Regardless of the intensity of the threat, threat becomes embodied, influencing the way we think about ourselves. Depending on how deep or intense the threat, these views can be temporary or more enduring. So, for example, if one loses a baseball game, one might think, "I didn't play my best today." However, if one plays the sport for many years without winning, one might eventually come to view oneself as a loser. When we think about the way threat influences how we perceive ourselves and others, it might be helpful to conceptualize this through a matrix. For example, when things are good, and there is either a low level of threat, no level of threat, or someone feels able to overcome the threat and supported by others in doing so, they may view themselves and others as positive. In contrast, when someone experiences a challenging situation that is caused by another person who is acting irresponsibly, or is treating the person negatively, the individual might come to view themselves as positive and the other person or other people as negative.

When the threat is overwhelming, or the person feels like they can't respond adequately to the threat, despite the support of others, the individual may come to view themselves as negative and others as positive. Finally, when someone is forced to endure a threat that they cannot overcome, and they have not received adequate support, or they feel like they have been threatened by others, it is conceivable that they might come to see themselves and others as negative. The ways that we view ourselves and others in relationship to the threat can have long-term consequences for our self-esteem, our views of ourselves in the world. When life is a constant struggle, these views become entrenched, shaping our outlook on the world and oneself.

Though it is possible for children to recover from experiences of negative stress and regain control of their behavioral responses through intervention and support, research (Obradović et al., 2010; van der Kolk, 2005) on the stress response suggests that children's behavior is not always under their control. However, the classroom environment, and the opportunity to interact with additional supportive adults and peers, can serve as a potential buffer against the negative effects of toxic stress (Wentzel et al., 2010). Research indicates that children who remain resilient in the midst of difficult experiences tend to enjoy school, even if they may not be exhibiting strong academic performance (Bergin & Bergin, 2009). In contrast, when children are punished at school for what they are doing to survive, their fears that the world is out to get them are only confirmed, and school becomes one more dangerous place where they need to protect themselves. As a result, the children most difficult to like almost always receive the worst treatment from peers and adults (Vlachou et al., 2011; Wright, 2010).

When we cast children's toxic stress responses as purely psychological or as behavioral problems, we shift the problem from what they are being forced to endure to how they act. Across 15 years spent working as a child trauma therapist, I have rarely, if ever, had a child referred to counseling because of what they may have experienced. Children are virtually always referred to counseling because of how they are behaving or performing academically. Framed less generously, children are usually referred for support because of how they make the adults in their lives feel versus for what they are being forced to experience. In supporting children and families who are struggling, we must address both the adverse circumstances of their lives and how they are responding to them.

THE STRESS RESPONSE SYSTEM

As just discussed, threat is the "human or embodied experience" underlying our encounter of challenging life circumstances. This felt experience both causes and is the result of a complex physiological and emotional reaction, known as the *stress response*. The stress response is the body's emergency reaction system, and its primary function is to keep us safe. The body's stress response is initiated in the amygdala, a part of the brain responsible for emotional processing. When the amygdala receives information from the body (usually from the eyes and/or ears) that signals a threat, it instantly sends a distress signal to the hypothalamus, our brain's command center. The hypothalamus then communicates this information to the rest of the body through the autonomic nervous system, which controls involuntary body functions, like breathing, blood pressure, heartbeat, and the constriction of key blood vessels and the bronchioles, small airways in the lungs. The autonomic nerve system consists of two components, the sympathetic nervous system and the parasympathetic nervous system. The sympathetic nervous system fuels the body with a burst of energy so that it may respond to perceived threats. The parasympathetic nervous system is the recovery system, calming our body down after the perceived danger has passed.

When the hypothalamus triggers the sympathetic nerve system, the adrenal glands respond by releasing epinephrine, also known as adrenaline, into the bloodstream. As adrenaline is pumped throughout the body by the bloodstream, it triggers a number of physiological changes: an increased heart rate that drives more blood to the heart, lungs, and muscles. As the pulse and heart rate increase, we begin to breathe more rapidly, which causes the bronchioles to open wider and increases the amount of oxygen we can inhale with each breath. This extra oxygen is sent to the brain and used to sharpen our senses, allowing us to become more vigilant. At the same time, epinephrine also catalyzes the release of fats and glucose (or blood sugar) into the bloodstream, which supplies the extra energy needed for all of these amped-up functions.

As the initial surge of epinephrine is diffused, the hypothalamus activates the second wave of the stress response system, the HPA-axis. The HPA-axis, made up of the hypothalamus, pituitary gland, and adrenal glands, uses hormonal signals to regulate the stress response, fueling the sympathetic nervous system as long as a perceived threat exists. When this occurs, the hypothalamus releases corticotropin-releasing hormone (CRH). CRH triggers the pituitary gland to release its own hormone, adrenocorticotropic hormone (ACTH). ACTH then catalyzes the release of cortisol by the adrenal glands. Cortisol is often referred to as the "stress hormone"—it provides the "amped-up" feeling and causes the body to sustain its vigilance. When the perceived danger finally passes, the parasympathetic nervous system moderates the stress response and helps the body return to a calmer state of functioning.

This stress response system is hardwired to respond to threat in one of three ways: fighting, freezing, or fleeing (van der Kolk, 1997). Sometimes these responses manifest literally, through physical violence, refusal to move, or running out of the classroom. Other times, the responses may express themselves less obviously. For example, rather than physical violence, a student might "fight" teachers in a different way, refusing assistance, dismissing feedback, or breaking classroom rules (Ford et al., 2000). "Freezing" often results in students appearing zoned out or frequently falling asleep in class (Cohen et al., 2006). And, though physically present, students may be "running" in their minds, distracted by traumatic flashbacks or consumed by fear. Consequently, students navigating toxic stress may seem off task, unsure of instructions, checked out, or disorganized in their thinking (Briere & Scott, 2012).

When the stress response system is activated, the brain usually hits the pause button on higher-order tasks, like learning math, thinking critically, or wondering how our actions will make another person feel, sending the extra energy to survival tasks (De Bellis, 2005). That is why traumatized students may find it impossible to sit down and pay attention (De Bellis & Van Dillen, 2005)—even if they are trying their best—and are more likely to struggle academically (Shonk & Cicchetti, 2001; T. Thompson & Massat, 2005) and socially (Kim & Cicchetti, 2010).

These physiological actions happen so quickly that we are not aware of them. So efficient is the stress response that the amygdala and hypothalamus are triggered before our brain's visual and auditory centers have had a chance to process the perceived danger. In other words, because pausing to think about how threatening something might be delays our reaction time, we frequently respond to a perceived threat *before* we fully understand what is happening or how we have acted. In acutely dangerous situations, such lightning-quick responses may mean the difference between life or death. That the stress response system responds first and ask questions later often leads children to seem impulsive or out of control (Alink et al., 2012). Likewise, as their challenging life experiences have taught them to be on guard and suspicious, children experiencing toxic stress are less likely to give new situations or relationships the benefit of the doubt (Daignault & Hebert, 2009). As a result, any new or unexpected stimuli—a book banging loudly on a table, an adult who raises her voice too loudly, an unexpected announcement booming over the intercom, the shame of being called a name by a classmate, or chaotic transitions between activities, for example—might trigger the child's stress response system. For the non-traumatized individual, these stimuli retreat into the background of life, but for the child living in fear, each could signal the beginning of the next bad experience.

For children who have experienced toxic stress, the stress response system can take over every part of their lives, even setting the structure for their brain development (Beers & De Bellis, 2002). When children operate in overwhelming states of stress, the stress response system may become the normal mode of functioning (Bremner & Vermetten, 2001). Consequently, even when actual dangers are not present, children may react to the world as if they are (Siegel, 2020). Unable to control their heightened levels of emotional response and arousal, children navigating perceived threats simply cannot turn off the survival strategies being employed by their brains (van der Kolk, 2006). This explains why our responses to perceived threats often happen before we even know what we are doing—we jump, run, punch, or yell instinctively. Because this happens automatically, it may also help explain why we sometimes have the feeling that "something isn't quite right," even if we are unsure why we are feeling this way. Our body may be responding to a perceived threat of which our conscious mind has not yet become aware. But in our daily lives, these impulsive stress response systems can work against us, turning on when we don't really need them.

Differentiating the Stress Response From "Bad Behavior"

Amazingly, the stress response happens automatically and beyond our intentional cognitive processing. In other words, stress responses and their related actions are not always intentional. Unlike behavior, which is willful action, stress responses are reactions, impulsive responses to an external stimulus. This is particularly true when we have felt helpless, hopeless, or the perceived threat is great. When experiencing these feelings, our body is hardwired to fight, flee, or freeze, to act first and think later. *This also explains why traditional behavioral approaches may not be effective in supporting children whose behavior is underlaid by threat or fear.* Behavioral management strategies typically rest on the assumption that behavior is about choices—as adults, we must take control of the situation and challenge or incentivize children to earn their "freedom" through demonstration of behaviors that we find pleasing. In other words, we wrestle children under control by demanding or incentivizing their compliance.

Given that the stress/trauma response is most likely to occur when children feel threatened or out of control, such compliance-driven or control-restricting approaches may actually exacerbate or trigger the very "behaviors" that we find challenging. The more we try to exert power over or take control away from the child, especially in moments when their stress response system has already been activated, the more threatened the child will feel. Rather than de-escalating the situation, allowing the child to take more responsibility for their actions and become more grounded, this increased level of perceived threat actually signals the body to "press the gas pedal" on the HPA-axis, releasing another dose of cortisol and amping up the body's reactivity and escalating the child's fight, flee, or freezing response.

Unfortunately, such escalation in the child usually results in our, the educator, feeling more out of control. This triggers our own stress response, and we become more reactive. As we begin to "feel" more unhinged, and therefore more threatening to the child, our own stress response actually triggers another dose of cortisol release in our student—resulting in the child becoming even more activated. As you can probably guess by now, our own stress response system will be kicked into overdrive by this escalation, and our HPA-axis will then release an even larger dose of cortisol to ensure that we are ready for "battle." Unfortunately, once our stress response system is activated, it becomes even more difficult for the child and us to think clearly and act intentionally. We become engaged in a cocreated "dance"—shifting and moving together in a ballet of fear and threat. Though we may be moving together, our steps clearly in time with each other, this is not how it feels. Inside of the experience, the participants feel more like they are engaged in a sword battle, two enemies swinging, dodging, and battling for control.

Given that this escalation is reactive and largely impulsive, traditional behavior interventions are not typically effective when supporting students who feel threatened. As discussed, approaches focused on power and control may actually intensify the behavioral responses of our students and exacerbate our own control-seeking behaviors. When they are effective, it is usually because we have rendered the child powerless and they comply as a "freezing" or safety response. In these cases, we have not changed their behavior; we have just scared them into paralysis. Similarly, when we only make sense of children's actions through the lens of behavior and behavior problems, we tend to assume those actions are more willful than they actually are, perceiving them as "disrespectful," "questioning our authority," or "challenging." Notice, all of these frames are oriented around *our* sense of safety and personal control. When we view the child's behavior as threatening us, we are more likely to engage in control-seeking behaviors ourselves, which are only more likely to trigger the child's sense of threat.

Time and time again, I have watched well-intentioned teachers inadvertently trigger the very behaviors in children that they dread the most. Similarly, I have watched children trigger the same behaviors in their teachers that make them feel most threatened. When we worry about losing control or that the other person may become out of control, we immediately become vigilant—even hypervigilant—about when the "bad" things could happen. Essentially, we signal ourselves to be on guard and make it more likely that our stress response will be triggered. When we have felt threatened, we learn to worry about what might happen. We feel stressed. As it turns out, this is a very unpleasant way to feel, and most of us hate existing in this purgatory of dread. As a result, one of the ways that we cope with the threat of danger is by provoking the thing that we fear. Especially for people who have had to defend themselves a lot in their lives, we become more comfortable in our fight, flee, or freeze responses than in dread or waiting. Likewise, individuals who have not yet had the opportunity to feel safe or hopeful always view the world as falling apart or about to fall apart. Since the waiting is so anxiety provoking, these people often inadvertently cause things to fall apart because they actually feel more comfortable operating in freefall.

The Ghosts in the Classroom

Sadly, even after the battle is over, such negative interactions may still leave the child and us feeling as if we are in a war with each other. Over time, the notion that one must be on constant guard becomes internalized, with many children coming to school every day in survival mode—watching their backs, ready to run out the door at the first sign of danger, or sitting quietly in the corner trying to remain invisible (Kim & Cicchetti, 2003). They anticipate that the classroom environment will be threatening and spend their days scanning for any warning of danger (van der Kolk, 2005). Though these traumatic responses are meant to be protective (Wright & Ryan, 2014), they have the potential to impact the key skills involved in learning, such as attention, organization, comprehension, memory, the ability to produce work, engagement in learning, and trust (Streeck-Fischer & van der Kolk, 2000), and are frequently viewed as behavior problems or as developmental deficits in the classroom (McFarlane et al., 2005; van der Kolk, 2005). In fact, teachers describe traumatized children as less ready than non-traumatized children to learn in school (Alisic, 2012) and as being more likely to demonstrate poor work habits (Nikulina et al., 2011).

When we have caused another person pain or made them feel threatened, their brains and bodies are hardwired to view us as potential threats. Similarly, when children have triggered us to feel threatened or out of control, our mind and body are programmed to remain guarded and vigilant around them, making it more likely for us to assume the worst of their intentions and perceive them as threatening. This is particularly true for children with whom we battle frequently. Frequently, our bodies become wired to become guarded, reactive, and to feel threatened by the very children who need our support the most. Similarly, despite our positive efforts on their behalf, when we battle with a child, we become one more person who has the potential to hurt them. Because the stress response system is preconscious—designed to respond to threats before we can even comprehend them—we may develop "hard feelings," "feel distance," or put up our guard with children without even realizing it. And they are likely doing the same with us.

For better or worse, the stress response system is wired to generalize, encoding signs of potential threat. These "signs" are rooted in our own life experiences and what we are taught to fear. For children who have been hurt by another adult, any adult might be perceived as threatening. Likewise, when we have students who trigger us to feel out of control, we might find it more challenging to let our guard down with any student, especially those who remind us of or share similarities with the one who challenged us initially. Even thinking about threatening events from our past or anticipating scary things in our future can trigger a stress response, leading us to feel and act as if we are under threat when we are not. As a result, children living with painful memories or growing in the midst of stressful circumstances often feel "haunted" by these difficult experiences. Even when they cannot put their finger on what is bothering them or explain why they feel angry and ready to fight, we can see their difficult past stirring in them. Such hypervigilance serves to prime their stress response system, ensuring that they can fight, flee, or freeze on a moment's notice, at the same time, keeping them anchored to experiences that they would probably rather forget.

I have come to think about such hypervigilance as the ghosts in our classroom. Even though we may not be able to know, see, or understand the painful memories haunting our students, we can still feel their presence. Rather than pretending that they aren't there, I have learned that acknowledging these ghosts has helped my students and me feel less afraid and less at odds with each other. I sometimes say, "I can tell that you have something on your mind," or "It feels like your thoughts are pulling you in another direction," or "I'm here to watch over you and keep you safe now. It's okay to focus on your learning. Nothing is going to happen on my watch." Recognizing these ghosts has helped me to become more patient with children and individuals who are struggling, and to take their mistrust and fear responses less personally. While it still hurts when children seemingly mistrust me or respond to me out of anger and fear, I no longer get defensive or assume the child is being disrespectful or defiant. I try my best to see that they feel unsafe, threatened, and scared, responding to these needs rather than my ego's experience of them.

DIFFERENTIATING BRIEF STRESS, ADVERSITY,
TOXIC STRESS, AND TRAUMA

Given that the body's physiological response is designed to accommodate the perceived level of threat, the stress response system may be conceptualized along a continuum of brief stress, adversity, toxic stress, and trauma. Understanding the relationship among brief stress, adversity, toxic stress, and trauma—and also their distinctions—is critical for educators and anyone interested in supporting children and families.

At the low end of the continuum exists brief stress, or the momentary disappointments or difficulties of life. For most children, this would include taking a test, a disappointing performance, an argument with a friend, or missing the bus. While these daily stressors may cause momentary frustration or self-doubt, we generally overcome them in short order and move on with the regular demands and joys of living. In terms of the stress response, these events cause mild elevations in stress hormone levels and brief increases in heart rate. Brief stress is unpleasant, but it does not blow us off course. Metaphorically, it is a stumble but not a fall.

Moving along the continuum of threat, adversity is the messy, or challenging, circumstances of life. Examples of adversity might include navigating the death of a loved one, divorce, learning challenges, or failing to meet a major life goal. Adversity might cause moments of frustration, doubt, and pain. These are life moments when we feel tripped up, and maybe even fall down, but soon get back up again. Physiologically, adversity causes serious, temporary stress responses; however, these are generally buffered by supportive relationships and/or the development of our own coping skills.

In contrast, when adversity overwhelms our capacity to cope, we experience toxic stress. Toxic stress is a physiological and psychological response to adversity with implications for emotions, behavior, learning, physical health and well-being, self-understanding, and relationships. Toxic stress is characterized by prolonged activation of our stress response system in the absence of effective supports, maladaptive coping skills, and/or protective relationships. Toxic stressors make us fall down and keep pushing us back down until we begin to question if we can or want to get back up again. In the midst of toxic stress, we often feel afraid and doubt our ability to overcome the challenges we are facing. Anecdotally, toxic stress is the experience of "almost drowning," as if we are barely managing to keep our head above water.

At the extreme end of the continuum is trauma. Trauma is the experience of panic that occurs when we are not sure that we can or want to survive. Trauma is a reflexive physiological response to extreme toxic stress that triggers a survival response, with more pronounced implications for each stress response domain. Trauma occurs when an external event overwhelms one's ability to cope, leaving us feeling temporarily helpless (Terr, 2008) or hopeless. If we do not fear for our survival—or doubt our will to survive—then we have not experienced trauma, we have navigated toxic stress and/or adversity.

Traumatic events are typically unexpected and uncontrollable, fill victims with terror, and force them to confront just how fragile they are (Terr, 1991, 1995; van der Kolk, 2005). Events that occur once (suddenly and unexpectedly) are often referred to as short-term or Type I traumatic events (Terr, 1991). Included in this category are natural disasters (e.g., tornados, hurricanes, and earthquakes), accidents (e.g., motor vehicle accidents, fires, explosions, dog bites, or falling), and tragic human-made events (e.g., bombings, shootings, rape, kidnappings, robbery, and industrial accidents). Type II traumatic events (Terr, 1991) typically involve chronic, repeated, and/or ongoing exposure such as chronic illness, child abuse, child maltreatment, domestic abuse, and imprisonment. Increasingly, trauma researchers recognize that stress associated with chronic poverty and ongoing exposure to neighborhood violence may result in symptoms consistent with post-traumatic stress (stress response system et al., 2011). The constant strain caused by Type II trauma can make it difficult for children to imagine a positive future and cause them to lose hope that their circumstances might change (De Bellis & Van Dillen, 2005).

The impact on children of feeling threatened is influenced by the nature and severity of the stressful experience (D. J. Thompson et al., 2015); characteristics of the child (Ingram, 2012); and the way the family, school, and community respond (Bonanno et al., 2010). Given that toxic stress and trauma are determined by how one copes with a stressful experience, rather than the details of the event itself, it is important to keep in mind that what may be traumatic to one child may not be traumatizing to another. Children in the same family or classroom who have experienced the same thing may be impacted very differently, their reactions varying as a result of their individual coping skills. Similarly, because adults typically possess more advanced coping skills, we often underestimate the impact of life challenges on children, who may be experiencing a particular adversity for the first time. Likewise, when working with children and families from different sociocultural or experiential backgrounds, teachers may over- or underestimate the impact of particular events on their well-being. When we evaluate how someone is functioning through the lens of our own experiences, we are frequently wrong about how they are being impacted.

For example, I recently supported a 9-year-old child experiencing symptoms of post-traumatic stress disorder following the death of his beloved parakeet. Because the child's parents and teachers were not equally impacted by the event, they feared that his sudden bouts of anger, sleepless nights, hopelessness, separation anxiety, grief, and malaise were the result of hidden abuse or onset of an acute mental health disorder. Though the child could not stop talking about how much he missed his bird, the family viewed this as obsession rather than fear and heartbreak. However, for my client, the bird both represented the pain of loss and challenged him to realize how little control he had over some aspects of his world. As he explained to me:

Losing [my bird] made me think about what would happen if I lost my mommy and dad. I am just a kid—who would take care of me?. . . No matter how much I love them, they can be taken away. . . . I feel so helpless and afraid.

As an example of emotionally responsive teaching, realizing that losing the parakeet had led the child to feel helpless and hopeless, I began to consider his response through the frame of traumatic stress and came to see that his attitudes and behaviors were consistent with feeling threatened and vulnerable. Because this child had enjoyed a life of privilege and endured very little adversity, he had not developed coping skills for the level of grief, loss, and vulnerability that losing his parakeet had evoked. Over time, the child did come to terms with the loss and began to feel more confident in his ability to cope with future life challenges. As his ability to cope increased, his traumatic symptoms decreased.

In many cases, such as the one just presented, brief stress and adversity function as "positive" or "optimal" stressors. It is in the process of meeting the demands of these challenges that we build adaptive coping skills, increase our competence, and become more self-confident. By overcoming these manageable threats, we begin to see how strong we are and learn to trust in our ability to cope with difficult experiences. The belief that we are going to be able to meet the challenges of life fosters a sense of self-efficacy, allowing us to pursue loftier goals and better tolerate feelings of vulnerability. It is only through taking such risks that we develop our capacity for resilience. Just as steel is forged in fire, our strength is best developed in situations that challenge us to become stronger.

In contrast, toxic stress and traumatic events are negative stressors. In feeling helpless or hopeless, these overwhelming threats cause us to doubt ourselves, become less trusting of others, and have a negative effect on our physical and emotional health. The skills that we use to cope with negative stressors are generally maladaptive in more normative environments, pervasive, and longer term. Put simply, toxic stress and trauma are the physical and psychological embodiments of the overwhelming circumstances around us, the conversion of fear and injustice in the world into intrapersonal suffering. Far too often, we forget that stress and trauma are the symptoms of adversity and that the root causes of such toxic stress are those things that lead us to feel terrified, helpless, or hopeless.

SUMMARY

Haunted by challenging life circumstances, many children with messy lives spend their days trapped in fear, reliving their worst experiences or running from terrifying events that may not yet have happened. In this chapter, I defined adversity, stress, and trauma, and detailed the impact of messy life circumstances on children's development and schooling. Centrally, I indicated the importance of differentiating between challenging life experiences and traumatic responses, casting the stress response as a physiological and psychological reflex to threat as opposed to challenging behavior or behavior problems. I shared the impact of my daughter Olivia's traumatic experience to illustrate the profound consequences of trauma on children and their families—and the possibilities for healing and growth in overcoming such struggles.

CHAPTER 6

Too Scared to Learn

The Impact of Fear on Development and Learning

In my experience, educators typically think about the consequences of trauma and toxic stress almost exclusively through the lenses of behavior problems and social–emotional challenges. Because we tend to view our primary responsibility as supporting children's learning, I often hear colleagues describe the behavioral, social, and emotional needs of children with messy lives as distractions from or getting in the way of their learning and our teaching. Exasperated, teachers often describe working with such children as "out of my wheelhouse" or feeling like "I can't teach until the child is ready to learn." Many times, I've had teacher colleagues say to me, "He doesn't need a teacher, he needs a therapist" or "I can teach her math, but someone else is going to have to help her deal with those behaviors." Implicit in these comments are the assumptions that adverse experiences manifest only through how children feel and behave and that teachers may not have a unique role to play in supporting children experiencing them. In other words, these views suggest a belief that if children could just regulate and pay attention, they would learn and engage the curriculum in exactly the same way as children developing in more normative circumstances—that when children are ready to learn, we will be ready to teach them. However, supporting children in building the skills to cope with such challenges and equipping them to learn in the midst of adversity are central to emotionally responsive teaching.

Traditional instructional models focus on learning standards and normative developmental trajectories, often assuming certain types of prior knowledge, learning dispositions, values, and experiences. Yet chronic stress, trauma, and messy life circumstances have profound consequences for children's psychological, cognitive, and academic development. Children growing up in the midst of such adversity must often develop different types of knowledge, values, and dispositions to survive and may not share many of the same experiences as children growing up in less challenging contexts. In my observations, early childhood educators typically draw on positive experiences when providing examples or illustrating concepts for their students, referencing a big birthday party, friendly community helpers, a summer vacation, or the best day ever. However, for children with difficult lives, such notions may be outside of or in conflict with their experiences. I have known many children whose birthdays were forgotten or disappointing, who viewed police officers suspiciously, who never had a vacation, and who rarely experienced good days. Not only might such examples trigger feelings of sadness, disappointment, or being left behind for children, but lacking such prior experiences makes it difficult for them to understand the concepts we are trying to teach.

Consequently, traditional models may not be well aligned with the ways highly stressed children learn, view the world, and process information. Toxic stress and trauma fundamentally reorganize not only one's physiological systems, but also cognitive, emotional, and social development. As a result, such children often arrive in the classroom with different sets of resources, assumptions, and prior knowledge and sometimes lack the skills and knowledge on which much of our typical instructional and pedagogical practices are predicated. For example, children growing up in unpredictable environments may be less attuned to following classroom routines, connecting their behavior with its consequences, orienting positively to authority figures in the classroom, or knowing how to cooperate with peers. Understanding these differences is essential in tailoring an instructional approach that provides appropriate learning support and underscores the fact that teachers have an essential and unique role to play in supporting children with challenging lives.

In this chapter, I detail the implications of messy life circumstances for learning and development and offer suggestions for providing more responsive instructional support. In the first section, I focus on how messy life circumstances may change our view of the world. In the following section, I will examine how such adversity impacts our view of ourselves. In the final sections of this chapter, I will focus on how adversity impacts learning and development.

A SHIFT IN WORLDVIEW

Of all the impacts of chronic stress, perhaps the most fundamental are shifts in one's worldview and self-concept. The way we view the world has implications for virtually every aspect of our personality and development. How we feel about the world and ourselves are the first impressions we form in our lives and become the lenses through which everything we think about others and ourselves is perceived. If we view the world as filled with possibility, we will likely become optimistic, more physically and intellectually engaged in exploration and knowledge building, more content, and more emotionally invested in relationships with others. In contrast, if we assume that the world is dangerous, we will likely become more aggressive or inhibited, hunker down to protect ourselves and our belongings, binge and hoard out of fear that our needs won't be met in the future, and avoid or mistrust others.

Adversity has the potential to transform one's positive self-concept and optimistic outlook to viewing oneself and the world as negative and filled with danger. Once we have felt threatened, we must forever live with the knowledge that we might be hurt. Once we have been hurt, we may no longer believe that we are invincible or that others may be trusted to keep us safe. In such circumstances, our view of ourselves shifts from feeling safe and in control to feeling threatened and powerless, and our view of others shifts from assuming care and respect to assuming menace and neglect. Navigating these painful realizations is the very essence of trauma and chronic stress.

The developmental stage in our lives when we confront existential threats informs both the scope and severity of their impact. As infants, we are totally helpless, depending on others to meet our every need. When these needs are met for us, we develop a deep inner sense that we are important, that others may be trusted, and the world is good. This sense of well-being and positive outlook becomes embedded deep in our psyche and lays the foundation for the development of trust, optimism, agency, self-efficacy, hope, and faith in others. When we have been well loved and our basic needs have been met early in our lives, we develop a positive orientation to the world, a foundation of goodness, and reservoirs of love for ourselves and others to draw from in challenging times.

If we are born into a scary world or one that does not meet our needs, our earliest sense is that others are neglectful, punishing, and/or disinterested in us. In such a chronically deprived environment, we do not develop a positive orientation to the world and are likely to become mistrustful of others. We may come to view others as threats to our well-being and safety and become self-focused, trusting only ourselves to act in our best interests. When caregivers are emotionally distant, children experience disorganized attachment, needing care but unable to attract it; this leaves children feeling distrustful of adults (Craig et al., 2021). Rather than a psyche infused with optimism and the assumption of others' goodness, we may internalize a deep sense of rage, sadness, hunger, or numbness, so overwhelming are our emotions that we cannot bear to feel them. For children such as these, it is essential that they have a chance to experience unconditional positive regard—though they may feel deeply threatened by it and have no concept of the care that they are receiving—in order to challenge their view of the world and to begin imagining the possibility that there may be people who will care for them and parts of the world that may be safe.

When life challenges occur after infancy, they may not set the foundation on which our worldview is built, but they call what we thought we knew into question, leading us to feel as if our lives are falling apart, helpless and out of control. This is also why life's challenges are sometimes experienced as a crisis of faith, challenging our very assumptions about the goodness of the world, how we think of others, and what we believe about ourselves. In one tragic moment, such as in a traumatic incident or discovering what we thought about some aspect of our life to be a lie, we may shift from feeling like nothing can really hurt us to wondering if we will be able to survive. Of events like this, it may be difficult to trust that the universe has our back, that others can keep us safe, or that we are somehow protected. We may start to believe that others do not care about us or perceive that they may even be out to get us. Though the seeds of hope and trust may have been planted in us initially, they may become dormant in the midst of overwhelming circumstances.

In the classroom, such a wounded worldview often presents as negative expectations and assumptions. For example, on a recent classroom visit, I greeted Jeremiah, an 8-year-old experiencing grief and loss after the death of his beloved grandmother, by saying, "Hi! My name is Travis and I am excited to get to know you." His response was, "Don't bother. You're not going to like me." So depressed was Jeremiah that his sadness had begun to orient him to others and his expectations of the world. As I spent more time in the classroom, I observed Jeremiah greet each new experience with such negativity. When his teacher shared that the class would enjoy a walk to the neighborhood splash pad later in the week, Jeremiah said, "It's probably going to rain." As I encouraged him to reengage with a class assignment, Jeremiah replied, "I hate this. . . . I'm not good at it. . . . Who cares anyway?" Coming to understand that Jeremiah's grandmother had stepped in after his mother had been unable to care for him, becoming his primary caregiver and cheerleader, helped me to appreciate his despondency. Beyond the simple weight of grief, Jeremiah must have wondered why such tragedies continued to befall him. In attempting to reconcile such early loss, perhaps Jeremiah had come to assume that he is cursed or deserving. In the egocentric mind of the child, perhaps Jeremiah even feared that his actions had somehow contributed to his grandmother's passing and his mother's abandonment, perhaps worrying that he had been "too much" for them. To cope with such hurt—and to steel himself against the pain of future losses—Jeremiah had adapted by expecting disappointment and abandonment. By not allowing himself to become invested in the possibilities of hope or connection, he would not have to endure the sting of disappointment or loss. But, in doing so, he risked missing out on the very connections that would allow opportunities for healing.

Children who did not enjoy a healthy attachment process when young have reduced capacities for self-regulation, empathy, and perspective taking (Henschel et al., 2020; Joireman et al., 2002). For some children, such as Jeremiah, feeling hopeless or out of control presents as overwhelming despair and pessimism that circumstances can or will change. These children may have difficulty forming personal attachments, instead developing relationships based on fear and insecurity. Children who experienced insecure attachments early in life may avoid direct contact with teachers, resist compliance in class, and seek attention from the educator (Craig, 2016). They are more likely to become bullies or to be bullied, and they may either seek attention to control the environment or withdraw and garner as little attention as possible. Similarly, these are the children who may constantly vie with us for power and control, challenging or undermining our authority, or become perfectionistic, seeking to avoid any judgment or fearful that a mistake will result in negative consequences.

Children growing up in the midst of threatening circumstances typically develop a siege mentality, assuming that anyone who attempts to get close is an enemy until proven otherwise. From the perspective of self-preservation, such suspicion and skepticism are more likely to keep them safe. Children subjected to overwhelming trauma or ongoing adversity live in a state of constant alertness, or hypervigilance, and develop an extraordinary ability to scan the environment for warning signs of attack. They learn to recognize subtle changes in facial expression, voice, and body language as evidence of imminent danger. When threat is relentless—or perceived to be—this siege mentality becomes one's dominant view of others and the world. Over time, they may lose the ability to self-regulate or be unable to turn off the survival strategies they have been conditioned to employ.

While protective in dangerous circumstances, such a stance also makes it more difficult to recognize that a threat may have passed or that an ally has arrived to assist us. As teachers, we have to navigate this difficult terrain, recognizing that children may be viewing us as potential threats while we begin to convince them that we are there to help. Teachers must use "playfulness, acceptance, curiosity, and empathy" to engage these children (S. E. Craig, 2016). Their goal is to form caring relationships with children that promote earned secure attachment, neural integration, flexible affect management, improved self-regulation, and problem solving (S. E. Craig, 2016). For example, in attempting to build relationships with children who seem suspicious or shy, I often prefer a less direct approach to developing a connection. A favorite strategy is to engage children in a project—art materials or building blocks are typical. While they are working away, I ask questions about their work, compliment their efforts, and/or sit quietly in close proximity. Allowing them the opportunity to tolerate my presence before making any demands or asking direct questions, instead using comments to reassure and affirm them, often helps to smooth the process of becoming acquainted.

As in the real battlefields of life, sometimes we have to wave a white flag—saying out loud that "I am not here to hurt you"—proceed with caution, and avoid making any fast movements, frightening sounds, or doing anything else that could be perceived as threatening. Eventually, when the children come to understand that we will sit next to them in their scary moments, they will come to view us as a trusted ally. In this place, we can help them see that while there may be threats to confront and dangers to avoid, there are people who will be there to support them. Over time, the hope is that they will begin to internalize that they are worth fighting for.

The goal of supporting children with challenging lives is not to convince them that the world is all good, that they are totally safe, that all people can be trusted, and that they are perfect just as they are. Children that have endured the dark sides of life have already learned that this is not the case. To convince them otherwise would require them to let go of all the trust and knowledge they have gained in their lives and ask them to be vulnerable in ways that would most certainly place them at risk. As a matter of their survival, it would not be fair or responsible to try to convince them that "it's all good." Rather, the goal of this work is to help children who understand how bad things can be to know that sometimes, and in some places, life can be better— and to support them in developing the knowledge, skills, values, and resources to seek out these environments and relationships and be successful in them.

Inner Badness: A Shift in Self-Concept

In the same way that adverse experiences may lead children to view the world negatively, they may also lead children to view themselves negatively. For me, this is the most tragic and insidious consequence of toxic stress and trauma. Not only do victims lose faith in others, they almost always lose faith in themselves as well. As in the case of messy circumstances or toxic stress, one may start to view oneself as helpless or becoming hopeless—feeling that no matter how hard one works, they cannot seem to make things better. Though the individual may have previously thought of themselves as capable and competent, such circumstances may eventually lead to self-doubt. In life as in the ocean, even the best swimmer can only keep their head above water for so long, eventually tiring and starting to panic. Each of us has an endurance threshold, and when pushed near the point of breaking, we must confront our limits and vulnerability.

Likewise, when bad things happen to us, it is normal to wonder why. For younger children, whose limited experiences in the world have been mostly framed around themselves, it is cognitively challenging for them to differentiate how something makes them feel from their responsibility for it. If they feel bad, they internalize this sense as "I am bad." For example, I once worked with a child whose father's involvement in his life was inconsistent and often chaotic. Rather than externalizing his feelings and being mad at his father for such ongoing disappointment, the child had come to view himself as a disappointment and the "kind of kid that dads don't really want to be around." In other words, his feelings of being disappointed had become internalized as "I am a disappointment" rather than as "My father disappoints me." Sadly, children who navigate chaos, experience abuse, or who are deprived often come to believe that bad things happen to them because they deserve it. For many victims, it is too scary to believe that the world is out of control or that the people who are supposed to protect them are capable of causing them harm or are unable to protect them. So, if those who have been hurt need to believe that the world and the people around them are good, the only way to justify the bad things happening to them is to believe that they themselves are bad. This bad feeling then becomes internalized as the reason the abuser hurts them or why the world around them seems to be falling apart. Sadly, they may start to feel that the abuse is warranted and actually act out in order to be treated the way they expect to be treated.

One way of understanding this is that even in the midst of life challenges, most of us are wired to see the best in others and to feel hope in the world. In order to maintain this positive outlook, we often sacrifice the goodness that we might believe in ourselves. Similarly, we need the world to make sense somehow, and deciding that we are bad and deserve the bad things that happen to us is one way to find logic in the abuse. This may be especially true for children who have experiences of being told that they have done something wrong or out of limits.

When children endure negative circumstances for too long or the traumatic events are too severe, it may erode their early foundation of trust and self-confidence. But hope is not lost. As long as the seeds of hope have been planted with children having the opportunity to experience respect, trust, care, and love, they may grow into trust and self-worth. When the conditions for growth are not optimal, hope and self-esteem may go dormant to survive—but this does not mean that they are dead. If we create the conditions for growth, they may sprout and reach for the light once again.

ADVERSITY AND LEARNING

Growing up in adverse circumstances, and especially traumatic ones, affects child development and later learning. The correlation between chaos and trauma and subsequent learning problems is strong and persistent (Briere & Scott, 2012; Cloitre et al., 2019; Larson et al., 2017; D. L. Perry & Daniels, 2016; Schore, 2001). Here, I discuss the most common learning effects associated with messy life circumstances and trauma: language and communication skills, forming attachments and perspective taking, problem-solving and analysis, recognizing cause and effect, organizing narrative materials, paying attention and engaging the curriculum, regulating emotions, and maintaining executive function (see also Cole et al., 2005). Though each of these may be positively influenced by therapeutic supports, these learning needs are best addressed through the support of teachers and skilled instruction.

Language and Communications Skills

Neglect, trauma, and challenging life circumstances are detrimental to the development of expressive and receptive language in children (Culp et al., 1991). Language is the most fundamental way of communicating with others, used to express thoughts, feelings, ideas, and knowledge. It is the primary way by which people create and share meaning and an important tool for communicating social identity and self-expression. When children struggle with language and communication skills, each of these essential human functions are also impeded.

Unfortunately, when kids are overwhelmed, they struggle to communicate. Children may not be able to express how they are feeling or understand what others are communicating. Sometimes they do not actually have the language to express what they see or feel. Further, instead of using language to build bridges with others on the basis of mutual understanding, some traumatized children use language to build walls between themselves and those they regard as potentially threatening (Coster & Cicchetti, 1993). Children who have been hurt or who are afraid may use their language to keep other people at bay. They need educators who can help them build both the trust to begin communicating openly and the vocabularies and communication skills to do so.

When parents and caregivers are highly stressed and/or depressed, they may be less likely to engage in rich, reciprocal conversations with their children, negatively impacting the child's vocabulary and communication style. For example, when a caregiver only gives orders or commands, and doesn't elicit thoughts, feelings, or opinions, children may internalize a predominantly instrumental understanding of language, meaning that language is used primarily as a way to communicate the speaker's purpose to the listener. In such a communication pattern, language does not become viewed as a means of explaining, reflecting, or reciprocating; it is a tool for demanding or communicating a unilateral perspective. Such communication may actually reinforce the child's sense of powerlessness and promote their compliance, foreclosing the possibility of critical thinking and development of personal agency.

In highly directive classrooms, where teachers issue mainly commands and directives, this communication style becomes reinforced and may actually support the child in associating the fear that they may have internalized in other parts of their life with their teacher. Often, I have observed that children living in overwhelming circumstances, especially those with dominant and anxiety-provoking caregivers, respond most comfortably to such dictatorial communication styles in the classroom. However, we must not confuse compliance with learning or the best interest of the child. Rather than reinforcing such instrumental and intimidating use of language, we should endeavor to support children in developing rich expressive language and create opportunities for them to use language for multiple purposes (see Figure 6.1).

Halliday (1975) established seven language roles for children in their early years: instrumental, regulatory, interactional, personal function, heuristic, imaginative, and representational (see Figure 6.2). The first four functions allow the child to meet physical, social, and emotional needs. The other three functions help a child adapt to new environments. As discussed previously,

Figure 6.1. Examples of Intimidating Versus Encouraging/Expressive Language

Intimidating Language	Encouraging and Expressive Language
Sit down.	I really like the way you. . . .
Be quiet. Or, shut your mouth.	I see how hard you are trying to. . . .
Don't make me. . . .	Wow! You are really good at. . . .
You are making me angry.	It makes me smile when I remember the time you. . . .
There will be consequences.	It is special when you. . . .

Figure 6.2. Examples of Halliday's Seven Language Roles

Language Role	Description	Example
Instrumental	Used to get things done or to have needs met.	"I want candy." "I need help going to the bathroom."
Regulatory	Used to control the behaviors of others.	"Please stop." "This needs to be finished."
Interactional	Used to define and/or initiate interactions with others.	"Hello" "You and me" "May I play with you?"
Personal Functions	Used to express awareness of self and personal preferences.	"Here I come." "I am wearing yellow pants."
Heuristic	Used to explore and/or acquire information.	"Explain to me why." "How did that happen?" "How do you make green?"
Imaginative	Used to express creative language.	"I want to walk on the moon!" "I want to eat an ice cream as big as a building."
Representational	Used to share information.	"I'll tell you." "I know. . . ." "I made a fort."

instrumental language is used to achieve a certain result. Regulatory language is used to maintain proper physiological states, or managing stimuli, and is used to control the behavior of another person. Interactional language is the communicative use of language, when we learn to put our thoughts and ideas into words so that others might understand them.

Personal function of language means information about people and their relationships, such as "me," "you," and "I." Heuristic refers to how our brain organizes and processes information, and heuristic language refers to the use of language to help people make decisions. An example of heuristic language is, "Tell me why you made that choice?" Imaginative language is the ability to represent mental images. Representational language is the ability to establish a connection between an object and that object's name. Representation is the basis for linguistic understanding and knowledge acquisition, helping us to form meaning from our experience by linking names with objects we have seen before. In responsive classroom environments, children will have the opportunity to engage and build appropriate skills in each of these language domains.

Social and Emotional Communication

In addition to receptive and expressive language challenges, messy life circumstances and other types of adversity may greatly impact the development of children's social and emotional communication skills. Frequently, these negative effects are the result of challenges in children's relationships with their caregivers, whose mental health also suffers due to adversity and high-stress environments. When caregivers are anxious or depressed, they tend to present with flat affect, demonstrating little emotion on their faces and communicating in a dull, flat tone. In such cases, children are not exposed to a range of emotions—usually only numbness, sadness, or anger. Depressed and/or anxious caregivers are also less likely to demonstrate positive emotions, like joy, happiness, or curiosity. As a result, their children do not develop the nuanced ability to differentiate emotional experiences for themselves or others—or to recognize or communicate these emotional experiences. Likewise, when children learn to spend most of their time navigating the emotions of their caregiver or others versus having their own emotional experiences validated, they learn to overemphasize the needs and preferences of others and to minimize their own wants and needs. Similarly, when a child must assess the mood of their parent before deciding if it is safe to express a personal preference, they cannot fully develop a sense of self. This can result in an inability to trust oneself and maintain personal boundaries, which can lead to difficulty making independent choices. This difficulty has serious academic consequences; deficits in this area can make it hard to solve a problem from a different point of view, infer ideas from text, participate in social conversation, and develop empathy in relationships.

Given that relationships require interpersonal reciprocity, if children have only been interacted with unilaterally, they will not have learned to care about another person's feelings or to interpret them. While they may be very attuned to what others need—and may do their best to meet these needs in order to keep the peace or to feel safe—it does not mean that they will necessarily care or feel empathy toward the person whom they are helping.

Children navigating messy lives often experience fear, anxiety, irritability, helplessness, anger, shame, depression, and guilt, but their ability to identify and express these feelings is often underdeveloped and poorly regulated. Some of these children may express emotions without restraint and seem impulsive, under-controlled, unable to reflect, edgy, oversensitive, or aggressive. They may overreact to perceived provocation in the classroom and on the playground. Other traumatized children block out painful or uncomfortable emotions; they may appear disinterested, disconnected, or aloof. For them, the consequence of not knowing how to communicate or interpret emotions is the dampening or constricting of their feelings. Another group of traumatized children protects themselves from unmanageable stress and anxiety by dissociating—that is, by completely disconnecting emotions from the events with which they are associated.

In a world filled with frustration and despair, almost everything feels angry, sad, or anxiety provoking. Regardless of what else children may be thinking or experiencing, each emotion is "felt" against a backdrop of one or more of these negative emotions. This creates an emotional feedback loop where virtually everything starts to feel negative. Similarly, when children feel overwhelming anger or sadness, other, more positive emotions are crowded out. As a result, children may find it difficult to feel or name positive emotions. Unless this knot of negative emotion is loosened, eventually children will start to feel hopeless or helpless, and the traumatic stress response will be triggered to help overcome these emotional threats. Children will fight, flee, or freeze, often from themselves, with self-harm, self-sabotage, or harming others as possible outcomes.

Similarly, depressed or distracted caregivers may overlook their children's behavior or emotional protests until they feel out of control or overwhelmed by them—then overreacting with their own anger or rage. Children growing up in the midst of such a dynamic typically become hyperattuned to these powerful negative emotions as they are the only ones with any real consequence for them. As a result, these children become wired to assume that any strong display of emotion will be negative and potentially dangerous or punishing to them.

These triggers often manifest in the classroom as inappropriate responses to the positive emotions of teachers and other students. Time and again, I have watched children "freak" with fear or panic when teachers raise their voices with praise, clap with excitement, or wear an elated expression on their faces. Just last year, I witnessed a 2nd-grader run across the room, screaming for his life, and hide in the dramatic play area when his teacher jumped for joy when he finally achieved one of his academic goals in the classroom. For students who have only seen adult faces enlivened with anger, any strong emotion can only be perceived as menacing. Sadly, teachers often misinterpret students' fear-based reactions as disrespectful, undermining, or being out control and respond to them accordingly. Such a negative response only reinforces the child's belief that the emotion was indeed a menace.

In some cases, children may associate this outburst with care, or even love, as this is the emotion that is connected with being noticed. Some children who are denied positive attention will choose to accept, and seek out, such negative attention, preferring this type of acknowledgment to no attention at all. This cycle may not only reinforce children's feeling of inner badness, but also the perception that anger and rage are emotions with power. For children who are struggling to feel in control of their lives or to identify with those whom they love, learning the language of rage may come to feel empowering and also a way to maintain connection to the one who intimidates them. In misguided efforts to feel connected to us, they may even choose to misbehave in order to seek out our attention.

Cruelty, adversity, and other types of threatening circumstances may undermine a child's ability to form new relationships that are essential to healing and learning. Individuals with trauma or those afraid to trust may vie for power in relationships since they only feel safe when they control the environment. Children who have experienced instability may manifest behaviors that get in the way of relating to others. They struggle to form personal attachments in their relationships, basing the relationships on fear and insecurity. They often spend so much effort scanning the environment for the next bad thing to happen that they find it difficult to focus on regulating themselves, being aware of their bodies, or noticing how their actions might be affecting others. Such children have difficulty understanding their own perspective and communicating it and a much harder time recognizing another person's perspective and taking it (Sorrels, 2015).

When children lack the ability to manage strong feelings, it often manifests behaviorally through reactivity and impulsivity (B. D. Perry, 2007). They are on guard, hypervigilant. They may become defiant or aggressive as a way to protect themselves by keeping others away, or they may withdraw to achieve the same goal. This is a particular challenge for children who have experienced chronic stress because they are too hypervigilant, or busy trying to anticipate violence, to recognize or regulate their emotions. When a child's stress response system has been activated, their bodies work hard to make them overreact. The ability to modulate emotions is a predictor of academic and social success, and it is a foundational skill for a number of other critical abilities, such as impulse control, regulating aggression, interpreting emotions of others, and a predictable sense of self (Cole et al., 2005; Sorrels, 2015).

To support children in overcoming these social and emotional communication challenges, it is important for them to learn how to experience, identify, and express a broad range of emotions. Similarly, focusing explicitly on building skills in the area of perspective should be a top priority when supporting children with challenging lives. Being able to take one's own perspective as well as the perspectives of others and coordinate them in increasing complexity are the essential skills for social coordination and relationship development. Being able to negotiate such interpersonal understanding is foundational to developing friendships, mentoring and learning relationships, and eventually intimacy with another person.

One simple way to improve children's capacity for social–emotional language is to build their vocabulary and understanding of different emotions, including how to identify and express feelings. Many classrooms have a chart called "The Little Faces of Feelings," which is a helpful tool in this regard, as is modeling a range of emotions in our classroom and being explicit in naming the feeling and in drawing children's attention to how we are expressing it on our face and with our body. Because any strong emotion will often be perceived as negative by traumatized children, despite its actual valence, it is helpful to preview what we are feeling to the child and then say, "I'm going to show you what this feeling looks like on my face and my body." Without being explicit about our intention when demonstrating strong emotions—even positive ones—we might inadvertently be terrifying students who have been conditioned to assume the worst. As well, we must be sure to praise children for desirable behaviors and connect with them outside of punishment or negative reinforcement. If children come to realize that they will receive more of our attention for being their best, they will come to spend less energy trying to meet our negative expectations of them.

Problem-Solving and Analysis

Children developing in chaotic circumstances may have difficulty solving problems. From a lived perspective, this makes sense. If a child's life is chaotic and they cannot figure out how to have their needs met, everything may come to seem capricious—like life just happens randomly, with good or back luck falling from the sky. In a world such as this, there is no semblance of natural consequences, and what happens is often unrelated to what one deserves. Often, children have shared with me just this type of perspective: "I'm doing everything I'm supposed to do and we still lost our house," "I try my best to be a good kid and my dad still hits me," or "I thought I was going to get in trouble for failing my test, but mom was passed out on the couch and didn't say anything." In situations such as these, children may have limited experience using verbal problem-solving methods and little exposure to adults who encourage the kind of self-reporting of ideas or feelings often expected in a classroom setting. Children being raised by highly stressed or neglectful caregivers may also have had limited experience engaging in complex communications and may find it challenging to extract key ideas embedded in lengthy narratives, making it challenging for them to conceptualize the problem that needs to be solved.

Contributing to problem-solving challenges is the fact that children affected by chaotic circumstances may have trouble recognizing cause-and-effect relationships, connecting the problem with the solution. In chaotic circumstances, where they constantly feel as if things just keeping happening out of the blue, children may not develop the sense of order and predictability to notice which and how various actions and their consequences are related. This challenge has profound implications for many aspects of learning, impacting children's ability to identify patterns, order, and sequence; make predictions and inferences; and connect symbols and sounds—essentially the building blocks of reading, math, and spelling!

This dynamic is often evident in the context of behavior and consequences as well. Children growing up in environments with little consistency or structure, where behaviors may be ignored one day and punished the next, may not internalize the relationships among the rules, their actions, and the punishment they receive. Though as teachers, we may discuss class rules and provide consequences for children who do not follow them, children with messy lives may not connect our expectations, their actions, and the consequences. Unfortunately, when children do not understand the consequences of their own actions, their view that they are being punished capriciously and unfairly—that we are out to get them—is only reinforced. I have learned that when children start complaining that teachers are out to get them or they feel they have been treated unfairly, it is important to consider both if this might be true and also if the child understands the connection between the rules and their actions.

Problem-solving is essential to learning and academic success, and typically requires the complex integration of multiple skills. Such integration may be especially challenging for children exposed to chronic stress and/or trauma, whose brains are forced to spend much energy on splitting and fragmentation in order to maintain some semblance of balance. For example, children with positive experiences of the world and positive self-esteem are likely to approach new tasks thinking, "I got this!" Such confidence permits them to focus on the task, spending little to no energy self-soothing.

In contrast, children who have learned to assume the worst may approach the task thinking, "Is this teacher trying to make me look stupid," or "This is going to be hard!" In order to engage the task at hand, these children must recall the required knowledge and skills while also expending energy buffering their self-esteem and trying to convince themselves that they should and can attempt the challenge. From a cognitive perspective, rather than an integrated sense of self—"I am good and I can do this"—children navigating negativity must fragment contradictory self-understandings in order to engage the problem—"I'm probably not going to be able to do this, but I will get in more trouble if I don't try." Such inner conflict siphons a great deal of emotional energy from the problem-solving task, with each new challenge in the process potentially overwhelming the child's self-confidence and raising the level of anxiety. Put simply, for some children, this process feels like trying to learn math in a pressure cooker.

From a cognitive perspective, children who are overstimulated and overwhelmed often process inputs as discrete pieces of information. As the brain uses contrast and comparison to organize information and to create knowledge maps to support our recall and understanding, information that is processed in such individual units may be more difficult to recall or file appropriately in the brain's repository. In other words, when children are not supported in recognizing the relationship between various pieces of information, they may not develop complex cognitive schema, or mental structures for organizing knowledge and behavior, that places pieces of information in conversation with each other. This cognitive skill is essential in building the cognitive capacity necessary to solve complex problems and other forms of critical thinking.

Supporting children in strengthening their problem-solving skills is essential. To start, it is important to be explicit in naming the relationship between cause and effect, problems and solutions, and behaviors and consequences. Rather than assuming that children understand, even if they say yes when we ask them directly, it is important to provide opportunities for them to rehearse and repeat to help them internalize these relationships. Teaching children how to use context clues to make predictions and inferences is particularly important, as this is a critical skill for building vocabulary and improving reading comprehension. Likewise, it is also important to teach the following skills explicitly, in order to ensure that children develop the building blocks for more complicated problem-solving: identifying patterns, ordering and sequencing, making predictions and inferences, and connecting symbols and sounds. Art projects, making music, teaching children the alphabet and common expressions in sign language, and line dancing are all engaging strategies that may be used to introduce and reinforce these skills. One of my favorite activities is to divide the class into small groups, working with each to develop a mystery for classmates to solve. In crafting the mystery, students must construct a "problem" that needs to be solved, develop a narrative about the problem (order and sequence), generate clues that allow classmates to make predictions and inferences, and create logical connections between clues and the context of the story. In deciding how to share (or act out) the story for peers, children must develop a sequence of events. This enjoyable activity engages them in a multisensory learning experience, provides an opportunity for collaboration, and is fun!

Organizing Narrative Materials and Reading Comprehension

Figuring out how to build narratives is a challenge for children, even if everything in their life is stable. Imagine how much harder it is to learn how to put things together in a sequence if everything in your life feels out of order or disjointed. Organizing narrative material is especially difficult if a child is distracted or hyper or getting sensory inputs from lots of different directions, such as in a chaotic classroom. This is especially true for children who are traumatized or navigating overwhelming life circumstances, who may be experiencing anxiety internally at the same time—worrying about the past, present, and future. For example, while listening to you read a story or attempting to read a passage on their own, the traumatized child may be experiencing flashbacks or worrying about what's going to happen when they leave school all at the same time. For such children, it is challenging to differentiate among the past, present, and future—and even more challenging to craft a linear narrative that places these tenses in an ordered relationship with each other. When one is experiencing such distraction, it can be especially difficult to attend to context clues, which are essential for inferring meaning, building on prior knowledge, and interpreting meaning. In addition to creating challenges organizing or tending to the present narrative, disturbances in these important areas also make it harder to read or listen for meaning and to decode new vocabulary.

Supporting children in feeling grounded and nurturing their ability to remain in the present moment are essential in building their ability to organize narratives and the related skills of reading comprehension and language acquisition. Implementing these practices is critical in laying the foundation for children to develop a better sense of the relationship among past, present, and future. When children are able to feel less anxious and more organized internally, they will be better poised to narrate their experiences and feelings in a more coordinated fashion as well.

Creating experiences and processes in the classroom that have a beginning, middle, and end can be powerful in helping children to build narrative skills. Frequently, we ask children to draw on prior knowledge from outside the classroom to practice their narrative skills. For example, we may ask, "What did you do this weekend?" For children with scary weekends or difficult pasts, asking them to go back there can invite the painful memories into the classroom that they are trying to forget, making it even more challenging for them to concentrate. When children have waited all weekend to return to the safety of the classroom—or to flee a place that has been difficult for them—that is the last thing they want to be asked about it. One approach is to begin each morning by reading a book aloud, so that everyone has something shared to talk about together in the morning meeting. This also allows children to hear your voice in a calm, soothing tone and in a way that is not immediately directive or unilateral, which can be an important antidote/reframe for a weekend that may have been filled with yelling and punishing.

When I am supporting children with challenging lives who may have had a difficult weekend, the first thing I do on Monday morning is to invite the class to take a stroll around the school grounds, observe the clouds and weather through the window, or to notice how the class plant or pet may have changed during the time away. Following the experience, you might ask, "Where did we go? What did we see? What did we do?" In addition to organizing the narrative linearly for them, this approach also helps the children to reconnect with the class environment and draws their attention away from stress or worry that they might be carrying with them. This also reinforces for the children a sense of boundaries, that this is our place and that you are safe here now.

In addition to supporting children in remaining grounded and having experiences that allow them to internalize a sense of beginning, middle, and end, there are several teaching strategies that will support children in strengthening their narrative and comprehension skills. First, we must use narratives in teaching children. Most basically, we must use sequencers—words like *first, next, then, after that,* and *finally*—to explicitly support children in building their understanding of the narrative process. It builds that schema and helps them start to set that structure for organizing material. Second, we should develop explicit processes for students to follow in our classrooms and should be explicit in narrating processes for students to follow. This orients children to the importance of structure and planning. Third, modelling "self-talk" can be an important strategy for students who may not be used to processing information in order to arrive at their own perspective. When teaching children new skills, modeling how to process something that happened, or previewing how they might address a new challenge, you might consider speaking aloud your internal thought process as a way to model for students how they might organize their perspective.

For example, before transitioning to the cafeteria, you might speak aloud, "Wow, I am suddenly feeling a little nervous about walking into that big room with so many loud noises. First, I'm going to remember to breathe as a way to calm myself. Second, I'm going to find my friend and sit with him. Third, I'm going to remember to ask my teacher for help if I start to feel upset." Modeling self-talk in this way supports children in organizing their thinking and coordinating their emotions and responses. This type of narration can also help children remain oriented to the present and pay more attention to the processes that are going on around them.

It is essential that children hear stories in our classrooms—this allows them to build listening skills and orients them to narrative as a way to communicate complex and sequential information. Narratives also allow children to develop complex schema for organizing information, as they must sort and integrate various aspects of the story in order to track and understand it. Many children are taught information and skills discretely—that is, what to think and how to do something may be taught independently of each other. Particularly in environments that prioritize high-stakes testing, children may be taught using a "drill and skill" approach, prioritizing rote memorization and discrete knowledge. This undermines their ability to tend to complex narratives and to synthesize them for themes and understanding. Without these skills, children may be more challenged to curate their own complex stories.

Finally, children should be provided with many opportunities to narrate their own perspectives. If they are to become more skilled at organizing their perspectives and generating narratives, they must be provided opportunities to do so. We should create opportunities in our classrooms for children to respond to open-ended questions and to generate stories from their imaginary or real lives.

Show-and-tell is a classic and wonderful way for children to narrate something that is important to them. Inviting children to give tours of their classroom to guests, asking them to make up tall tales, and inviting them to create inventions or stories are all powerful ways for them to make meaning of the world around them and organize their thoughts into narrative. Arts-based activities may be helpful ways for all children to practice communicating both their thoughts and feelings. This is especially true for children who may feel inhibited or who lack the vocabulary or language skills to communicate the complexity of their perspectives orally. In the same way that children might be asked to speak a story, they may instead be given the opportunity to illustrate one—inviting them to be mindful of creating a beginning, middle, and end.

Many teachers have used playwriting and acting very powerfully in this regard. Children may be invited to tell a story, one that is make-believe or from their personal life. Other children may then be asked to act out the story as the child narrates. This allows the narrator to understand the importance of providing context and transitions for the narrative and forces them to think about how others might be understanding (or not) what they are saying. Children who are acting or in the audience may be given opportunities to ask questions of the narrator, which support the child in learning to fill in the gaps and further communicate their perspective. Older children may be asked to first draw or write the story as a way to practice written communication skills and to anticipate how they might be interpreted in action. There are many variations on this general approach, but in skilled, intentional hands I have watched children's communication skills, self-esteem, and classroom relationships blossom through investment in such an approach.

While writing this, I can still see the gigantic grin that spread across a child's face when he received a standing ovation from his classmates on re-enacting a scene from his life that he directed. In having a child walk around the room with an empty leash, Ricardo had managed to communicate that the sadness and loneliness that he experienced when his dog died was similar to the feelings he had when transitioning to our classroom following an unexpected family move. Using his play to show us things about himself that he felt we might not have had a chance to see, like enjoying soccer, listening to music, and playing with Pokémon cards, Ricardo communicated with his classmates that he would like to know them and invited them to know him as well. In his final scene, he presented his fantasy that he would score the winning goal for his school's soccer team and everyone would cheer for him. When his classmates shouted "Bravo" and clapped for his play, Ricardo managed to experience some of the recognition and celebration that he craved so deeply.

Executive Function and Self-Regulation

Executive functioning is the mental processes that enable us to plan, focus attention, remember instructions, and juggle multiple tasks successfully. The brain requires this skill set to manage impulses, set and achieve goals, plan and prioritize tasks, filter distractions, and anticipate consequences. Executive functioning depends on three types of brain functioning: working memory, mental flexibility, and self-control. Working memory is the ability to remember and manipulate pieces of information over short periods of time, such as working math problems in our heads, processing a friend's story, or reading for comprehension. Mental flexibility is what allows us to sustain or shift attention in response to what's happening in our environment and apply different rules in different settings. Self-control enables us to resist impulsive actions and to set priorities. Supporting children in building each of these skills is necessary to the development of their executive functioning.

Executive functioning is essential to academic and life success. Completing homework, working toward a goal, dreaming of college or a better life, following classroom procedures—all of these require executive function. Yet children with messy lives, especially those who have experienced trauma, often struggle to develop high levels of executive functioning. They may lack the optimism or sense of efficacy necessary to plan; they may be stuck in reactive mode. When children and their families struggle—experiencing homelessness, navigating abuse or addiction, or worried about how to put food on the table or pay bills, for example—it may feel to the child that life is like a minefield, dodging one dangerous obstacle after another. A child who resides in such a constant state of reaction or is being raised by someone struggling to set goals or navigate systems does not learn to think in a linear way. They react more than plan.

Such reactivity both sets the structure of brain development and is also reinforced by it. The prefrontal cortex, where executive function resides, may be damaged by trauma (De Bellis, 2005; Mezzacappa et al., 2001) or subverted by the brain structures associated with the stress response system. When our brain is in panic mode, energy is actively directed away from the prefrontal cortex and executive function because stopping to think, plan, and consider consequences may make us more vulnerable when we need to fight or flee. Likewise, when we do not have an opportunity to self-regulate, plan, or receive positive reinforcement, the brain is less likely to reach its full capacity for executive function.

Executive function challenges also impact children's attitudes toward incentives and achievement motivation. Frequently, teachers and schools focus on future achievement—college, money, career, and especially how ready children will be to meet the demands of the next grade level—to encourage children's academic engagement and persistence. Even more proximal incentives—field trips, rewards, or extra computer time—often require children to delay instant gratification for some eventual gain. Though these are important future life possibilities and the ability to delay gratification is a key predictor of future life success and well-being, they are not typically aligned with the needs and perceptions of children enduring high levels of chronic stress. When children experience chronic deprivation, struggle to have their most basic physical and emotional needs met, and feel they must constantly compete with others for attention and validation, the idea that good things will happen in their future often feels unbelievable, and the idea that they should forego something they want or need in the present seems irrational. When children are barely making it in the present, it is almost impossible for many of them to imagine a future, particularly one that is fulfilling.

Consequently, it is important to provide more immediate rationales, incentives, and encouragement for children with messy lives in addition to these longer-term rewards. It is important for them to have things to look forward to and incentives to work hard; they should hear high expectations for their futures. However, children with low self-esteem and/or poor executive functioning may need extra scaffolding to work toward and sustain the behavior necessary to achieve those expectations.

In my own work, I have found encouragement and praise to be two of the most important and immediate supports. Research suggests that children with low self-esteem and/or poor impulse control require approximately six praise statements every 15 minutes and a ration of four praise statements for every one reprimand in order to feel affirmed and supported (Fredrickson & Losada, 2005). Children struggling with an academic or social task may require even more immediate and higher amounts of praise in order to persist through the challenging task. When supporting a child in developing a new skill or investing in a particular behavior, praise should be provided immediately when the child demonstrates the requested response. I like to ask children their favorite ways to receive praise and encouragement and respond accordingly, with high fives, fist bumps, and words of affirmation being common choices. But children can be very creative—I've also learned to clap hands like a seal, puff out my cheeks like a puffer fish, and walk around in circles like a penguin. Whatever it takes to get children excited about engaging and persisting with their learning is fine by me! Providing positive descriptive feedback to promote child engagement in classroom and social expectations fosters metacognition, or higher-order thinking; emotional control; goal-directed persistence; and organization; and strengthens self-reflection and self-monitoring skills.

Executive functioning develops through experiences and practice. Adults set up the framework for children to learn and practice these skills over time by establishing routines, breaking tasks into smaller pieces, and encouraging games that promote imagination, role-playing, following rules, and controlling impulses. These skills typically develop rapidly between the ages of 3 and 5 years, followed by another spike in development during the adolescent and early adult years. However, children may build and enhance these skills at any time! It takes a lot of practice to develop executive functioning, but as children become more skilled at planning, executing, and managing their emotions, they become more capable of functioning independently and more confident in their own abilities. Executive functioning may even improve children's health outcomes, helping them to stick to healthy habits and reducing their overall stress.

Targeted instructional strategies can also be very helpful in fostering the development of executive functioning. Providing children with engaging learning activities supports them in sustaining attention and remaining persistent in pursuit of a goal. A balanced schedule of activities that minimizes the time children are not engaged in learning also contributes to time management skills and attention. In addition to the benefits discussed previously, engaging in supportive conversations with children not only expands their communication skills, but also promotes cognitive flexibility and emotional control, and it stimulates development of working memory. Explicitly teaching children the rules and expectations of the classroom also supports their higher-order thinking and impulse control, as does structuring transitions to decrease the likelihood that challenging behaviors might occur.

Play is also very important for the development of executive function as it provides opportunities for children to plan, initiate, respond to feedback from peers, and calibrate behavior and expectations; it also supports cognitive flexibility. Games are also terrific ways to support the development of executive function. For example, Memory and other matching games require working memory skills; strategy games, like checkers and chess, promote cognitive flexibility; and both winning and losing promote emotional control and impulse inhibition.

Routines are very important in supporting executive functioning, allowing children the predictability and structure necessary to internalize expectations and classroom process. Routines and schedules promote organization, planning and prioritization, and time management. Using a visual schedule for younger children or a written planner for older ones may prove incredibly helpful for children who struggle with executive function. As children with executive function challenges often struggle with working memory, it may be difficult for them to remember assignments or classroom tasks, follow through with homework, or return permission slips. Unfortunately, children who struggle to remember may also forget that they won't remember if they do not write things down, so challenges with working memory tend to snowball. Planners and visual organizers can help children navigate these challenges, but they must be taught and reinforced to use them. Ensuring that parents and guardians have ways to access and monitor what has been assigned their children is also important, providing children with executive dysfunction one less thing to try to remember.

Children with executive dysfunction often struggle to identify the steps necessary to complete a task. Often, these children will become so frustrated by the decision-making process that they never begin, or they may stop and restart throughout as they think of different ways to accomplish the task. Working with the child to develop a checklist, or providing them with one in advance, often makes the task less overwhelming and more achievable. When making a checklist, or assigning a task, it is a good idea to assign a time limit for each step, particularly if there are multiple steps. Providing them with such clear directions helps them understand and respond to expectations and promotes their ability to plan and prioritize, initiate tasks, and support their working memory. Finally, while it is important for them to have choices, too many choices can become overwhelming for children struggling with executive dysfunction. Limiting the number of options available to them may help, as will remembering that they may need some scaffolding to be able to make choices for themselves. Similarly, children may become angry or sullen when faced with too many options—experiencing the fear of missing out for those in which they could not partake.

Attentiveness to Classroom Tasks and Engaging the Curriculum

For all of the reasons that we have discussed previously, it may come as no surprise that children navigating toxic stress and other messy circumstances often struggle to attend to classroom tasks, engage the curriculum, and perhaps even find meaning in school attendance. Traumatized children can be distracted or lack focus in the classroom because they are preoccupied by anxiety and fear: Kids "do not pay attention because they are unable to distinguish between relevant and irrelevant information. They tend to misinterpret innocuous stimuli as traumatic, and if not interpreted as traumatic, they tend to ignore sensory input" (Streeck-Fischer & van der Kolk, 2000). Children may be busily interpreting the moods of others, or disassociating; they may act out because they are lost in the academic activities. Traumatic experiences can deplete motivation and internal resources for academic engagement. Academic engagement, or self-initiated and -regulated learning for competence, is a powerful predictor of academic success (Shonk & Cicchetti, 2001). Yet their engagement may be compromised for trauma-affected children. Often, these difficulties are compounded by children's inability to regulate their emotions and behavior in the school setting.

Children filled with frustration, anger, grief, or loss may have difficulty imagining the future or feeling hopeful about it. They're not working for the future; they're working on surviving. They may need help to feel satisfaction or a sense of joy and purpose, being in the here and now. For children confronting their very survival—or the well-being of those they love—the typical concerns of the classroom may pale in comparison. For example, if a child is worried about what they might eat or where they might sleep after school, learning a letter sound or remembering a rule of grammar may seem insignificant in comparison. For the child grieving the loss of a loved one, a teacher's expectations may seem inconsequential. If a child is hungry or sleepy, it may be hard for them to manage their emotions or focus on learning activities. It can be difficult to be happy for peers or celebrate their achievements when one's own life feels empty or devastated. Children may feel even more isolated when teachers talk only about good news and happy stories, feeling like their life isn't represented in or welcomed into the conversation.

Again, teachers may play an important role in helping children care about and engage their schooling. First and foremost, we can ensure that the classroom is a safe and comfortable place for children. Providing a safe and predictable environment allows the sense of security necessary for successful behavior change and investment in learning to occur. We must be careful not to confuse how children perform with how important school is to them. In my own work, I have observed that children who struggle outside of school often like school, even if their academic performance is lagging. When we only praise children for their performance or communicate with them about their academic needs, they may come to feel that they matter only for what they do, not because of who they are. As in other parts of their life, children who may be struggling academically will have one more reason to believe that they are less than others. When children doubt themselves, it will only be harder for them to invest in their learning.

We can ensure that the curriculum, including the stories we tell, the questions we ask, and the projects we assign, are meaningful to our students. It is important to incorporate aspects of their lives and communities into the classroom, valuing their identities and cultures. It is important not to avoid discussion of challenges and disappointments. If children do not feel that we can understand or handle their challenges, they will not share them with us. While it is important to ask children about their hopes and dreams, it is also important to allow them to speak about their disappointments and fears.

Perhaps in addition to writing a story about their best day ever, we might invite them to reflect on their biggest regret or disappointment. Sometimes, it may be helpful to share our own struggles or frustrations—in a way that is child centered, developmentally appropriate, and respectful. For example, if we made a bad grade on a test, lost a relative, experienced bullying as a child, our parents divorced, or we are worried a great deal about making friends, we might say so. Some children may find it helpful to hear that we, too, experienced difficult things and managed to get through them. Books may also be a helpful way to incorporate exploration of children's fears and frustrations; reading about a child's bad day, fight with a friend, or feeling like a "fourth-grade nothing" can be powerful for children navigating similar feelings and situations.

Schools are just beginning to consider how to leverage more fully the resources and resilience that children navigating adversity have developed to survive. At the same time, children developing in the midst of challenging circumstances sometimes struggle to develop key skills necessary to engage the curriculum in a more prosocial or developmentally appropriate way. For example, children growing in unpredictable or chaotic environments do not have the same opportunity to internalize the sense that the world is an orderly and predictable place, which impacts their ability to recognize repeating patterns, identify cause-and-effect relationships, or draw connections between actions and their consequences. In turn, such circumstances often manifest through children as language and communication deficits; social–emotional communications gaps; and challenges solving problems, organizing narratives, and recognizing cause-and-effect relationships. These capacities are fundamental to learning, and almost everything taught in school builds on them. So basic are these abilities that most instruction assumes that kids have them. However, for children with messy lives, we must foster these foundational skills specifically.

Because our behavioral management strategies are often ineffective in addressing children's fear responses, sometimes even making them worse, we may become frustrated and feel disempowered in our efforts to support children with messy lives. As these children struggle to engage the curriculum, stay focused on their work, or yield to our requests, we decide they are not ready or interested in learning. We may think things like, "This child isn't ready to learn," "This child needs a therapist, not a teacher," or "I'm not going to work harder for him than he's willing to work for himself." Over time, we may come to believe that some children cannot be successful in school or that we cannot teach a child until their other needs have been addressed and they are ready to learn. We buy into the belief that children navigating toxic stress need stable lives and calm and peaceful bodies before they are ready to learn.

However, nothing builds competence and confidence like learning. When children's lives are out of control or threatening, acquiring new knowledge and being successful in school may help them feel capable, confident, and proud. If school becomes a place in the world that feels good when other parts of life feel bad, then schooling becomes a resource, a stabilizing influence, and a haven that children will turn to time and again when they need a positive outlet for their struggles. In helping children to recognize that learning makes you feel bigger rather than smaller and that schools may provide a positive escape from life's challenges, we will have provided a safe place to for children and will have reinforced the power that education has to help them take control of their lives and plan an escape from difficult circumstances. In this way, outside of their families, school has the potential to be the single most important support for children navigating difficult lives.

Certainly, school represents society's greatest investment and best chance to provide an anchor for children whose family and/or community lives may be in turmoil. For children trapped in the middle of toxicity, school may be the only place in their lives where they might come up for air. Sadly, for many children, school does not feel like an escape; rather, it reinforces their inferiorities, induces guilt and shame, feels threatening and scary, and/or affirms their beliefs that others will not look for the best in them, will overlook them, or will try to keep them in their places. Educators who understand how adversity impacts children's development, behavior, and learning have a chance to play an essential and unique role in children's healing, equipping them with the skills necessary to feel competent and pursue life paths with less struggle.

SUMMARY

Traditional instructional approaches may not be well aligned with the ways highly stressed children learn, view the world, and process information. Not only do toxic stress and trauma fundamentally reorganize one's physiological systems, they have profound consequences for the ways we think, feel, relate, and learn. As a result, children with messy lives often arrive in the classroom with different sets of resources, assumptions, and prior knowledge, sometimes lacking the skills and perspectives on which much of our typical instructional and pedagogical practices are predicated. Understanding these differences is essential in cultivating an emotionally responsive approach to teaching that provides appropriate learning support. In this chapter, I detailed the implications of messy life circumstances for learning and development and offer suggestions for providing emotionally responsive teaching support.

CHAPTER 7

Cultivating Emotionally Responsive Teaching

In this chapter, I will provide several frameworks and many suggestions for cultivating an emotionally responsive teaching practice. I use the terms *cultivate* and *practice* very intentionally to underscore that emotionally responsive teaching (ERT) is more than a collection of strategies to be implemented. ERT requires us to invest in, tend to, reflect on, and continually refine our efforts to meet children and families where they are and support them in growing into what they might become. Consequently, ERT is as much about who and how we are with children and families as what we do with them. If your head and heart are not in a responsive place, then your environment, relationships, and instruction will not be either. ERT recognizes that this alignment requires time to develop and effort to sustain, and that all days and all relationships with children and their families are not the same. The practice of ERT is not simply about the application of specific strategies in a precise manner.

Yet, while essential, attitudes and perspectives are not enough to meet the learning needs of children, especially those who are struggling to engage or remain present in their learning because of stressors in other parts of their lives. As teachers and counselors, we must understand how to create learning environments that help children feel safe, provide instruction that is effective in building their competency, build relationships with families successfully, and advocate for our students, for example. Successful teachers understand our craft and have invested the time necessary to learn how children learn, filling our teacher tote with many tools of the trade. ERT is about growing in our ability to use as many tools as possible as flexibly as possible to engage children and their families as meaningfully as possible. In this way, ERT is absolutely about instruction and strategies, but these alone are not enough to be successful for children with messy lives. ERT is about creating both the conditions required for growth and providing the support and instruction necessary for it to occur.

In the following section, I will present a framework I devised, the anchors of emotionally responsive teaching, and suggest strategies that might be used as a foundation for your ERT practice. Next, I will discuss how to use knowledge, skills, values, and resources (KSVR) as a framework to help you figure out where to start with a child or family member and support ongoing assessment and planning.

THE ANCHORS OF EMOTIONALLY RESPONSIVE TEACHING

Emotionally responsive teaching is enacted through the cultivation and practice of four main elements, or anchors, in our teaching relationships with children and families. These anchors are:

1. safety
2. connections
3. instruction
4. affirmation

I have chosen to refer to them as anchors because these elements offer stability and confidence in otherwise uncertain situations, providing a firm foundation for our teaching practice. When walking with children or families through the messy circumstances of life, it is easy to become buffeted by the storms they are experiencing, potentially allowing ourselves to get blown off course. Returning to these four anchors, remaining true to them in our teaching practice, will allow us to regain our footing and return to a place of stability and effectiveness in our classrooms. In the following sections, I will define each of the anchors and share suggestions for fostering them in our work with children.

Safety

In ERT, safety has two components: (1) protecting children and their families from situations that are likely to cause danger, risk, or injury, and (2) creating the conditions that allow children and families to experience the feeling of safety in our classroom and during our interactions with them. By definition, trauma and adversity leave us feeling unsafe. Such perceived vulnerability triggers a cascade of reactions that make learning more challenging and connections more threatening. Unless children, families, and teachers are supported in feeling safe in the school environment, learning, growth, and healing cannot occur. Fear is the enemy of learning and relating.

Protection

Typically, when trauma-informed approaches are discussed, the implicit assumption seems to be that children who struggle in our classrooms are presenting with *post*-traumatic stress. However, we should not assume that all traumatic stressors are in the past, as many children and families are certainly experiencing difficult lives in the present. Trauma-informed approaches are meant to help children cope with the consequences of trauma, learning to regain their footing and self-regulate following adversity. However, these strategies are likely to be ineffective, or certainly much less so, when children and families are still fighting or fearing for their lives. If we are doing our best to provide emotionally responsive teaching support and children and families are not able to respond adaptively, it is likely that overwhelming or otherwise messy circumstances are still present in their lives.

Consequently, the first and most important thing that we can do as emotionally responsive teachers—and caring human beings—is to help our children and families find safety and security. If we allow children and families to continue suffering—especially when they know that we can see their struggles—it is unlikely that they will be able to trust us when we say that we care about them, have high expectations for learning, or tell them that they matter. At worst, such indifference normalizes their suffering and affirms that perhaps they are being treated as they deserve. Our inaction confirms a child's internalized belief that they are bad or may not deserve better. So often when I have supported children and adults who are working through painful parts of their pasts, I hear them wonder, "How could no one see what was happening?," or "Why didn't they help me when they knew that I was suffering? How could I believe that anyone cared when no one offered to help me?"

One of the most difficult parts of being a teacher is worrying about children and families who we know are struggling; one of the most uncomfortable challenges is knowing what to do when we are concerned about their safety or well-being. Yet we must be willing to respond when children and families are telling and/or showing us that they are distressed. In my experience, both children and adults are reluctant to share with us their deepest struggles, threats, or injuries, either because they have been threatened into secrecy, are consumed by shame and guilt, or are uncertain about the consequences of sharing. My work has taught me that even young children have a deep sense that secrets should be hidden and that things that make us feel yucky should not be named. Perhaps because many of the bad things that happen to them are not spoken—only being done to them in silence or under threat—means that children do not develop a vocabulary to discuss them. Regardless, across 20 years spent working with children and families who have experienced very difficult things, my sense is that silence, not speaking, is the norm. Thus, when children and families allow us to see that they are unsafe—through their words, actions, or injuries—we must respond.

This is especially true when the violence, abuse, or trauma have become so severe that they may no longer be hidden. While bruises and scars are certainly part of this manifestation, so are behaviors and attitudes. If children cannot do better or feel better despite how hard they or we may try, we must view such actions as potential pleas for help. I sincerely believe that each of us is born with the ability to keep our heads above water. When we cannot, we must first consider what is underneath the surface pulling us down. Sadly, far too often, it feels like the first question that is asked of the child or family who is struggling is, "What is wrong with them?"

Again, across my career, I can think of very few times when children or families were referred for clinical support because of what they have experienced. Rather, individuals are almost always referred for counseling because of how their actions (usually behaviors and attitudes) are affecting others. In other words, people are almost always provided support because of how they make others feel rather than for how they may be feeling themselves. For example, when I ask parents or teachers why they may be seeking counseling for one of their children, they frequently begin by saying, "They are driving me crazy!" Or "I'm so frustrated with the way they are acting." Or "I'm really worried." Notice, these concerns are mainly self-referential. While it is true that we should pay attention to how others are making us feel as a window into what may be happening between us or within them, care is best provided and empathy most clear when it arises from an awareness and primary focus on the other. This focus on what might be going on in the other—the child or family—is at the heart of ERT.

In my experience, violence, abuse, and other forms of chaos escalate until the situation receives the necessary level of support. Sadly, violence often become the language to communicate such struggles. Many years ago, while working as a school-based counselor, Lisa, a mother with physical, mental health, and economic challenges, shared with me that she was struggling to manage her children at home and was feeling overwhelmed about how she would cope with them full-time during the summer. She explained that despite her challenges, she had managed to shelter and feed her children and develop a positive connection with each of them.

As I built a relationship with Lisa, I learned about her own trauma history and the ongoing abuse that she was experiencing in a romantic relationship that she was struggling to escape due to her personal challenges and the economic support she was receiving. Lisa had begun to recognize that she might not be able to protect her children from her partner's abuse any longer, especially when they would be around more often during the summer, and she was concerned that her own mental health and patience were declining. Lisa saw the children begin to struggle even more at school and wished more stability for them than she was able to provide currently, her depression contributing to her own outbursts and inability to flee her present circumstances.

I spent 6 weeks trying to find a summer placement for Lisa's children, tracking down school, camp, and community-based options. Because of the level of support required for the children to be successful (given unique learning and behavioral support needs), each program that I contacted indicated that they did not have adequate resources or structures to support them. To say that I left it on the mat was an understatement. I tried to cash in every cent of goodwill that I had developed with the various programs and agencies in the city. Despite my best efforts, I was unable to find a space for the three oldest children.

On the last day of school, the oldest child entered the building with a fresh bloody nose. He calmy explained that his mother had given it to him just before sending him to school that morning. As I was able to piece it together, Lisa had convened the children in a family meeting of sorts, explained to them that she was trying to keep them safe for the summer, and needed the school to help her. She told her children that she had done everything possible to find them a safe place to be, but no one would listen. Lisa had become convinced that the only way her children would be removed from her home—and the struggles that she knew they would face there—was for her to be viewed as an abusive mother. She told her children she loved them and that she would do everything possible to create a safe place to which they could return, but that she had to get them protected now. Lisa pulled her eldest close, asking the 9-year-old to be "her little man," and explained that what she was about to do was for his safety and to help his younger siblings. Lisa then hit him in the nose with a hairbrush and told him to find Mr. Wright when he arrived at school.

I was devastated when I saw the bloody nose. After consoling the child and asking him what happened, I knew that I would need to inform the school principal and was mandated to report the incident to Child Protective Services immediately. However, since the children were now safe, I convinced our school leader to first allow me to contact Lisa to better understand what had happened.

When Lisa answered the phone, she said, "Well, did you see? Guess you've probably already called the cops. But I didn't know what else to do."

I responded, "I have seen and I am very worried about your children and you. We both know I have to call CPS (Child Protective Services). But I'd much rather you come down here, call the authorities yourself, and share what you did and why. I know you tried to find help another way. I want to support you in receiving it now." I went on to explain my belief that she would be more likely to receive help and support by taking responsibility and explaining how things had become so unmanageable. I also expressed my desire to support Lisa in making changes in her life rather than simply buying into the assumption that she was bad and abusive.

Though I hoped she would, I was still a bit surprised when Lisa decided to take me up on my offer. In 15 minutes, she was at the school placing the phone call. The principal and I joined on speaker. Clearly, it is never acceptable for children to be harmed, and the system responded as the mother expected and the children deserved. The police and CPS arrived at the school within the hour, interviewing the children and removing them from the home. They spent their summer separated from each other and in various foster care placements. Though I tried to maintain contact with each, I only managed to keep track of two as they navigated the system that summer. However, I did stay in touch with Lisa throughout, eventually supporting her as she transitioned into a domestic abuse shelter, received treatment for her mental and physical conditions, and entered a job training program. Over the next year, Lisa transitioned out of the abusive relationship, reunited with her children, and was accepted into a community housing program that provides support for single mothers with young children in the form of mentoring, parent coaching, mental health services, educational advocates for the children, and guaranteed housing. Lisa and her children were reunited and, until I lost contact with them a couple of years later, were beginning to thrive.

This experience complicated the way I have understood and responded to children and families since. It taught me that families (and children and teachers) can do bad things and still be good people. Working with Lisa helped me to appreciate that it is possible to do the best we can and that it not be good enough. Let me write this again: *It is possible to do the best one can AND it not be good enough.* Both can be true simultaneously. In fact, in supporting others who struggle—and ourselves—we must be able to hold both truths simultaneously to maintain the connection necessary to help people change and to provide them with the information and resources needed to do better.

If Lisa had thought I was out to get her and perceived her to be a villain, she might have used me to have her children removed from the home, but would not have allowed me to support her in doing her own work to change the situation. Previously, my experience had been that families reported for abuse or neglect typically left the school and dropped off my radar when I had to report concerns about their children's safety. At this moment when children clearly needed stability and support, perhaps being more vulnerable than ever, they were often spirited away, hidden. Though my intention was always to provide support, I came to be viewed as an enemy by the family and lost my connection with them and their children.

My sense is that Lisa allowed me to provide her with support—and to hold her accountable for her actions—because she knew that I saw what she might become and believed in her despite the horrible thing that she did to her son. More than once, I found the courage to say, "I can see how much you love your children and have come to believe in your strength. However, it also feels like you are stuck and afraid that you cannot make changes. If you are willing to give it a try, I will do everything I can to help. But if you want things to change, you are going to have to be willing to change." Because I had developed a relationship with Lisa, I knew that she loved her children the best she could, even though she was not always able to meet their needs the way she would have liked or the way I would have wished. When I focused solely on what she had done, I, too, felt hopeless in the situation. But when I could remain connected to why she did it—using the only tool she felt she had to receive the support she needed for her children and to avoid things getting worse—I remained hopeful that with appropriate support she would have available and be able to make different types of choices.

It was not easy for me to get there. Given my own personal history, it was challenging to be sympathetic to a parent who seemed unable to create a safe, predictable environment for her children at home, ultimately harming one of them physically. Initially, I could not understand her decision as anything but selfish and weak. However, when I managed to set aside the wounds from my own past and reflect on the action in context—giving myself permission to view what happened through a systems perspective rather than just the lens of character—I began to see the mother's action in more complicated ways. Instead of viewing Lisa only as a perpetrator of child abuse, I could also see that she too had experienced abuse as a child and as an adult. I began to recognize that she had proactively asked for help and that the system was unable or unwilling to respond. I could see that the family was denied services in part because of their level of need and lack of resources, rather than being supported because of them. From this perspective, I could begin to see how the mother felt forced to use the language of violence to receive the help and support that she knew her children (and she) needed. It wasn't until Lisa actually harmed her children—becoming criminal and being willing to risk her relationship with them for their own best interest—that she received the help that she sought earlier. In other words, in this particular case, society had developed a system for intervention but not for prevention. Time and again, I have reflected on this, watching families and children struggle, increasing in intensity, consequences, and harm, until they can no longer be ignored. If we had only taken the first cry for help seriously, how much damage might have been prevented and how many resources focused on growth rather than healing?

Hopefully, you will never face such a situation in your own teaching life. My role in this situation was as the school counselor, which is why I was seeking summer school placements, for example. This would not be a task that I would have taken on while working as a classroom teacher. Yet, while my role and responsibilities in the situation were different, I can certainly imagine being confronted with similar circumstances while I was teaching. I am certain that you will encounter moments when you will become aware of things that are making children and families unsafe. But—how to respond?

First and foremost, though you would be considered a mandated reporter (just as I was in this episode), please know that you do not have to make such decisions alone. Reach out to your school's administrators, social workers, or others in the school building or school system who may be more familiar with the resources that might be activated to support your student and their family. Ask them to help you develop a response plan and to provide support for the family, child, and you. In complicated situations, it is likely that there will need to be multiple levels of support put in place to support the child and family in establishing safety.

As the one on the front line—the one closest to the child and family and the one they entrusted with their pain—the most important thing that you can do is to ensure that others and the system pay attention and take seriously the child and family's distress. It may have taken the child and family all of the emotional energy they could muster to ask for help one time—especially if their earlier pleas had fallen on deaf ears or if they only allowed you to see their suffering in a moment when they could hide it no longer—so taking each request seriously and continuing to advocate are the most important things we can do. As emotionally responsive teachers, we do not have to solve or carry the emotional burden of our children and families' suffering, but we are responsible for providing the support that we can in our classrooms and advocating so that their needs are seen and addressed by others.

Forming partnerships with families, supporting them in advocating for themselves, can be a powerful way to empower them and also support them in developing the skills of self-advocacy. Similarly, when institutional racism, bias, and other forms of stigma may be impacting the way systems view and respond to children and families, standing alongside families that are struggling is a powerful way to leverage our own privilege as educators. Such advocacy and collaborative support may be provided through offering to participate in conferences with school administrators or community agencies as allies, calling on resource providers jointly, or writing letters of support or offering to serve as references for families as they engage various support systems. Or, as in the case of Lisa, support may be provided through our willingness to walk with children and families as they navigate broader systems of support.

Fostering a Sense of Safety in the Classroom. Unfortunately, despite our best efforts to support them, some families and children will continue to struggle. Many challenges are simply beyond our control or outside the scope of our support. Some adversities are impossible to predict or contain: Natural disasters, the loss of relatives, divorce, job loss, mental health issues, to name but a few, are simply part of the human experience. While we would like for the children and families in our classrooms to avoid such struggles, it just is not possible. Sometimes the best and most important thing that we can do is to ensure that our classrooms become a haven in the midst of life's challenges, allowing our children and families to experience safety and security when things may feel less so elsewhere. In so doing, not only will we allow them some respite from their troubles, but we will also be allowing them the space to learn how to navigate calmer waters. If children only build the skills to survive turmoil, they will not know how to thrive when conditions are more stable.

Outside the immediate family, the school setting is the most consistent institution in the lives of children (Cicchetti & Toth, 2005; Garbarino et al., 1992). Children who remain resilient in the midst of adverse experiences tend to enjoy school, even if they may not be exhibiting strong academic performance (Werner, 2000). There is abundant evidence of the protective nature of high-quality school environments for children at risk of failure in academic and social domains (e.g., Areba et al., 2021; Catterall, 1998). Research has found consistently that the effects of stress at home can be mediated by children's positive experiences in the classroom (Wall, 2021; Wright, 2010). Positive school experiences may serve as a protective factor against the effects of challenging life events by increasing children's sense of self-worth and control over their life (Llistosella et al., 2022).

To support children and families in viewing the school and classroom as distinct from the challenging parts of their lives, we must be explicit in naming the physical and psychological boundaries of these environments. In other words, we must be very clear in differentiating "in here" from "out there." The primary purpose of setting such clear boundaries is to reinforce that the classroom exists outside of the challenges they may be experiencing in other parts of their lives. When we are navigating tough moments or overwhelming feelings about one big thing in our life, it is very easy for this to shape the way we perceive and experience the other parts of our life as well. For example, conflict with our significant other in the morning may weigh on us all day, making it difficult to concentrate on work or be as patient with our students. Helping children realize that what's going on at home does not have to shape how they feel or who they get to be with us or in our classrooms is essential if they are to benefit from the environment that we have created to nurture them. Consequently, naming that "in here" things may not be the way they are at home, on the playground, or in other parts of your life may be a powerful invitation for children to explore different ways of engaging the world.

At the same time, we do not want to devalue, judge, or minimize what children are experiencing "out there." The goal of establishing such boundaries is not to create a hierarchy, leading children to believe that inside our classroom is better than their lives outside. Rather, the purpose is to simply model for children that different parts of our lives may have different rules, opportunities, types of relationships, or demands. In reality, what may work for children in our classrooms may actually place them at risk in other parts of their lives. Time and again, children have shared with me their perception that they will get beaten up if they are viewed as being "nerdy" as a defense against my academic expectations of them. I do not doubt that this may be the case for many of them in some parts of their lives. To deny it would be deceptive at best and to place them in the midst of harm at worst. Yet, if children are to engage their academic work meaningfully, they need a way to live with this duality. This is where I find distinguishing "in here" from "out there" most helpful. Rather than dismissing their fears of being nerdy, I usually say something like, "I get that it makes sense not to act nerdy out there. But in here, learning and taking pride in your work is what will let you feel smart and powerful. I want you to know what that feels like. How about you give that a chance when you're in here. I will trust you to decide how to act out there."

By helping children distinguish among the various environments, relationships, and expectations in their lives, we are empowering them to cope differently in different spaces. Not only does this reinforce that we have choices and flexibility in who we become, it also models that we can set boundaries for ourselves—defining who and how we want to be in various parts of our lives versus simply letting one part of our life define us. The idea that we can choose and be in control of our choices is not only empowering, but a powerful antidote to traumatic stress and adversity that lead us to feel out of control and powerless.

Creating a Supportive Learning Environment. Once children have internalized the sense that our classroom is bounded ("in here") and we have communicated our commitment to keep them safe, it is important to create a learning environment that reinforces this sense of security. Children feel competent and are able to succeed when the environment meets their physical, cognitive, emotional, and social needs. When children feel safe and are having their needs met, they are less likely to use challenging behaviors to regulate themselves or the classroom.

Given that children with challenging lives often assume the worst and experience anxiety in moments of uncertainty, ensuring that classrooms are structured and predictable are critical for children to feel safe and remain engaged. Helping children predict what will be happening next and anticipate what will happen throughout the day can go a long way in easing transition and minimizing traumatic responses. Posting an age-appropriate classroom schedule at children's eye level, adhering to the schedule, previewing new people and places before children are introduced to them, and maintaining a predictable routine are all important components of a supportive learning environment. Be sure to announce or count down times before the transition occurs to give children time to ready themselves and also find a stopping point in their present activity. It is important to establish classroom routines early in the year so that children experience clarity and predictability from the beginning of their time in your care. It is best to keep explanations of the routines brief and understandable.

A primary developmental task of early childhood is honing the ability to monitor, understand, and manage one's emotions in stimulating situations, such as those occurring during transitions inside the classroom. However, the impulsive nature of the body's stress response system sometimes makes it difficult for children living with adversity to regulate their emotions (Cloitre et al., 2019). Further, given the complexity of their emotions, children with trauma and other challenging life circumstances often struggle to understand and communicate their feelings (van der Kolk, 2006). This makes it difficult for them to develop an appropriate response to their feelings, and may lead to outbursts, withdrawing, or behaviors that are viewed as inappropriate. Additionally, trauma can negatively impact young children's capacity for creative play, an important way for many children to cope with problems in their everyday lives (Streeck-Fischer & van der Kolk, 2000).

To aid students in overcoming these challenges, educators can offer emotional supports by:

- teaching students how to identify and discuss their feelings by naming and validating emotions in the classroom;
- selecting books that showcase a variety of feelings;
- allowing students time and a safe space to calm down; and
- advocating for additional mental health, special education, and family support services when appropriate.

Managing Challenging Behaviors. Nothing undermines the sense that our classroom is safe and secure faster than a fellow student acting out in anger or when our own emotions feel out of control to students. Such outbursts may trigger anxiety and fear in other students, frustrate them, or distract from their learning. Similarly, when we become overwhelmed or overly emotional, and especially angry, this too can cause students to feel unsafe, threatened, and, especially, can trigger students who have been on the receiving end of other authority figures' anger. Developing effective behavior support strategies that are not based on power, control, and intimidation is essential in cultivating an emotionally responsive classroom.

When it comes to addressing behavioral challenges, prevention is much more effective than intervention. In other words, reducing the likelihood of behavioral triggers is a far better investment of time and energy than waiting until a child is in the midst of an emotional struggle, when it is virtually impossible for them to self-regulate. Working to prevent and/or minimize such behavioral challenges should be a priority for emotionally responsive teachers.

The stress response system may cause traumatized children to respond to various stimuli in unpredictable and unexpected ways. Mistakenly, many believe that traumatized children should be able to control these behaviors and simply make better choices. However, teachers and child-care providers should recognize that aggression, tantrums, clinging, inattention, withdrawing, irritability, and difficulty following directions are symptoms of traumatic stress that are sometimes beyond the child's control. Similarly, some traumatized children come from homes and/or communities where behavior is reinforced through power and violence rather than rules and incentives. Expectations may be inconsistent and not clearly communicated. It is important for these children to learn the difference between rules and discipline.

Teachers can consider the following strategies for creating a consistent and predictable classroom environment:

- Discuss, rehearse, and frequently revisit rules, expectations, and rewards.
- Discuss the rationale for rules, expectations, and rewards.
- Avoid threats, intimidation, and battles for control.
- Reinforce that schools are a nonviolent and safe place for children, both physically and emotionally.
- Integrate safety and conflict resolution skills throughout the curriculum.

Sometimes, despite our best efforts to prevent children from feeling frustrated, angry, or sad, their feelings get the best of them, and they explode in the classroom. It is important for us to understand that these are difficult moments and not bad children. When outbursts are rooted in fear—the manifestation of trauma and fighting, fleeing, or freezing—this is not behavior at all, but rather traumatic responses. In moments such as this, the child is reexperiencing a moment when they felt afraid for their lives, feeling totally out of control. When in the midst of such a struggle, children need support and the opportunity to feel more in control of themselves and the environment. As a result, typical behavior management strategies, which function by exerting more control over the child, usually exacerbate traumatic responses. As we attempt to "manage their behavior," the child will feel more threatened, and usually their behavioral response will become more extreme.

When we see that children are feeling afraid and out of control, we must provide them a safe place to regain their composure. After they have begun to return to the present, we can support them in taking control of their breathing by asking them to take several deep breaths, eventually holding the breath for a count of three and then exhaling to a count of three. As the child becomes more grounded in the present, we can say, "I'm sorry that was so difficult for you and that you had to feel so afraid. Can we talk about what happened?" Notice what the child shares, and together try to figure out what triggered such instability. Often the trigger is something very concrete—like a sound, a way that someone looked at the child, or a feeling they may have had in response to feeling overwhelmed by the new lesson, for example. The more you can understand what is difficult for the child, the better equipped you will be to tailor your efforts to minimize the likelihood of the same trigger moving forward.

Similarly, it is important to support the child in recognizing what it feels like just before the strong reaction occurs—and strategize about some ways they might take care of themselves before having a full-blown traumatic re-enactment. Sometimes children might find putting their head down on their desk for a minute, looking out the window and counting to 10, moving to their "safe space" in the classroom, or beginning to draw to self-soothe. When you notice them starting to engage in such agreed-on behaviors, this is also a sign for you to remember that the child is beginning to feel threatened and you might begin providing support more directly.

However, while much of the challenging behavior that I witness in the classroom may actually be rooted in traumatic responses, this does not explain everything that children do. Children do sometimes misbehave—to test boundaries, communicate frustration, out of boredom, and all the various reasons that any of us do things we should not sometimes. To address and minimize such behavior, it is important to keep in mind that behavior is always meaningful—and in children's behavior and responses we are able to learn something about how they see the world and themselves. The theory of functional behavior (Yoman, 2008) postulates three possible functions for behavior: (1) The child gets something (attention, access to object/activity, etc.), (2) the child avoids or escapes from something, and (3) the child changes the level of stimulation.

Once we understand what a particular behavior means to a child and how the behavior is intended to function, it is possible to support the child and shifting the behavior and/or developing a more prosocial way to cope. Functional behavior theory suggests three main strategies for responding to behavior challenges: (1) change the environment, (2) replace the challenging behavior with appropriate behavior that achieves the same outcome for the child more quickly and with less effort, and (3) ignore the challenging behavior as much as possible. Over time, as children develop more adaptive coping skills and begin to feel safer and more positive, their challenging behaviors tend to dissipate.

Connections

Positive, supportive relationships with teachers and peers are critically important for children navigating trauma and adversity, who frequently display early academic and behavior problems and who have difficulty forming trusting relationships (Kim & Cicchetti, 2010). Particularly for young children who have experienced trauma or other types of challenging circumstances, most negative life events are associated with relational disappointments or betrayals. People they know and love either hurt them or could not keep them safe. Consequently, children with messy lives often struggle to trust relationships with other adults and find it challenging to let their guard down with adults who seek to develop a relationship with them.

However, as children with challenging lives are supported in becoming more trusting, they frequently become more outwardly focused, less temperamental, and demonstrate more positive emotions (Wright, 2010). Soon, they begin to receive more positive attention from their teachers and peers, building additional social–emotional skills through interactions with them (Howes, 2000). As teachers begin to see these children in a different light, they often begin to enjoy them more, gain energy from their love and affection, and feel like they are making a difference. It is the important relationships in their lives that inspire traumatized children and sustain a support network for them—greatly improving the prospects of their futures.

The following strategies can assist teachers' work in building positive relationships with traumatized children:

- Recognize the self-protective and adaptive function of children's behaviors.
- Show interest in children's lives by asking questions and remembering details about their likes, dislikes, families, and activities outside of school.
- Engage regularly in warm, caring, one-on-one interactions.

A critical task of early childhood is mastering the ability to establish positive peer relationships, which are highly predictive of subsequent adjustment during adulthood (Masten & Coatsworth, 1998). Because of their focus on self-preservation, children with difficult lives, especially those who have experienced trauma, tend to be less skilled socially (Darwish et al., 2001) and are rated less well-liked by peers (Shaffer et al., 2009). Frequently, these children demonstrate challenges in understanding social situations, assume that other children are "out to get them" (Raine et al., 2006), and experience higher rates of behavior problems and aggression (Jaffee et al., 2002).

Teachers can support traumatized children's peer relationships by:

- offering structured opportunities for both group and individual play;
- creating quiet spaces for children to "take a break" throughout the day;

- modeling and role-playing strategies for joining in play and resolving conflicts; and
- recognizing and naming moments of positive social interaction.

These strategies can help honor children who may be afraid to trust or are overwhelmed by feelings of closeness, while allowing them opportunities to practice connecting with others, and space for respect and interdependence to emerge.

Fostering a Positive Social Climate. These caring connections may be greatly enhanced or impeded by the social climate of our classroom. The social climate is the general atmosphere of our classroom, including the customs, norms, and attitudes that prevail. For example, does the classroom feel warm and supportive or rigid and competitive? Are students motivated through support and encouragement or by threats and punishment? How it "feels" to be in our classroom and what type of behaviors and attitudes are rewarded profoundly influence how children see us, themselves, and how they interact with each other.

When considering the social climate of your classroom, it may be more accurate to think about "social climates." I use the plural form to indicate that it is possible that different children have radically different experiences of the classroom environment, each other, and you. While some children may be celebrated and supported in the classroom, others may feel marginalized or disregarded. We must be vigilant in ensuring that all children are treated similarly and valued equally; otherwise we may be inadvertently reinforcing some of the very same social dynamics that are harming children and families outside of school.

Children emulate the attitudes of teachers and other adults and are quick to pick up on which children we may favor or dislike. When we inadvertently establish a social hierarchy in our classroom, children will compete with each other for our favor, viewing each other as competition rather than as friends and resources. One way to tune into the possibility that you may be communicating such implicit bias is to notice if certain children in the classroom are becoming scapegoats or if children begin tattling on certain individuals in order to gain your favor. If you notice such dynamics emerging, it is important that you reflect on your actions and be proactive in reframing the targeted child as valued and as a resource in your classroom. As I have said elsewhere in this book, the children who need our support the most are often the most difficult to like. And it is even harder for the difficult child to experience care when it seems that others, including the teacher, do not like them. Pulling out of this dynamic—finding a way to value and respect the child—is critical for them to take academic and other positive risks in the classroom.

There are many ways to go about building a positive social climate in your classroom; however, there are some characteristics that most positive environments have in common:

- Incentives encourage children to work toward something and provide a positive focus for their efforts.
- Positive reinforcement, particularly in the form of verbal praise and encouragement, is essential in motivating students to persist in the midst of challenges.
- Inviting student feedback, allowing them to express preferences, and asking for their opinions about classroom activities communicate that their opinions are valued.
- Allowing students to work collaboratively and teaching them to provide supportive, constructive feedback to each other foster interdependence and builds connections within the classroom.
- As appropriate, allowing children to move freely around the classroom and to make choices about their learning activities fosters agency and trust, at the same time allowing them to feel more in control of their bodies.
- Positive environments also invite joy and appreciate humor— children are allowed to express delight and teachers engage with them in shared laughter. There is no better medicine for the human spirit than joy!

Instruction

There is no better way for children to feel powerful and in control of their life than learning. In order for them to feel hopeful about the future and positive about themselves, they must feel capable and competent. Especially for children with messy lives, learning and academic success can serve as powerful antidotes to chaos—providing a productive focus in the midst of adversity and allowing them to feel some mastery and goodness in the midst of situations that are less stable.

One of the most helpful insights that I have gleaned during my career is that children will almost always prefer to be viewed as "mean" rather than "stupid." Time and again, I have watched children act out, shut down, or misbehave when they begin to struggle academically. As I have shared this observation with children and reflected on their responses, my understanding is that behavior is viewed by them as being more external, something one does rather than something one is. Children seem to better tolerate being judged for how they act, which somehow cuts less deep than being seen as inadequate or deficient, which is how children experience feeling "stupid." When we struggle to learn, when teachers present information that we cannot quite grasp, we internalize the sense that we cannot understand, that we don't quite get it.

Likewise, when children are distracted by trauma and adversity, it can be difficult to focus on learning, leading them to feel like they've missed something or cannot understand what is being presented. This internalized sense of being deficient seems to reinforce the sense of inner badness that children often develop in response to trauma and other negative life circumstances. Consequently, learning can become very fraught—with children struggling to learn often feeling helpless and hopeless, ultimately presenting with trauma-like responses in the classroom—fighting, freezing, or fleeing learning activities. Likewise, children who have been traumatized may struggle to learn, which exacerbates their traumatic symptoms. As a result, effective instruction and appropriate instructional support are essential aspects of ERT.

Learning requires attention, organization, comprehension, memory, the ability to produce work, engagement in learning, and trust. Not surprisingly, traumatic experiences have the potential to negatively impact each of these important skills by undermining language and vocabulary skills and compromising the ability to complete learning tasks, making it difficult to organize and remember new information. Because traumatic circumstances are often unpredictable, traumatized children sometimes have difficulty understanding cause and effect relationships, recognizing sequences, and making predictions (Burt et al., 2008). The following strategies can support academic development for traumatized children:

- Emphasize causal and sequential relationships in classroom activities.
- Divide tasks and instruction into parts to help students feel less overwhelmed.
- Present information in multiple ways in order to reduce the likelihood of children missing important pieces of information and lessen the anxiety they experience when uncertain of classroom expectations.
- Because traumatized children often struggle to think abstractly, provide concrete examples, and use visual cues, physical movement,

and recall activities during instruction to help them stay focused and engaged.

- Utilize graphic organizers and physical manipulatives in academic lessons to help children organize new information.
- Create opportunities for children to repeat and rehearse instructions.
- Offer ongoing support and encouragement to support children in staying on task.

Please revisit Chapter 4 for a more detailed discussion of trauma and learning and for many additional suggestions for implementing emotionally responsive instructional strategies.

Affirmation

For children growing up in the midst of adversity and chaos, it is very easy to feel lost in the storms of their lives—invisible, deprioritized, or disregarded. Similarly, children who identify as victims of violence may work to fade into the background of life, seeking to avoid being caught in the crossfire of another's anger. It is difficult to feel seen, heard, understood, and valued when one is struggling for stability and security. As a result, children with difficult lives are often challenged to feel important and positive about themselves. It is this wound that persists long after survivors of challenging lives have regained safety, developed friendships and connections, and begun to feel competent. It is possible to sustain each of these dimensions and still believe that one is lucky to feel safe, to have friends, or be smart. A life built on a foundation of luck never feels quite stable, as those of us who have experienced life fall apart know that luck can change on a whim.

Supporting children in feeling understood and celebrated—valued because of who they are—is essential in allowing them to heal and feel hopeful about who they might become. It is only when one begins to trust that they matter and have value simply because they exist that the wounds of trauma transform into evidence of strength rather than reminders of weakness.

Seeing, understanding, and celebrating children for who they are and who they are trying to become is at the heart of such affirmation.

Seen, Heard, and Celebrated. My definition of affirmation is fostering in others the sense that they have been seen for who they truly are, that what they have been saying has been truly understood, and that they are being celebrated for who they truly are. Authenticity, the sense that one is being true to oneself, is an important aspect of positive identity. If children feel insecure, worried, or that they are hiding something about themselves, it is challenging for them to assume a positive identity. In being concerned that others would not like them if they knew the "real" me, even a child who is well liked, engaged, and seemingly together may struggle to feel positive about who they are. For this reason, it is essential that children be allowed to be themselves in our classrooms.

Instead of defining children by their experiences, social location, risk factors, or learning outcomes, we seek to understand their strengths, resources, and who they are and who they are trying to become. In ERT, individual identity is prioritized and understood to be influenced by multiple social identities. In other words, in ERT, the goal is to understand how each individual child wishes to be seen and understood. When thinking about who a child is, our understanding would begin with the child's hopes, fears, personality, preferences, knowledge, abilities, resources, values, and so on. In order to feel affirmed, children must feel known as an individual and celebrated for what is particular about them.

This framing is not meant to be at odds with other ways of conceptualizing who children are, such as through the lens of social identity. However, in ERT, these lenses are used by teachers as a way to understand how a child may be making sense of themselves and how the world may be imposing expectations and bias on them. For example, culturally responsive pedagogy (Ladson-Billings, 2014) is an approach to teaching that children's cultural strengths are identified and nurtured to promote their achievement and a sense of well-being about their cultural place in the world. In ERT, culture would be a lens through which children are viewed, and culturally responsive approaches would be incorporated into our instructional pedagogy. However, in ERT, culture would not be the only or primary lens through which the child's perspective or identity is considered. ERT would encourage educators to cultivate as many lenses as possible—cultural, gender, socioeconomic class, sexual orientation and identity, religion, and so on—through which children and families might be seen and heard. This knowledge should absolutely inform and space be made for these various social identities in our classrooms. However, in ERT, the ultimate aim of such perspectives is to help us see the individual child more clearly. If we cannot understand the child as a product of these various identities, the child will not feel seen, valued, and celebrated. Similarly, if we only view the child as the product of their social locations, then the child will also feel unseen, undervalued, and not affirmed.

To support children in feeling affirmed, it is important to know and celebrate their individual interests. Providing opportunities for children to explore and share these interests in the classroom is empowering and affirming. Show-and-tell, talent shows, art projects, and sharing stories are all ways to invite children's unique abilities into the classroom and to showcase them. Fundamentally, we should seek out opportunities for individual children to shine.

Another way to support children in feeling valued is to allow them a special "job" in the classroom. Allowing them to have jobs that they appreciate and that are valued by others can be powerful. Especially for children who are sometimes viewed as challenges in the classroom or who require a great deal of support in the classroom, jobs can be a great way for them to view themselves and to be viewed by others as a resource. Likewise, it is important that this job is not a reward or an incentive. Regardless of how the child has acted during the rest of the day, they should be allowed and expected to complete their job. This affirms that we will still count on them even when they struggle and allows them to repair any damage that they may have caused previously. Children should not have to earn the right to feel like they are contributing in meaningful ways; this should be presented as an expectation and opportunity.

Likewise, if a child has become invested in a particular job, and it is clearly meeting an important self-esteem need, they should not be required to give up or rotate jobs. However, if another child would really like to do the job, asking the current jobholder if they would be willing to share might be an opportunity to forge a collaboration. However, such an arrangement should not be forced. Remember, the purpose of the job is to help the child feel special, productive, and as if they are contributing something of value to the classroom community. From the child's perspective, such meaningful work may have come to be viewed as "their purpose" and a reason for making it to school each day, convinced that others are counting on them. To force the child to relinquish a responsibility that is making them feel so important could undermine everything else the job has afforded them. In my experience, as children come to trust their value and find other ways to feel successful in the classroom, they may defend the job less strenuously and be more willing to share responsibilities or consider another, expanded role.

In reading this section, I hope you have noticed that children should be affirmed both for what they do and who they are. They should feel that we are excited when they walk in the class just because we care about them. One of my favorite parts of teaching is greeting children and families in the morning. In addition to asking how they are doing as a way to assess their frame of mind, I like to find an individual quality to celebrate. For example, I might say, "How's my amazing artist today?" Or "How is my number one Pokémon card collector?" This is a quick way to affirm that I know you, I see you, I'm glad that you are here and bringing what is special with you to our classroom. Likewise, we should be intentional about praising children for actions and behaviors that we would like to encourage and reinforce.

Praise and Acknowledgment. For children who have been told or made to feel bad far too many times, praise is an important antidote to these negative messages. When praising children, it is important to praise specific actions and behaviors. For example, you might say, "You did a good job attempting every question on your assignment," or "I noticed that you took a positive risk by raising your hand to share during circle time." Please note that these are examples of specific recognition or acknowledgment of an important accomplishment. This is what counts when offering praise! Otherwise, children who feel bad about themselves may simply not pay attention to any positive thing that is directed at them, or they may dismiss general praise as perfunctory. When we focus specifically on something that a child does, it is not just praise, but also affirmation that "I see what you have done and I appreciate what it means for you."

Research has found that a ratio of 4:1 praise to reprimands is necessary in order to ensure an affirmative classroom environment (Fredrickson & Losada, 2005). Likewise, evidence suggests that students should hear approximately six praise statements every 15 minutes in order to feel encouraged and persistent. Praise should be given immediately, or as soon as possible after noticing the requested behavior, in order to provide immediate reinforcement. The rate of praise may be increased or decreased in order to maintain the desired behavior. For children who are really struggling to stay on task or navigate a tough situation, it may be necessary to remind them almost constantly, "You got this! Keep going! I'm here to help and believe in you!" However, as children achieve more success and begin to internalize that they can do challenging things, they will require less direct praise to keep trying and will better tolerate frustration.

I realize that not everyone agrees about praise, recognizing the concern by some educators that praise undermines intrinsic motivation. In other words, if children do something because it pleases someone else, the concern is that they may be less likely to do something because it is the right thing to do or because it is important to them. I can also appreciate the structural critique that children should not be taught to blindly seek the approval of those with power over them.

However, in my experience, when thinking about children who have been traumatized or who have been actively disempowered—children who have lost their self-confidence or been told terrible things about themselves—encouragement, praise, and affirmation are needed to counterbalance the negative messages that are constantly looping in the minds. Time and again, I have witnessed children try something because I think they can do it—long before they would ever have thought it possible for themselves. In a world that has often reminded them how vulnerable they are, it seems unrealistic to think that children would arrive in our classrooms automatically believing in their capacity for success. In my work, I have found praise to be essential in helping children feel better about themselves. Similarly, praise makes explicit what I am noticing about the child—and a way to see that I am looking for the best in them. This, too, is a challenge to the assumptions of many traumatized children that others are out to get them.

Affirmation in Challenging Moments. Children with difficult lives—and especially those with minoritized identities—are prone to have experienced much rejection and disappointment, often being made to feel less than others. Consequently, many children come to expect rejection and resist our efforts to get close to them to avoid such pain or to assert some control over the ability of others to hurt them. Children who have come to view the world in this way are especially sensitive to our responses, assuming that we may hurt or turn against them at any moment.

In order to overcome these expectations and to experience deep care and regard, children must feel that we are always working to pull them closer rather than hoping they might move further away. This is not always easy! Believe me, I understand! Seeing the best in a child who is doing everything possible to convince us that they are bad—or who may actually be calling out our worst qualities and insecurities—is often easier said than done. But it is the work that must be done. If children only feel accepted when they are perfect—engaged, calm, and compliant—then they will not internalize unconditional acceptance and positive regard.

The moments when children struggle the most—when they expect us to walk away and we do not—are our best chances to communicate our care and acceptance. This is why we should strive to keep our children in the classrooms when they are having a hard time or be very careful about any action that would seem like we are rejecting them for "being bad." Conventional wisdom has dictated that children should be sent out of the room, separated from the group, suspended, or expelled for misbehavior. However, this response says to the child, "You are not welcome here when you struggle," or "I cannot handle you or will not be with you in your difficult moments." For the child who already feels alone or damaged by others, such messages only confirm their suspicions about the world and themselves. Separately, if we keep sending away the children who most need the structure and support of the classroom, where will they have an opportunity to learn to self-regulate and lean on school for support?

Rather than sending children away, we should ask, "How can I help you be here?" When children are struggling, perhaps even shredding the room, it is okay to say, "Enough. You cannot hurt our room or make it feel unsafe." But we must also say, "I can see you are having a hard time and I am here to help you. You are not alone and let's get through this together." Perhaps the child will need to seek out a quiet corner or run to a favorite desk or computer in the classroom to save face and calm down. This is fine and what any of us might do in a moment of anger, embarrassment, or frustration. What is important is that the child is able to return to safety while remaining connected to us rather than feeling that they must flee from someone who is working to care for them.

Often, when I speak about finding ways to help children stay in our room, I will be asked what about the safety of the other children in the room or the impact of such outbursts on them? Obviously, we should never place any students in our classroom in harm's way. If they are being threatened or hurt by another student, we must be unequivocal in protecting them, and this cannot be tolerated under any circumstances. In such dire circumstances, it would be important to separate the children until tempers subside, and we must be very clear in indicating that we will not tolerate any physical or emotional threats in the classroom. In my experience, it is often more productive and easier to ask the children who are not upset to change their location in the classroom—moving away from the anger.

When the children are calmer, we can talk about what happened as a community. If the student in crisis is willing and able, they might be invited to share how they were feeling at the time. Likewise, other students may then have an opportunity to share how they felt when they saw their peer having such a hard time. (In my experience, these responses are often incredibly attuned—with children expressing frustration, fear, and compassion in equal amounts.) However, we must be careful to ensure that the comments don't become attacks. I encourage children to begin their comments with "I" statements. For example, rather than saying, "He was a bad kid," I would invite a child to say, "I felt afraid when he got angry." After everyone has had a chance to share, I might ask, "If we could turn back time and redo, does anyone have ideas for how we might have changed what happened?"

This allows children, and especially the child who struggled, to hear suggestions from peers about other ways they might have responded—broadening their repertoire and understanding of the situation and each other.

In ending the conversation, I ask if anyone would like to apologize, take responsibility, or make reparations to the group. This is an invitation and not an expectation, as it can be very difficult for a student who has been vulnerable to let their guard down even further. However, the questions communicate the expectation and model a path forward. I end the circle by saying, "I'm sorry that all of us have had to experience something difficult. It can be scary to feel so out of control. We all have hard times, and I'm glad that we can come together to understand and accept each other after difficult moments." Sometimes it is necessary to follow up this conversation privately with students who may have been most implicated in or affected by what happened. In these conversations, I coach students on what I hoped they heard from their peers and share any expectations or suggestions about how I would expect things to be different in the future.

This approach to navigating difficult moments in the classroom is meant to reinforce several important values and understandings. First, this "community approach to conflict" underscores that we rise and fall together and that we should support each other in hard times. For the child who expects disappointment and rejection, this approach communicates, "I am not giving up on you and that you matter here. I see your pain and I'm willing to support you in your struggle." Allowing children to voice their concerns and the negative impacts of difficult moments also indicates that our actions have consequences for others and that it is acceptable to share with others when they harm us. It is important to note that these conversations are not meant to facilitate shame and guilt, as these will only reinforce the negative sense of self that led to the outburst initially and lead the child to feel further disconnected from others. Inviting children to share their suggestions for how things might be handled differently in the future invites them to view each other as resources and reminds them that they have knowledge and skills to support them in moving through challenges.

I can imagine that some readers will find this approach unsatisfying. When people have expressed such concerns with me previously, it is often because they feel that the child who upsets the balance of the classroom "gets away with bad behavior." Often in discussions such as this, the other person feels strongly that children need consequences when they do bad things. I think of this perspective as seeking justice.

While I am not opposed to justice, I am not convinced that searching for justice is the best way to support a child who is likely well acquainted with the inequities of life. In my experience, children struggle in our class-rooms because they do not feel safe, have unmet needs, do not know how to respond differently, or because we or others may have led them to feel disrespected. Punishing a child for feeling angry may make us feel better, but in my experience, it only makes the child angrier, underscoring their outlook about the world and the intentions of others. Likewise, when children feel afraid or angry, it is usually care and safety that help them feel less so.

In other words, I think we help children change their behavioral responses to our classrooms by helping them feel safer, more cared for, and smarter. While punishing them may eventually lead them to be more silent or compliant, this does not necessarily mean that they feel better about themselves or the world. For the emotionally responsive teacher, our first priority must always be ad-dressing the child's unmet needs, helping them to feel valued and appreciated. In the long run, this will always yield the greatest benefit for the child and society.

I am writing this just days after a school shooting in the small community of Uvalde, Texas. Like most of us, I have been consumed with the tragedy—feeling brokenhearted for the children, teachers, families, and all impacted by the tragedy. I have also been reflecting on how this happened, how a young man could cause so much pain. As I've listened to descriptions of the perpe-trator, he is usually cast as the angry outcast—and surely, he was. One can only imagine what he must have experienced to cause him such inner turmoil and to become so fluent in the language of violence and the actions of hate.

Though it is uncomfortable to extend compassion and understanding to someone who did something so awful, I feel we must do so in order to figure out how to prevent such tragedy repeating itself. Peers and former teachers seemed to recognize his potential for violence over many years, indicating that he became increasingly isolated and dark. He was absent from school for most of his final year. Did anyone reach out to say that he was missed? While only the perpetrator can be responsible for what happened, I cannot help but think that maybe things would have gone differently if this young man had been able to establish a positive connection earlier in his life, one that had been nurtured and sustained as he traveled through the school system.

When I imagine what the shooter's life must have been like, I feel confident that as a student and as a child, he was punished, shamed, and excluded. What is less certain is how he might have been loved, valued, respected, and supported. We will never know if and how this might have made a difference in Uvalde—but I am convinced that responding to the emotional needs of this young man years before hate filled his core, shifting his view of himself and the world, would likely have changed the story. My experience tells me that this young man would not have destroyed a school and the innocence of so many childhoods if school had been a haven for him and his own innocence had been protected.

Becoming Anchored. These anchors are mutually reinforcing, meaning that change in one anchor is likely to foster change in each of the others. For example, as we strengthen our relationship with a student, they are likely to feel more safe, affirmed, and likely to engage our instruction. Likewise, if we take a step back in one area, the others are likely to be impacted as well. Again, if we fail to support a child in feeling competent or reinforce their belief that they are not smart through ineffective instructional practices, they are also less likely to feel affirmed, safe, or connected to us in our classroom. It is important to keep in mind that these are not direct relationships, such that a change in one anchor creates exactly the same change in the others. For example, it is possible for children to feel safe and connected even if they are struggling to learn. Yet, unless we find a way to help the child learn, they will likely feel bad about themselves or us over time, and our classroom will eventually be experienced by them as threatening. Ultimately, each anchor must be established if children in our classrooms are to become secure, well adjusted, and competent.

It is through this mutual reinforcement that these anchors become more firmly embedded, or rooted, in children's self-understanding and emotions over time. For example, as children begin to feel affirmed in our classrooms, they will also experience more safety and security. This will empower them to take more academic risks and to be more open to vulnerability in relationships with others. Experiencing more connection with others will allow them to broaden their perspective-taking skills and improve their communication abilities, which will allow them to trust themselves more (feeling safer) and also to feel more affirmed. This improved self-esteem will likely manifest through engaged learning, if the child is allowed appropriate learning opportunities. Thus, tending to each of these four anchors iteratively and over time will allow children to return to a place of stability and growth in their school lives. As school becomes a place where they feel anchored, it will provide a protective harbor for them in the midst of life's storms. When working with children or families, we should be aware of the anchors that are both least and most established, tailoring our approach accordingly.

Knowledge, Skills, Values, and Resources (KSVR)

In the same way that these anchors are mutually reinforcing, ERT posits that in order for individuals (children, parents, teachers, and counselors, e.g.) to accomplish any new task or assume a new perspective or aspect of their identity, they must know about and understand the new thing (knowledge), possess the skills necessary to implement or accomplish the task (skills), value what they are being asked to do or to view the change as consistent with their values (values/valuing), and possess the resources and support necessary to sustain the change (resources). I refer to these elements—knowledge, skills, values, and resources—collectively as KSVR. In this section, I will define each element of KSVR, present KSVR as a framework for support, and discuss how to use these developmental domains as the basis for developing a tailored support plan for individuals.

- **Knowledge** is the theoretical or practical understanding of a subject, and may be acquired through experience or education. In KSVR, knowledge refers to how we think about the thing that we are trying to do.
- **Skills** are the ability to use one's knowledge effectively in execution or performance. In KSVR, skills refer to how well one can "do" the thing that is being attempted, and what can be learned or strengthened in order to master the new developmental goal.
- **Value/Valuing** is the regard that something is held to deserve, including one's judgment of what is important in life. In KSVR, we focus both on the regard in which something is held by the individual and also the extent to which a particular value is shared among children, teachers, families, schools, and communities.
- **Resources** refer to the support, supplies, materials, and other assets that may be drawn on to accomplish the developmental goal and to function effectively. In KSVR, resources are the "things" that we have or need to implement the developmental goal.

However, it is not enough to simply possess knowledge, skills, values, and resources. Individuals must be able to integrate these elements in order to accomplish the new developmental task. In this way, development or growth in any developmental domain may be conceptualized as integrating KSVR in increasing complexity over time. In other words, when teaching or supporting children in developing any new capacity—learning to read, strengthening friendship skills, or beginning a hobby, for example—our support should be focused on ensuring that they have the requisite knowledge, skills, abilities, and resources to be successful, and that they receive instruction in and opportunities to practice how to integrate them to accomplish the desired goal.

KSVR—A Framework for Support and a Place to Start

Throughout this book, I have presented ERT as a paradigm and an ethic, shared research and strategies, indicated anchors for cultivating one practice of ERT, and discussed the importance of reframing the way we think about children and families and our work as teachers. I have attempted to expand the way you conceptualize your work, yourself, trauma-informed practices, and the ways we support children and families. I hope that you are excited about these possibilities, and I also imagine that you might be feeling quite overwhelmed at this point. Indeed, a reasonable question might be, "How do I pull it all together, for myself and in a moment with a child or family member?" KSVR is where I always begin with attempting to translate ERT into practice.

When beginning any piece of work with another person—working toward a behavioral change, developing a relationship, or planning instruction—I start by asking:

- What does this person know, and what do they need to know?
- What can they do, and what must they learn to do?
- What do they value, and what am I asking them to value?
- What do they have to accomplish this task, and what do they need?

In planning the path forward, I work to build on where the person is beginning in each KSVR domain and provide them with the KSVR necessary to accomplish the new goal.

For example, recently I was asked to help a 1st-grader, Jonathan, who was struggling with peer relationships at school. During my initial conversation with his teacher, Jonathan was described as being very guarded and selfish with his peers, sometimes lashing out and being unwilling to share. Jonathan's teacher indicated her concern that he was becoming increasingly isolated in the classroom. In talking with Jonathan, his family, and his teacher, I found that he was really good at interacting with his younger brother and sister and was invested in making friends at school. In teasing these observations apart in greater detail, I figured out that Jonathan **knows** how to play with children who are younger than him and who prefer to follow his lead and are more tolerant of unilateral actions. In turn, in order to build friendships with peers his own age, Jonathan **needs to build knowledge** around cooperative play and about the importance of reciprocity in peer interactions. With regard to **skills**, Jonathan is good at negotiating a shared play theme and going with the flow in terms of story line, and needs to **build skills** at taking turns and sharing toys. It is clear that Jonathan values making friends, but is having a hard time **trusting/believing** that peers will reciprocate. In terms of **resources**, Jonathan has peers in his class who are excited to be his friend, and he needs supported opportunities to practice with them. As illustrated in this example, KSVR is helpful in focusing on children's resources and needs, guiding the development of a plan for supporting their growth and development.

KSVR is also a helpful tool to guide our own reflection and personal development. When I am personally overwhelmed by a situation or trying to figure out a path forward, I often return to KSVR to help orient to the situation. Reminding myself what I know and need to know, what I can do and what I need to learn, what I care about and how my values might be in conflict with the new demand, and getting clear about what I have to work with and what I need to ask for to be successful almost always helps me get clarity about where I stand and what should be my next steps. KSVR may also be helpful in figuring out where we may be stuck or why we may be struggling on a particular path. For example, sometimes when I am struggling to make progress on a project, I find that while I might have the knowledge, resources, and skills required to do the new thing, maybe I am struggling to see the value in it. Or sometimes I value something so much that I have failed to realize that I might need more knowledge, skills, or resources to be successful. Regardless, KSVR often provides a helpful framework for reflection and planning. It is the frame that I always use first in planning for the growth of children, families, and myself.

In this chapter, I have offered several frameworks and many suggestions for cultivating your emotionally responsive teaching practice. Throughout this book, we have focused primarily on how ERT benefits children and their families. However, in the following, and final chapter, I will explore what is in it for us, as teachers and student support professionals. I realize that this work of ERT may seem overwhelming and require a great deal of our emotional energy. However, the potential rewards are equally great. I will also discuss the importance of responding to our own emotional and physical well-being and suggest strategies for sustaining ourselves as we walk through difficult moments with others.

SUMMARY

While an ethic of emotionally responsive teaching is as much about how we think about and who we are with children and families as what we do with them, the practice of emotional responsiveness does require the cultivation of strategies and approaches. In this way, ERT is about growing in our ability to use as many tools as possible as flexibly as possible to engage children and their families as meaningfully as possible. Emotionally responsive teachers understand that teaching is a craft and invest the time necessary to understand how children learn and develop a large toolbox of strategies that might be drawn from to support children's growth.

In this chapter, I provided two frameworks and many suggestions for implementing emotionally responsive practices in one's classroom. Emotionally responsive teaching is enacted through the cultivation of four main anchors in our relationships with children and families: safety, connections, instruction, and affirmation. These anchors are mutually reinforcing, meaning that change in one anchor is likely to foster change in each of the others. For example, as we strengthen our relationship with a student, they are likely to feel more safe, affirmed, and likely to engage our instruction. KSVR (knowledge, skills, values, and resources) is a framework for ongoing assessment and planning. In the same way that the anchors of ERT are mutually reinforcing, ERT posits that in order for individuals (children, parents, teachers, and counselors, e.g.) to accomplish any new task or assume a new perspective or aspect of their identity, they must know about and understand the new thing (knowledge), possess the skills necessary to implement or accomplish the task (skills), value what they being asked to do or to view the change as consistent with their values (values/valuing), and possess the resources and support necessary to sustain the change (resources).

CHAPTER 8

The Courage to Care

Almost 2 decades as an early childhood researcher, teacher, and mental health counselor have underscored for me that many children and families feel unseen or misunderstood at school and that many well-intentioned educators feel unprepared and under-supported to respond to the needs of children and families with challenging lives. It is this dual awareness that has informed my perspective in this book. Throughout, I have attempted to support you in broadening your perspective on the resilience of children, families, and teachers by reconceptualizing the possibilities and challenges of educating children with messy lives through emotionally responsive teaching. Such an approach is critically important because the necessity and potential consequences for children, families, and teachers are great— especially in this moment when teaching and learning are occurring against a backdrop of pandemic, war, gun violence, environmental threat, and po- larized politics. Now more than ever, we must find ways to help our class- rooms feel safe, support children and families in building connections across lines of difference, and prepare children to create a world that is more car- ing, sustainable, and just.

We must also be able to sustain ourselves, remaining hopeful, grounded, and healthy even while walking with children and families through chal- lenging times. It is pointless to work for the well-being of others if we can- not be well ourselves. Similarly, we might do amazing things in support of the families and children that we serve, but the cost is too great if it comes at the expense of our own children, families, and self. Learning to find and maintain such balance in the midst of chaos and instability is no easy task, and there will certainly be moments when we lose our equilibrium.

There have certainly been times in my career when I decided that it was worth giving more than 100% or invested a bit more energy than I really had to give in support of a student or family. Sometimes people just need a little extra—or a lot extra—to make it to where they are trying to get. Especially for children who have not been given enough support, love, or resources, sometimes it takes one or a few people giving extra to help close the gap. When I have been able, I have often tried. Yet these moments must be the exceptions and not the norms. We cannot help others see the best in themselves if we are unable to see the best in ourselves and preserve our own sense of stability, hope, health, and well-being.

In the same way that we must be mindful of caring for ourselves, it is important to remember that children and families will also be doing what they think best for themselves. Some of the most frustrating experiences of my teaching life occurred when I did not understand or agree with their choices. These moments taught me that when children and families are forced to choose between knowledge, skills, values, and resources that keep them safe and/or connected to those they love and others who may threaten these connections, they will most always choose safety and connection. In other words, children and families typically do what is required for survival in their immediate lives and to remain connected to those they know and love, even if these choices jeopardize their well-being and future prospects. Consequently, schools and teachers must not view ourselves as competing with children and family's lives. Rather than devaluing the parts of their lives children and families bring into our classrooms, we should find a way to honor and acknowledge them as valuable in some other part, building on them whenever possible to foster children's growth at school. Our failure to do so will likely induce shame and inferiority and push children and families further away from embracing schools as safe and emotionally protective. A child or family may not be or have all that we wish, but what they do have is the world to them—and in this is the fertile ground of hope. Unless we plant our seeds in a place where they might grow, our own dreams for the child will wither and die.

In this closing chapter, I will further discuss the importance of cultivating an emotionally responsive approach to teaching and present some final thoughts on deepening one's emotionally responsive teaching praxis. I will also discuss vicarious trauma and burnout as possible consequences of supporting children with messy lives and suggest strategies for self-care and continued personal growth.

ALL CHILDREN BENEFIT FROM EMOTIONALLY RESPONSIVE TEACHING

Though initially conceptualized to facilitate restorative learning experiences for children developing in the midst of adversity and other challenging life circumstances, the ERT approach is beneficial to all students. Occasionally, educators and administrators will ask me if trauma-informed approaches impede the learning of children who have not experienced trauma or high levels of adversity. Their concerns are rooted in the observation that some academic interventions—that are highly structured or may not allow students to work at different paces—actually hold back children who may not be struggling, limiting their learning opportunities. However, there is nothing in the ERT approach that will harm children who have not experienced trauma or adversity.

All children perform better academically and feel better about themselves when we look for the best in them and tend to their emotional well-being. While children who benefit from high levels of self-esteem and support outside of the classroom may "need" ERT less in order to engage the curriculum, make friends, or remain persistent, such attunement will reinforce and extend their personal resources. Similarly, classrooms that are not emotionally responsive may undermine the strengths and positive self-identity that children have developed elsewhere. I have sometimes watched as schools and classrooms become the greatest source of adversity in children's lives, causing otherwise happy, well-adjusted children to experience anxiety and self-doubt. Learning difficulties, bullying, shaming, social isolation, a competitive environment, negative relationships with teachers, and other challenges all undermine the strengths the children have developed to cope with life's difficulties. ERT is a powerful antidote to each of these challenges.

In this way, rather than being viewed as barriers to our success as teachers or drains on our emotional energy, children with challenging lives may be viewed as sentries for the well-being of everyone else in our classroom. In the same way that miners carried canaries into the coal mines to warn them of odorless gas leaks (their small lungs are more sensitive to the deadly consequences), children who have experienced trauma are more sensitive to the climate and consistency of our classrooms. Thus, what is required to make our classrooms safer and more productive for these children will result in *all* children feeling more supported, safe, and celebrated. Similarly, ERT provides models for all children in learning how to interact with others more respectfully and sensitively. Once again, children often learn much more from what we do and how we are with them than from anything that we might say.

Balancing Care and Instruction

The anchors of emotionally responsive teaching are meant to support you in balancing the sometimes competing demands of providing both academic and emotional support to children and their families. In a recent study (Wright, 2022) focused on the teachers of young children experiencing homelessness, I found that how teachers balance academic expectations and emotional support was the major contributor to how they perceived their students and evaluated themselves. Teachers holding low academic expectations for their students and who either felt that it was not their job to meet the support needs of students or felt ineffective in doing so described feeling ambivalent about their jobs and the children they were teaching. Many of these teachers left the teaching profession in the year following our conversation. Other teachers described holding high academic expectations for students, but did not express a commitment to or appreciation for student support needs. Overwhelmingly, teachers with this type of perspective described feeling frustrated in their work.

In contrast, the largest grouping of teachers in my study expressed a deep commitment to supporting the nonacademic needs of their students, but often at the expense of academic expectations. Such respondents would say something like, "He's not ready to learn! I'm just happy for him to come to school and be safe. I give him extra snacks and let him sleep as much as he needs. Poor baby!" Invariably, children in these classrooms started to fall farther behind in their learning, becoming more frustrated and irritable in the classroom. Frequently, such students used behavior as a way to avoid work and mask their insecurities about learning. One student in this type of classroom even shared with me, "My teacher doesn't think I'm smart because she never makes me do my work." These children and teachers allowed me to appreciate that our good intentions are not always good enough.

In order for children to feel smart and safe, experiencing agency and interdependence, they must experience both care and learning. This understanding led me to recognize a small, but powerful group of teachers who manage to respond to both their students' learning and support needs. These teachers articulated an integrated perspective on their work and how they understand the complex needs of their students. Virtually all of these teachers described periods during their careers where they may have focused too much on support or academics, experiencing both frustration and benevolence. But, over time, they came to realize that these two needs—care and learning—should not be viewed as being at odds with each other. Rather, these educators learned that care and teaching were two sides of the same coin, each necessary to support children in healing from trauma and adversity. To allow themselves to take academic risks, children need to know that we care for them beyond just their academic success. Likewise, it is difficult for children to feel that we care deeply for them if we are unable to help them learn.

ERT Is Teaching With an Awareness of Context

As we have discussed throughout this book, balancing care and instruction requires an understanding of the world, community, and household—or contexts—in which children are growing. ERT begins with and is grounded in the understanding that how we make sense of children and their families and how they are perceiving us is influenced by the social context in which we are relating. For educators, what we know of children and families—and how they see us—occurs largely in the school environment. This means that we will mainly view children and their families through our expectations for what it means to be a good student and engaged parent, including the standards and values that the broader society has tasked us with imposing on or developing in our students. This also occurs in reverse, with children and parents comparing teachers with their own ideas about what good teachers and good schools should be like.

Context is also meant to imply the various social identities and social forces that influence what teachers, students, families, and communities bring with them to both interpersonal and collective interactions. We must recognize that both how we present ourselves to others and how we respond to the ways they present themselves (and reflect back how they see us) are by our own individual and social identities. Similarly, social policies, the economy, and other external events, for example, also shape how we interact with each other and in schools. We must always be aware that what we know of children and their families—and what they know of us—is limited by what we can know of them. We must never believe that we know "the truth" about a child of family, or about ourselves for that matter. However, this does not mean that we cannot come to understand each other better, developing a shared understanding of each other and ourselves.

Lastly, context also includes the messiness that children, families, and we bring to our work and interactions each day. Though we prioritize teaching and learning in the educational environment, these are not the only concerns that we bring with us to school. Each child and adult also bring hopes, dreams, life circumstances, individual concerns, and interpersonal drama, for example, into the classroom. Just as do we. Recognizing that there may be things going on in children's and families' lives—and our own—outside the classroom is essential in being attuned and responsive to each other. It is in this context of complexity that emotionally responsive teaching is practiced.

SUSTAINING THE EMOTIONALLY RESPONSIVE TEACHER

As stated previously, ERT is as much an ethic, or way of being a teacher, as it is a series of steps or strategies to be implemented. Consequently, in becoming an emotionally responsive teacher, we have to be willing to change how and who we are in children's lives as much as we commit to changing what we ask them to do in our classrooms. To help children feel cared for, we have to care for them. To help children acquire greater mastery of their learning, we have to hold higher expectations of them. To allow a child the possibility of different learning outcomes or more positive relationships with their peers or us, we must imagine that change is possible and be willing to interact with the children differently so that they might respond differently.

Balancing care and instruction, what children experience inside and outside our classrooms, their individual identities with their social identities, our view of the child and their view of us, is no easy task. I have found that changing how I see my students and their families and how I view myself has been far more difficult than changing my instructional strategies or approach. Yet cultivating an emotionally responsive teaching practice requires us to understand our students more deeply and respond to them more thoughtfully. To accomplish this, we must also be willing to better understand our own emotional needs and reactions.

Critical reflection, or examining our actions, attitudes, and assumptions to better understand our investment in them and how they may be impacting others, is essential in cultivating such personal transformation. It is important to carve out time every day, if only 5 or 10 minutes, to think about what worked well and what did not. I've found it especially important to pay attention to both the best and most challenging moments during the day—considering what happened before, during, and after. Often, such reflection will allow me to identify patterns, triggers, and causes of challenging behavioral responses as well as my efforts that worked. If we are mindful of doing more of what worked and less of what did not the following day, over time we will be able to cultivate a classroom environment and instructional program that works for our children, families, and us.

When we think about professional development and growth, our minds often turn to coaching, trainings, coursework, or curricular design. Yet I have found such daily reflection—paying attention to how children and families respond to my actions and being much more aware of my intentions and actions—the single most impactful tool in my personal growth and development. Daily reflection has allowed me to fine-tune my approach and make changes in my attitude and teaching approach much more quickly, becoming more attuned to my students and families, intentions, and actions in the process. Such contemplation has become a spiritual practice of sorts.

In addition to considering what I did and could have done during a particular interaction, I have also begun focusing on how I would like for a particular child or family member to feel when we interact. I allow myself to imagine what I would need to feel or communicate in order for this person to experience our interaction in this way. Over time, this mental exercise has changed the way I interact with children and families, helping me shift from a place of reactivity to communicating from an awareness of my hopes and expectations for them. As my children and families have begun to experience more trust in my care and positive expectations for them, they have become more vulnerable in inviting and accepting my constructive feedback and support.

Reflection has also taught me that teaching—and relationships—are ultimately a collection of moments. Allowing myself to identify opportunities for growth and trying them out as soon as my next interaction with a child or family has often allowed me to remain more open, flexible, and hopeful in my teaching life. This insight has also allowed me to focus on the possibilities of the next interaction or the next day rather than becoming overwhelmed by the circumstances or needs of a child or family's whole life. When the world seems to be crashing down around us, it is very easy to feel overwhelmed by everything that can happen and how little it feels like we can change. Yet the only way to change anything in our lives is by putting one foot in the front of the other—doing the next thing that needs to be done. This is the very structure of survival, making it from one moment to the next, and I've found such an approach very resonant with children and families navigating adversity. Time and again I've said to them, "If we can just do our best to do better and to make the best decision possible the next time we have to decide, things will eventually be better. We can't solve everything now—but if we can solve the thing in front of us, that is one less thing to worry about."

Creating opportunities to reflect with trusted colleagues can also be extremely helpful in gaining perspective and experiencing support. There is no way for any of us to be successful doing this work alone. As the old saying goes, "It takes a village to raise a child." Likewise, it takes a community to nurture a teacher. When we get too close to a situation or caught up in a power struggle with a child or family, it can be incredibly challenging to gain perspective on what may be happening. In such moments, trusted colleagues, supervisors, and mentors are essential in gently pointing out our blind spots, offering suggestions, and encouraging us in our efforts. Inviting others into our work—and supporting them in their own—is an essential aspect of emotionally responsive teaching. It is impossible to see all of the possibilities and perspectives in a situation in which we are so deeply embedded. The eyes and wisdom of others are essential in expanding our understanding and remaining grounded while investing so deeply in the lives of others.

Burnout and Compassion Fatigue

Though I have devoted much time focusing on the importance of supporting children and families, it is essential that you also develop a support network for yourself. Teaching children and families with difficult lives—who arrive in our classroom angry, overwhelmed, frightened, or sad—is sometimes difficult for us as well. Beyond being on the receiving end of angry complaints, emotional outbursts, or power struggles in the classroom, bearing witness to the struggles that families—and especially our young children—face can be heart-wrenching. I cannot count the number of nights that I have lost sleep worrying about a child or family in the midst of turmoil. I have gotten angry at school systems, insurance companies, police departments, politicians, parents, colleagues, and others who have turned a blind eye to the needs of one of my students or families. I have felt shame and guilt about my own inability to provide adequate support for a child and family, and even more during times when, for whatever reason, I was not able to do my best. I have pushed too hard when slowing down and providing additional support would have been better, and underestimated how much a child was struggling when they said everything was okay.

Watching how society treats vulnerable children and families has challenged my faith in our basic goodness and the decency of our social institutions. I have felt powerless to make a difference and confronted greed and self-interest at the individual level on up to the corridors of power. I have felt rage at those who hurt their children or those belonging to others. I have also felt afraid. As a gay man working in early childhood education, I have experienced discrimination, suspicion, and stigma. Only a few years ago, the director of a child-care center refused to allow me to conduct a therapy session with one of her students without a chaperone because she said that it wouldn't "look good." This happened despite the fact that it was her supervisor who asked me to do the consultation, and female providers were allowed to see children alone in the therapy suite all the time.

Losing children and families to illness, violence, and tragedy has been devastating. Listening to a child as they describe the horrible things that have happened to them, or seeing the bruises on a child's body, are equally painful. I have loaded children's backpacks with extra food for the weekend, knowing it might be the only thing they will have to eat. Many times, I have cried on my way home from work, worried about a family living in their car, struggling with addiction, or who have simply disappeared. Sometimes the difficult moments can be overwhelming, and it is easy to lose hope and become defeated. It is also easy to become numb and exhausted from the weight of worry and frustration.

Burnout and compassion fatigue are real, and I have experienced both. Burnout is a natural reaction to prolonged or chronic job stress, and compassion fatigue is burnout caused by caring too much. The symptoms of burnout are physical and emotional exhaustion, cynicism, and increased self-doubt and sense of failure. Burnout can also present as feeling helpless, trapped, or defeated. Typically, in the throes of burnout, one might feel alone in the world, a loss of motivation, and decreased satisfaction. In order to help others, our cup must be full enough to overflow—but when in the midst of burnout, we simply feel empty.

Walking with children and families through scary things and overwhelming circumstances can also lead us to develop vicarious trauma, feeling helpless and hopeless because of what others are experiencing. Vicarious trauma is also known as *secondary traumatic stress* and refers to the indirect trauma that results when we are exposed to difficult stories or disturbing images secondhand. Symptoms of vicarious trauma may include lingering feelings of anger, rage, and sadness about what children or families are experiencing; experiencing bystander shame, guilt, and feelings of self-doubt; having horror or rescue fantasies; difficulty in maintaining professional boundaries with our children and families, such as overextending ourselves to help them; distancing, numbing, and detaching; staying busy to avoid connecting with our children and their families; and feeling hopeless or helpless.

Taking care of yourself is essential to avoid or overcome burnout or vicarious trauma. In the same way that we cultivate emotionally responsive practices for our children and families, we must also cultivate emotionally restorative practices for ourselves. It is important to engage in relaxing and self-soothing activities. Some people love yoga, massage, or meditation. Others find peace in exercise, hiking, or spending time with friends or a beloved pet. It is important to be realistic about what you can accomplish and to avoid wishful thinking. Allow yourself to remember that it is not your job to take responsibility for the well-being of your children and families, but to supply them with the tools to look after themselves.

Developing a cadre of supportive colleagues is essential in maintaining balance and perspective. Seek support from colleagues and family members, asking for advice and debriefing with peers and supervisors when needed. Taking advantage of training opportunities can be a great way to increase our sense of efficacy and knowledge. Friends and colleagues can also help divert our attention on work-related stress. Fun outings, potlucks, happy hour, or shared lunches are great ways to come up for air in the midst of difficult work days. Dancing always does my heart good—and when I was a classroom teacher, a group of colleagues and I made it a point to hit the dance floor at least once per month. We always said, "Teachers that can boogie together, can change the world together!" And for some children, we did.

Whatever your passion, it is important to have interests and relationships outside of your workplace and students. Investing in things outside of work helps us to maintain boundaries and provides a positive escape from work stress. In my own life, for example, I decided to pursue a lifelong passion of becoming a shepherd and began raising sheep. For the past 10 years, I have begun and ended each day in the barn, tending to my flock. Caring for my animals requires me to slow down, pay attention, and exercise. Connecting with the animals pulls me out of my head, and they reward my care with affection, wool, and contentment. I am a far better educator—and human being—because of the time that I invest in shepherding. I have become far more gentle, patient, and attentive. The delight of lambs racing in the fields, the ewes' contentment as they graze green pastures, and the excitement of lambing season ground me, allowing me to experience the rhythms of nature and remain connected to the earth even when the chaos of the workday leaves me feeling unhinged. Doing something that I love is restorative and gives me a place to retreat when I feel drained in other parts of my life. When I feel hopeless, I can always shovel manure or stack hay. Though the tasks are stinky and mindless, the sense of accomplishment that I feel when I finish helps restore my sense of order and reminds me that I can accomplish things through hard work. It doesn't matter what you do—and there are thousands of ways beyond raising sheep to find similar meaning—but you must do something that helps you feel excited and alive in order to maintain your equilibrium while walking through adversity with others.

Finally, please allow yourself to take advantage of counseling when needed or when you are looking to focus on your own growth and well-being. There is no shame in reaching out for help or seeking the support of a mental health counselor to gain perspective and regain your balance. The type of self-examination that comes with ERT can be difficult at times as we are prone to see things that we may not like about ourselves and/or confront experiences from our past that may be painful. Counseling can be a powerful way to assert control over parts of our life that have left us feeling disempowered. Developing a new perspective on some aspect of our lives can free us to move forward in new directions. In contrast, when we avoid looking at ourselves or reflecting on our actions, we remain trapped in the past and miss the opportunity to grow, both with others and within ourselves.

Healing and Growing Through Emotionally Responsive Teaching

During my career in early childhood education and counseling, I have become increasingly aware of how my own experiences, understandings, and biases have shaped my perspective of others and myself—a dynamic that has proven both helpful and stifling at times. For example, the experience of being abandoned by my own father has made me particularly sensitive to children's anxiety around transition and loss. Drawing on the wisdom I gleaned from my personal journey, I have become skilled and empathetic when supporting children in the midst of these challenges. However, my personal experiences have sometimes gotten in the way of my ability to appreciate that others may have been impacted differently by the same experience. I have learned that not every difficult emotion experienced by children (or myself) is the result of abandonment. In my evolution as an emotionally responsive teacher, my reflections and observations have helped me to better differentiate my experiences from those of the children and families I seek to support and allowed me to remain more open to alternative interpretations of their actions and my own.

Becoming a stable, supportive figure in the lives of other children has allowed me to feel some power and control over my own early losses. In providing stability and support for others, I have felt less vulnerable and experienced greater connection. For example, parents sharing their struggles with me has helped me to find more compassion for my father and the challenges he faced in being present for my family. Having another child's father share with me that he often thinks about leaving because he thinks his child's life might be better if he did was pivotal in being able to imagine that perhaps my father's actions were not entirely selfish. Regardless, learning to accept that others do the best they can even when it isn't good enough has helped me to extend the same generosity to those in my personal life and myself.

Allowing my students to experience a broader range of emotions and connection has allowed—and required—me to do the same. For example, when I entered the world of teaching, I was uncomfortable with play and with receiving affection, letting my guard down, or not being perfect. I took life way too seriously and sometimes struggled to trust that others could accept me for who I am. Yet, in supporting children and families in facing challenges in their own lives—providing them with necessary support and reassurance, asking them to trust me, and accepting them for their imperfections—I also became more skilled and comfortable in extending this same acceptance to myself. Learning that I could walk with children and families through really hard things allowed me to become more confident in standing up to my own fears and confronting painful parts of my life. In turn, healing the wounded parts of myself has allowed me to become more responsive to the healing process of others.

My work has taught me to navigate cultural, educational, racial, ethnic, and class differences, which has similarly underscored the importance of remaining open-minded, reflective, and aware of the potential for misinterpretation and misunderstanding. While bridging such sociocultural divides in my interactions with children and families has been challenging at times, it has not proven impossible. Much of what we have been able to accomplish together has been through resolving misunderstandings about each other and the world. For example, working as a male in early childhood education has often challenged children, families, supervisors, and myself to cultivate a broader perspective on nurturing that provides permission for men to be connected and responsive to as well.

Interactions with children and families have taught me to question lessons I learned a long time ago. Familiar refrains from my childhood— "Don't cry," "Keep it to yourself," "Be tough," "Only sissies make tears," and "Don't be afraid to finish a fight"—now seem insidious. In learning to become more understanding and responsive to children in my care, I have been challenged to confront the ways I traversed the confusing terrain of masculinity. My relationship with my students has underscored for me that becoming a boy—becoming a man—is a difficult journey. Independence, resisting one's desire for connection, and demonstrating fewer emotions— traits deemed necessary to become the strong, independent man so celebrated by society's dominant culture—are acquired at great sacrifice. For boys who experience early loss, like being abandoned by their father or having their dad be incarcerated, the demands of learning to be strong and independent are particularly costly. My work with young boys has allowed me to recognize how this conflict has played out in my own life, understanding that in the midst of needing reassurance, support, and stability, many boys—especially those in the midst of challenging life circumstances— confront a world that pushes them away, expecting them to be "little men." Taking on the challenge of emotionally responsive teaching—caring about and tending to such needs—has helped me to imagine broader possibilities for connection, responsiveness, and strength in a boy's journey toward becoming a man. Though you may be called to learn different lessons than these in your teaching life, walking with others through their challenges will certainly provide an opportunity for you to grow similarly.

An Invitation

Given that this work is difficult—and that you may already be bruised or otherwise exhausted by your attempts to support children and families who are struggling, possibly doing so in environments that may not yet be fully supportive—you may be asking yourself, "Why do this?" While ultimately this is a question that you will have to answer for yourself, I can share the three answers that underscore my own commitment to this work.

First, I have navigated challenges in my own life, particularly as a child, and understand firsthand the importance of quality education and supportive adults in helping children make it through hard times. I know deep in my heart that this work matters because it made a difference for me, and I want to pay it forward. I suspect that many of us are called to this work because it cuts close to our own experiences.

Second, I want to make the world a better place and believe deeply that ensuring children have the opportunity to develop a positive sense of self through learning and support is the single most important investment in creating a more just, compassionate, and joyful world. And, finally, learning to see the best in others—even when it is difficult to see—has allowed me to become more accepting of myself and those around me. As I have become more oriented to the resilience that emerges in the midst of risky situations, learning to see the beauty in the struggle, I realize that I am better able to sustain hope in all the parts of my life. Appreciating that children with broken hearts can still jump rope, that a parent who did not do a good enough job still did their best, and that school can be the best part of a child's day even when they aren't doing well has helped me to understand in a deeper way that life can be complicated, ugly, and beautiful all at the same time. Learning that I can walk through such ambiguity—that I can stand in the fire with others facing circumstances far more challenging than anything I have experienced—has helped me realize that I am stronger than I ever imagined I could be. Time and again I have been reminded that strength is not about always having the answer; it is often about showing up, bearing witness, and helping someone else realize that they have known what is best all along.

All of this is to say, learning to love in one part of our life can help us give and receive love better in all the parts of our lives. Learning to love children and families who make it difficult to like them has stretched my capacities for patience, acceptance, and imperfection. Seeing the strength in a child who is struggling has resulted in more compassion for my husband, children, and friends. Learning to look for what children and families might become rather than focusing only on their struggles has led me to see more possibilities for myself and those in my personal life. Appreciating that I am stronger than I ever realized—knowing that I can keep showing up even when it is hard—has allowed me to provide more stability and security for my own children. Continuing to open my heart to children and families, even after it has been broken by others, reminds me of my capacity to heal. Knowing this has allowed me to build a life with another person, providing me with a level of security, acceptance, and love that I could never have imagined.

Learning to trust that I will be okay and accept my best even when I failed or the situation did not get better has freed me to love, take risks, and embrace the possibilities of life with more courage and abandon. This is the deepest promise of this sometimes challenging work. I cannot guarantee that every moment in an emotionally responsive approach will be easy; there will be moments of doubt, frustration, and even brokenheartedness. But I can promise that if you decide to open yourself to the possibility of this work, doing what you might simply because it needs to be done and even when it is difficult, your view of yourself and the world will be transformed. Knowing that you have made a difference in the lives of others will forever be a source of pride and protect you from the regret that perhaps you wasted your journey. And I know that you will find space in your heart that you never knew existed.

SUMMARY

In this closing chapter, I discussed the importance of cultivating emotionally responsive teaching and considered the ethical and personal dimensions of such a stance. Here and throughout this book, I have drawn on my personal experiences to share the heartbreaks and unexpected benefits of teaching children with messy lives with one's whole heart. I also discussed vicarious trauma and burnout as possible consequences of supporting children with life challenges and suggested strategies for self-care and continued personal growth.

References

Alink, L. R. A., Cicchetti, D., Kim, J., & Rogosch, F. A. (2012). Longitudinal associations among child maltreatment, social functioning, and cortisol regulation. *Developmental Psychology*, 48(1), 224–236. https://doi.org/10.1037/a0024892

Alisic, E. (2012). Teachers' perspectives on providing support to children after trauma: A qualitative study. *School Psychology Quarterly*, 27(1), 51–59. https://doi.org/10.1037/a0028590

Annalakshmi, N. (2019). Resilience and academic achievement among rural adolescents at-risk: Role of self-regulation and attachment style. *Indian Journal of Positive Psychology*, 10(4), 260–266.

Areba, E. M., Taliaferro, L. A., Forster, M., McMorris, B. J., Mathiason, M. A., & Eisenberg, M. E. (2021). Adverse childhood experiences and suicidality: School connectedness as a protective factor for ethnic minority adolescents. *Children and Youth Services Review*, 120. https://doi.org/10.1016/j.childyouth.2020.105637

Ayoub, C. C., & Fischer, K. W. (2006). Developmental pathways and intersections among domains of development. In K. McCartney & D. Phillips (Eds.), *Blackwell handbook of early childhood development* (pp. 62–81). Blackwell Publishing. https://doi.org/10.1002/9780470757703.ch4

Ayoub, C. C., O'Connor, E., Rappolt-Schlichtmann, G., Fischer, K. W., Rogosch, F. A., Toth, S. L., & Cicchetti, D. (2006). Cognitive and emotional differences in young maltreated children: A translational application of dynamic skill theory. *Development and Psychopathology*, 18(3), 679–706. https://doi.org/10.1017/S0954579406060342

Ayoub, C. C., & Rappolt-Schlichtmann, G. (2007). Child maltreatment and the development of alternate pathways in biology and behavior. In D. Coch, G. Dawson, & K. W. Fischer (Eds.), *Human behavior, learning, and the developing brain: Atypical development* (pp. 305–330). Guilford Press.

Beers, S. R., & De Bellis, M. D. (2002). Neuropsychological function in children with maltreatment-related posttraumatic stress disorder. *The American Journal of Psychiatry*, 159(3), 483–486. https://doi.org/10.1176/appi.ajp.159.3.483

Bergin, C., & Bergin, D. (2009). Attachment in the classroom. *Educational Psychology Review, 21*(2), 141–170. https://doi.org/10.1007/s10648-009-9104-0

Berryhill, J., Linney, J. A., & Fromewick, J. (2009). The effects of education accountability on teachers: Are policies too stress-provoking for their own good? *International Journal of Education Policy and Leadership, 4*(5), 1–14. https://doi.org/10.22230/ijepl.2009v4n5a99

Bettini, E., & Park, Y. (2021). Novice teachers' experiences in high-poverty schools: An integrative literature review. *Urban Education, 56*(1), 3–31. https://doi.org/10.1177/0042085916685763

Blank, M. (2007). Posttraumatic stress disorder in infants, toddlers, and preschoolers. *British Columbia Medical Journal, 49*(3), 133–138.

Bonanno, G. A., Brewin, C. R., Kaniasty, K., & La Greca, A. M. (2010). Weighing the costs of disaster: Consequences, risks, and resilience in individuals, families, and communities. *Psychological Science in the Public Interest, 11*(1), 1–49. https://doi.org/10.1177/1529100610387086

Bremner, J. D., & Vermetten, E. (2001). Stress and development: Behavioral and biological consequences. *Development and Psychopathology, 13*(3), 473–489. https://doi.org/10.1017/S0954579401003042

Briere, J., & Scott, C. (2012). *Principles of trauma therapy: A guide to symptoms, evaluation, and treatment*. SAGE Publications.

Bruno, P., Rabovsky, S. J., & Strunk, K. O. (2020). Taking their first steps: The distribution of new teachers in school and classroom contexts and implications for teacher effectiveness. *American Educational Research Journal, 57*(4), 1688–1729. https://doi.org/10.3102/0002831219882008

Burt, K. B., Obradović, J., Long, J. D., & Masten, A. S. (2008). The interplay of social competence and psychopathology over 20 years: Testing transactional and cascade models. *Child Development, 79*(2), 359–374. https://doi.org/10.1111/j.1467-8624.2007.01130.x

Burton, B. A. (2020). Resiliency and academic achievement among urban high school students. *Leadership and Research in Education, 5*(2), 106–141.

Busette, C., & Elizondo, S. (2022, April 27). Economic disparities in the Washington, D.C. metro region provide opportunities for policy action. *Brookings.* https://www.brookings.edu/blog/how-we-rise/2022/04/27/economic-disparities-in-the-washington-d-c-metro-region-provide-opportunities-for-policy-action/

Catterall, J. S. (1998). Risk and resilience in student transitions to high school. *American Journal of Education, 106*(2), 302–333. https://doi.org/10.1086/444184

Chang, J. (2011). A case study of the "Pygmalion Effect": Teacher expectations and student achievement. *International Education Studies, 4*(1), 198–201.

Christian-Brandt, A. S., Santacrose, D. E., & Barnett, M. L. (2020). In the trauma-informed care trenches: Teacher compassion satisfaction, secondary traumatic stress, burnout, and intent to leave education within underserved elementary schools. *Child Abuse & Neglect, 110*(Part 3). https://doi.org/10.1016/j.chiabu.2020.104437

Cicchetti, D., & Toth, S. L. (2005). Child maltreatment. *Annual Review of Clinical Psychology, 1*(1), 409–438. https://doi.org/10.1146/annurev.clinpsy.1.102803.144029

Cloitre, M., Khan, C., Mackintosh, M.-A., Garvert, D. W., Henn-Haase, C. M., Falvey, E. C., & Saito, J. (2019). Emotion regulation mediates the relationship between ACES and physical and mental health. *Psychological Trauma: Theory, Research, Practice, and Policy, 11*(1), 82–89. https://doi.org/10.1037/tra0000374

Cohen, J. A., Mannarino, A. P., Murray, L. K., & Igelman, R. (2006). Psychosocial interventions for maltreated and violence-exposed children. *Journal of Social Issues, 62*(4), 737–766. https://doi.org/10.1111/j.1540-4560.2006.00485.x

Cole, S. F., O'Brien, J. G., Gadd, M. G., Ristuccia, J., Wallace, D. L., & Gregory, M. (2005). *Helping traumatized children learn: Supportive school environments for children traumatized by family violence. A report and policy agenda.* Massachusetts Advocates for Children. https://traumasensitiveschools.org/wp-content/uploads/2013/06/Helping-Traumatized-Children Learn.pdf

Collie, R. J., Perry, N. E., & Martin, A. J. (2017). School context and educational system factors impacting educator stress. In T. M. McIntyre, S. E. McIntyre, & D. J. Francis (Eds.), *Educator stress: An occupational health perspective* (pp. 3–22). Springer International Publishing AG. https://doi.org/10.1007/978-3-319-53053-6_1

Coster, W., & Cicchetti, D. (1993). Research on the communicative development of maltreated children: Clinical implications. *Topics in Language Disorders, 13*(4), 25–38. https://doi.org/10.1097/00011363-199308000-00007

Craig, F., Tenuta, F., Rizzato, V., Costabile, A., Trabacca, A., & Montirosso, R. (2021). Attachment-related dimensions in the epigenetic era: A systematic review of the human research. *Neuroscience & Biobehavioral Reviews, 125,* 654–666. https://doi.org/10.1016/j.neubiorev.2021.03.006

Craig, S. E. (2016). The trauma-sensitive teacher. *Educational Leadership, 74*(1), 28–32.

Culp, R. E., Watkins, R. V., Lawrence, H., Letts, D., Kelly, D. J., & Rice, M. L. (1991). Maltreated children's language and speech development: Abused, neglected, and abused and neglected. *First Language, 11*(33, Pt 3), 377–389. https://doi.org/10.1177/014272379101103305

Daignault, I. V., & Hebert, M. (2009). Profiles of school adaptation: Social, behavioral and academic functioning in sexually abused girls. *Child Abuse & Neglect: The International Journal, 33*(2), 102–115. https://doi.org/10.1016/j.chiabu.2008.06.001

Darwish, D., Esquivel, G. B., Houtz, J. C., & Alfonso, V. C. (2001). Play and social skills in maltreated and non-maltreated preschoolers during peer interactions. *Child Abuse & Neglect, 25*(1), 13–31. https://doi.org/10.1016/S0145-2134(00)00228-3

De Bellis, M. D. (2005). The psychobiology of neglect. *Child Maltreatment, 10*(2), 150–172. https://doi.org/10.1177/1077559505275116

De Bellis, M. D., & Van Dillen, T. (2005). Childhood post-traumatic stress disorder: An overview. *Child and Adolescent Psychiatric Clinics of North America, 14*(4), 745–772. https://doi.org/10.1016/j.chc.2005.05.006

Dewitt, E. (2020, November 11). *States where high schoolers are least likely to graduate.* Stacker.Com. https://stacker.com/stories/1925/states-where-high-schoolers-are-least-likely-graduate

Diament, M. (2022, June 24). *Across US, special education enrollment on the rise.* Disability Scoop. https://www.disabilityscoop.com/2022/06/24/across-us-special-education-enrollment-on-the-rise/29920/

Eklund, K. M., Torppa, M., & Lyytinen, H. (2013). Predicting reading disability: Early cognitive risk and protective factors. *Dyslexia: An International Journal of Research and Practice, 19*(1), 1–10. https://doi.org/10.1002/dys.1447

Engel, G. L. (1981). The clinical application of the biopsychosocial model. *The Journal of Medicine and Philosophy: A Forum for Bioethics and Philosophy of Medicine, 6*(2), 101–124. https://doi.org/10.1093/jmp/6.2.101

Eslinger, J. C. (2014). Navigating between a rock and a hard place: Lessons from an urban school teacher. *Education and Urban Society, 46*(2), 209–233. https://doi.org/10.1177/0013124512446221

Fang, Z. (1996). A review of research on teacher beliefs and practices. *Educational Research, 38*(1), 47–65. https://doi.org/10.1080/0013188960380104

Fearon, R. P., Bakermans-Kranenburg, M. J., van IJzendoorn, M. H., Lapsley, A.-M., & Roisman, G. I. (2010). The significance of insecure attachment and disorganization in the development of children's externalizing behavior: A meta-analytic study. *Child Development, 81*(2), 435–456. https://doi.org/10.1111/j.1467-8624.2009.01405.x

Fischer, K. W., Ayoub, C., Singh, I., Noam, G., Maraganore, A., & Rayà, P. (1997). Psychopathology as adaptive development along distinctive pathways. *Development and Psychopathology, 9*(4), 729–748. https://doi.org/10.1017/S0954579497001429

Ford, J. D., & Kidd, P. (1998). Early childhood trauma and disorders of extreme stress as predictors of treatment outcome with chronic posttraumatic stress disorder. *Journal of Traumatic Stress, 11*(4), 743–761. https://doi.org/10.1023/A:1024497400891

Ford, J. D., Racusin, R., Ellis, C. G., Daviss, W. B., Reiser, J., Fleischer, A., & Thomas, J. (2000). Child maltreatment, other trauma exposure, and posttraumatic symptomatology among children with oppositional defiant and attention deficit hyperactivity disorders. *Child Maltreatment, 5*(3), 205–217. https://doi.org/10.1177/1077559500005003001

Fredrickson, B. L., & Losada, M. F. (2005). Positive affect and the complex dynamics of human flourishing. *American Psychologist, 60*(7), 678–686. https://doi.org/10.1037/0003-066X.60.7.678

Furrer, C. J., Skinner, E. A., & Pitzer, J. R. (2014). The influence of teacher and peer relationships on students' classroom engagement and everyday motivational resilience. *Teachers College Record, 116*(13), 101–123. https://doi.org/10.1177/016146811411601319

Garbarino, J., Dubrow, N., Kostelny, K., & Pardo, C. (1992). *Children in danger: Coping with the consequences of community violence.* Jossey-Bass/Wiley.

Giordano, K., McKeating, E., Chung, D., & Garcia, V. (2022). Expulsion from community childcare centers during the COVID-19 pandemic: A review of one state's practices. *Early Childhood Education Journal.* https://doi.org/10.1007/s10643-022-01312-7

Gonzalez, A., Peters, M. L., Orange, A., & Grigsby, B. (2017). The influence of high-stakes testing on teacher self-efficacy and job-related stress. *Cambridge Journal of Education, 47*(4), 513–531. https://doi.org/10.1080/0305764X.2016.1214237

Halliday, M. A. K. (1975). *Learning how to mean: Explorations in the development of language.* Edward Arnold Publishers.

Henschel, S., Nandrino, J.-L., Pezard, L., Ott, L., Vulliez-Coady, L., & Doba, K. (2020). The influence of attachment styles on autonomic correlates of perspective-taking. *Biological Psychology, 154.* https://doi.org/10.1016/j.biopsycho.2020.107908

Herman, J. L. (1992). Complex PTSD: A syndrome in survivors of prolonged and repeated trauma. *Journal of Traumatic Stress, 5*(3), 377–391. https://doi.org/10.1002/jts.2490050305

Herrenkohl, T. I., Hong, S., & Verbrugge, B. (2019). Trauma-informed programs based in schools: Linking concepts to practices and assessing the evidence. *American Journal of Community Psychology, 64*(3–4), 373–388. https://doi.org/10.1002/ajcp.12362

Howes, C. (2000). Social-emotional classroom climate in child care, child-teacher relationships and children's second grade peer relations. *Social Development, 9*(2), 291–204. https://doi.org/10.1111/1467-9507.00119

Ingram, B. L. (2012). *Clinical case formulations: Matching the integrative treatment plan to the client* (2nd ed). John Wiley & Sons.

Jaffee, S. R., Moffitt, T. E., Caspi, A., Taylor, A., & Arseneault, L. (2002). Influence of adult domestic violence on children's internalizing and externalizing problems: An environmentally informative twin study. *Journal of the American Academy of Child & Adolescent Psychiatry, 41*(9), 1095–1103. https://doi.org/10.1097/00004583-200209000-00010

Joireman, J. A., Needham, T. L., & Cummings, A.-L. (2002). Relationships between dimensions of attachment and empathy. *North American Journal of Psychology, 4*(1), 63–80.

Kim, J. (2013). Confronting invisibility: Early childhood pre-service teachers' beliefs toward homeless children. *Early Childhood Education Journal, 41*(2), 161–169. https://doi.org/10.1007/s10643-012-0529-6

Kim, J., & Cicchetti, D. (2003). Social self-efficacy and behavior problems in maltreated children. *Journal of Clinical Child and Adolescent Psychology, 32*(1), 106–117. https://doi.org/10.1207/15374420360533103

Kim, J., & Cicchetti, D. (2010). Longitudinal pathways linking child maltreatment, emotion regulation, peer relations, and psychopathology. *Journal of Child Psychology and Psychiatry, 51*(6), 706–716. https://doi.org/10.1111/j.1469-7610.2009.02202.x

Kira, I. A. (2001). Taxonomy of trauma and trauma assessment. *Traumatology, 7*(2), 73–86. https://doi.org/10.1177/153476560100700202

Koplow, L. (1996). *Unsmiling faces: How preschools can heal.* Teachers College Press. https://search.library.wisc.edu/catalog/999779156702121

Koplow, L. (2002). *Creating schools that heal: Real-life solutions.* Teachers College Press. https://search.library.wisc.edu/catalog/999932126302121

Koplow, L. (2021). *Emotionally responsive practice: A path for schools that heal, infancy–grade 6.* Teachers College Press.

Kwon, K.-A., Jeon, S., Castle, S., & Ford, T. G. (2021). Children's behavioral challenges in Head Start classrooms: Links to teacher well-being and intent to leave. *Early Childhood Education Journal, 50*, 1221–1232. https://doi.org/10.1007/s10643-021-01253-7

Ladson-Billings, G. (2014). Culturally relevant pedagogy 2.0: A.k.a. the remix. *Harvard Educational Review, 84*(1), 74–84. https://doi.org/10.17763/haer.84.1.p2rj131485484751

Ladson-Billings, G. (2021). *Culturally relevant pedagogy: Asking a different question. Culturally sustaining pedagogies series.* Teachers College Press.

Lai, I., Wood, W. J., Imberman, S. A., Jones, N. D., & Strunk, K. O. (2021). Teacher quality gaps by disability and socioeconomic status: Evidence from Los Angeles. *Educational Researcher, 50*(2), 74–85. https://doi.org/10.3102/0013189X20955170

Larson, S., Chapman, S., Spetz, J., & Brindis, C. D. (2017). Chronic childhood trauma, mental health, academic achievement, and school-based health center mental health services. *Journal of School Health, 87*(9), 675–686. https://doi.org/10.1111/josh.12541

Lawrence-Lightfoot, S. (1983). *The good high school: Portraits of character and culture.* Basic Books. https://search.library.wisc.edu/catalog/999531840502121

Lawrence-Lightfoot, S. (1997). *The art and science of portraiture.* Jossey-Bass. https://search.library.wisc.edu/catalog/999822086302121

Lelli, C. (2021). *Trauma-sensitive schools: The importance of instilling grit, determination, and resilience.* Rowman & Littlefield.

Lewis, S. J., Koenen, K. C., Ambler, A., Arseneault, L., Caspi, A., Fisher, H. L., Moffitt, T. E., & Danese, A. (2021). Unravelling the contribution of complex trauma to psychopathology and cognitive deficits: A cohort study. *The British Journal of Psychiatry, 219*(2), 448–455. https://doi.org/10.1192/bjp.2021.57

Llistosella, M., Castellvi, P., Limonero, J. T., Pérez-Ventana Ortiz, C., Baeza-Velasco, C., & Gutiérrez-Rosado, T. (2022). Development of the Individual and Environmental Resilience Model among children, adolescents and young adults using the empirical evidence: An integrative systematic review. *Health and Social Care in the Community, 1.* https://doi.org/10.1111/hsc.13899

Lu, P., Oh, J., Leahy, K. E., & Chopik, W. J. (2021). Friendship importance around the world: Links to cultural factors, health, and well-being. *Frontiers in Psychology, 11.* https://doi.org/10.3389/fpsyg.2020.570839

Lubeck, S., & Garrett, P. (1990). The social construction of the "at-risk" child. *British Journal of Sociology of Education, 11*(3), 327–340. https://doi.org/10.1080/0142569900110305

Marcionetti, J., & Rossier, J. (2021). A longitudinal study of relations among adolescents' self-esteem, general self-efficacy, career adaptability, and life satisfaction. *Journal of Career Development, 48*(4), 475–490. https://doi.org/10.1177/0894845319861691

Masten, A. S. (2014). *Ordinary magic: Resilience in development.* Guilford Press.

Masten, A. S. (2021). Resilience in developmental systems: Principles, pathways, and protective processes in research and practice. In M. Ungar (Ed.), *Multisystemic resilience: Adaptation and transformation in contexts of change* (pp. 113–134). Oxford University Press. https://doi.org/10.1093/oso/9780190095888.003.0007

Masten, A. S., Best, K. M., & Garmezy, N. (1990). Resilience and development: Contributions from the study of children who overcome adversity. *Development and Psychopathology, 2*(4), 425–444. https://doi.org/10.1017/S0954579400005812

Masten, A. S., & Coatsworth, J. D. (1998). The development of competence in favorable and unfavorable environments. *American Psychologist, 53*(2), 205–220. https://doi.org/10.1037/0003-066X.53.2.205

Masten, A. S., Lucke, C. M., Nelson, K. M., & Stallworthy, I. C. (2021). Resilience in development and psychopathology: Multisystem perspectives. *Annual Review of Clinical Psychology, 17,* 521–549. https://doi.org/10.1146/annurev-clinpsy-081219-120307

McFarlane, J. M., Groff, J. Y., O'Brien, J. A., & Watson, K. (2005). Behaviors of children following a randomized controlled treatment program for their abused mothers. *Issues in Comprehensive Pediatric Nursing, 28*(4), 195–211. https://doi.org/10.1080/01460860500396708

Mezzacappa, E., Kindlon, D., & Earls, F. (2001). Child abuse and performance task assessments of executive functions in boys. *The Journal of Child Psychology and Psychiatry and Allied Disciplines, 42*(8), 1041–1048. https://doi.org/10.1111/1469-7610.00803

Nakkula, M. J., & Ravitch, S. M. (Eds.). (1998). *Matters of interpretation: Reciprocal transformation in therapeutic and developmental relationships with youth.* Jossey-Bass.

National Center on Early Childhood Health and Wellness. (n.d.). *Understanding and eliminating expulsion in early childhood programs.* ECLKC.

Retrieved September 4, 2022, from https://eclkc.ohs.acf.hhs.gov/publication /understanding-eliminating-expulsion-early-childhood-programs

Naveed, M. (2017, December 15). Income inequality in DC highest in the country. *DC Fiscal Policy Institute.* https://www.dcfpi.org/all/income-inequality -dc-highest-country/

Nikulina, V., Widom, C. S., & Czaja, S. (2011). The role of childhood neglect and childhood poverty in predicting mental health, academic achievement and crime in adulthood. *American Journal of Community Psychology, 48*(3–4), 309–321. https://doi.org/10.1007/s10464-010-9385-y

Nurmohamed, S. (2020). The underdog effect: When low expectations increase performance. *Academy of Management Journal, 63*(4), 1106–1133. https://doi .org/10.5465/amj.2017.0181

Obradović, J., Bush, N. R., Stamperdahl, J., Adler, N. E., & Boyce, W. T. (2010). Biological sensitivity to context: The interactive effects of stress reactivity and family adversity on socioemotional behavior and school readiness. *Child Development, 81*(1), 270–289. https://doi.org/10.1111/j.1467-8624.2009.01394.x

Paley, V. G. (1986). *Mollie is three: Growing up in school.* University of Chicago Press. https://search.library.wisc.edu/catalog/999568770502121

Paley, V. G. (1991). *Bad guys don't have birthdays: Fantasy play at four.* University of Chicago Press. https://search.library.wisc.edu/catalog/9910773390502121

Paley, V. G. (2001). *In Mrs. Tully's room: A childcare portrait.* Harvard University Press. https://search.library.wisc.edu/catalog/999918703902121

Paley, V. G. (2005). *A child's work: The importance of fantasy play.* University of Chicago Press. https://search.library.wisc.edu/catalog/9910819822202121

Perrotta, G. (2020). Psychological trauma: Definition, clinical contexts, neural correlations and therapeutic approaches recent discoveries. *Current Research in Psychiatry and Brain Disorders: CRPBD-100006.*

Perry, B. D. (2007). Stress, trauma and post-traumatic stress disorders in children. *The Child Trauma Academy, 17,* 42–57.

Perry, D. L., & Daniels, M. L. (2016). Implementing trauma-informed practices in the school setting: A pilot study. *School Mental Health, 8*(1), 177–188. https://doi.org/10.1007/s12310-016-9182-3

Powell, B. J., Patel, S. V., Haley, A. D., Haines, E. R., Knocke, K. E., Chandler, S., Katz, C. C., Seifert, H. P., Ake, G. I., Amaya-Jackson, L., & Aarons, G. A. (2020). Determinants of implementing evidence-based trauma-focused interventions for children and youth: A systematic review. *Administration and Policy in Mental Health and Mental Health Services Research, 47*(5), 705–719. https://doi.org/10.1007/s10488-019-01003-3

Raine, A., Dodge, K., Loeber, R., Gatzke-Kopp, L., Lynam, D., Reynolds, C., Stouthamer-Loeber, M., & Liu, J. (2006). The reactive–proactive aggression questionnaire: Differential correlates of reactive and proactive aggression in adolescent boys. *Aggressive Behavior, 32*(2), 159–171. https://doi.org/10.1002 /ab.20115

Rausch, T., Karing, C., Dörfler, T., & Artelt, C. (2016). Personality similarity between teachers and their students influences teacher judgement of student
achievement. *Educational Psychology, 36*(5), 863–878. https://doi.org/10.1080
/01443410.2014.998629

Redding, C. (2019). A teacher like me: A review of the effect of student-teacher
racial/ethnic matching on teacher perceptions of students and student academic
and behavioral outcomes. *Review of Educational Research, 89*(4), 499–535.
https://doi.org/10.3102/0034654319853545

Rist, R. C. (2000). Student social class and teacher expectations: The self-fulfilling
prophecy in ghetto education. *Harvard Educational Review, 70*(3), 266–301.
https://doi.org/10.17763/haer.70.3.1k0624l6102u2725

Rivera Rodas, E. I. (2019). Separate and unequal—Title I and teacher quality. *Education Policy Analysis Archives, 27*(14). https://doi.org/10.14507
/epaa.27.4233

Rowe, W. G., & O'Brien, J. (2002). The Role of Golem, Pygmalion, and Galatea
effects on opportunistic behavior in the classroom. *Journal of Management
Education, 26*(6), 612–628. https://doi.org/10.1177/1052562902238321

Schore, A. N. (2001). The effects of early relational trauma on right brain development, affect regulation, and infant mental health. *Infant Mental Health Journal,
22*(1–2), 201–269. https://doi.org/10.1002/1097-0355(200101/04)22:1<201::
AID-IMHJ8>3.0.CO;2-9

Selman, R. L. (1975). A structural-developmental model of social cognition; implications for intervention research. *The Counseling Psychologist, 6*(4).
https://doi.org/10.1177/001100007700600403

Selman, R. L., Watts, C. L., & Schultz, L. H. (Eds.). (1997). *Fostering friendship:
Pair therapy for treatment and prevention.* Aldine de Gruyter.

Shaffer, A., Yates, T. M., & Egeland, B. R. (2009). The relation of emotional maltreatment to early adolescent competence: Developmental processes in a pro-
spective study. *Child Abuse & Neglect, 33*(1), 36–44. https://doi.org/10.1016/j
.chiabu.2008.12.005

Shonk, S. M., & Cicchetti, D. (2001). Maltreatment, competency deficits, and risk
for academic and behavioral maladjustment. *Developmental Psychology, 37*(1),
3–17. https://doi.org/10.1037/0012-1649.37.1.3

Siegel, D. J. (2020). *The developing mind: How relationships and the brain interact
to shape who we* (3rd ed.; 2020-23051-000). Guilford Press.

Sleeter, C. E. (1995). Reflections on my use of multicultural and critical pedagogy
when students are white. In C. E. Sleeter & P. L. Mclaren (Eds.), *Multicultural
education, critical pedagogy, and the politics of difference* (pp. 415–437).
SUNY Press.

Sorrels, B. (2015). *Reaching and teaching children exposed to trauma.* Gryphon
House. https://search.library.wisc.edu/catalog/9912146974502121

Steele, W., & Malchiodi, C. A. (2011). *Trauma-informed practices with children and
adolescents* (1st ed.). Routledge.

Streeck-Fischer, A., & van der Kolk, B. A. (2000). Down will come baby, cradle and all: Diagnostic and therapeutic implications of chronic trauma on child development. *Australian and New Zealand Journal of Psychiatry, 34*(6), 903–918. https://doi.org/10.1080/000486700265

Suldo, S. M., & Shaffer, E. J. (2008). Looking beyond psychopathology: The dual-factor model of mental health in youth. *School Psychology Review, 37*(1), 52–68. https://doi.org/10.1080/02796015.2008.12087908

Swadener, B. B., & Lubeck, S. (1995). *Children and families "at promise": Deconstructing the discourse of risk.* State University of New York Press.

Swann, W. B., & Bosson, J. K. (2010). Self and identity. In S. T. Fiske, D. T. Gilbert, & G. Lindzey (Eds.), *Handbook of social psychology* (Vol. 1; pp. 589–628). Wiley.

Szumski, G., & Karwowski, M. (2019). Exploring the Pygmalion effect: The role of teacher expectations, academic self-concept, and class context in students' math achievement. *Contemporary Educational Psychology, 59.* https://doi.org/10.1016/j.cedpsych.2019.101787

Terr, L. C. (1991). Acute responses to external events and posttraumatic stress disorders. In M. Lewis (Ed.), *Child and adolescent psychiatry: A comprehensive textbook* (pp. 755–763). Williams & Wilkins Co.

Terr, L. C. (1995). Childhood traumas. In G. S. Everly & J. M. Lating (Eds.), *Psychotraumatology: Key Papers and Core Concepts in Post-Traumatic Stress* (pp. 301–320). Springer US. https://doi.org/10.1007/978-1-4899-1034-9_18

Terr, L. C. (2008). *Too scared to cry: Psychic trauma in childhood.* Basic Books.

Thompson, D. J., Weissbecker, I., Cash, E., Simpson, D. M., Daup, M., & Sephton, S. E. (2015). Stress and cortisol in disaster evacuees: An exploratory study on associations with social protective factors. *Applied Psychophysiology and Biofeedback, 40*(1), 33–44. https://doi.org/10.1007/s10484-015-9270-4

Thompson, T., & Massat, C. R. (2005). Experiences of violence, post-traumatic stress, academic achievement and behavior problems of urban African-American children. *Child and Adolescent Social Work Journal, 22*(5–6), 367–393. https://doi.org/10.1007/s10560-005-0018-5

Ueland, B. (1938). *If you want to write.* G. P. Putnam's Sons. https://lapl.overdrive.com/media/131370

Valencia, R. R. (Ed.). (1997). *The evolution of deficit thinking: Educational thought and practice.* Falmer Press/Taylor & Francis.

van der Kolk, B. (2000). Posttraumatic stress disorder and the nature of trauma. *Dialogues in Clinical Neuroscience, 2*(1), 7–22. https://doi.org/10.31887/DCNS.2000.2.1/bvdkolk

van der Kolk, B. A. (1997). The psychobiology of posttraumatic stress disorder. *The Journal of Clinical Psychiatry, 58*(Suppl 9), 16–24. https://pubmed.ncbi.nlm.nih.gov/9329447/

van der Kolk, B. A. (2005). Developmental trauma disorder: Toward a rational diagnosis for children with complex trauma histories. *Psychiatric Annals, 35*(5), 401–408. https://doi.org/10.3928/00485713-20050501-06

van der Kolk, B. A. (2006). Clinical implications of neuroscience research in PTSD. In R. Yehuda (Ed.), *Psychobiology of posttraumatic stress disorders: A decade of progress* (Vol. 1071; pp. 277–293). Blackwell Publishing.

Vlachou, M., Andreou, E., Botsoglou, K., & Didaskalou, E. (2011). Bully/victim problems among preschool children: A review of current research evidence. *Educational Psychology Review, 23*(3), 329–358. https://doi.org/10.1007/s10648-011-9153-z

Wall, C. R. G. (2021). Relationship over reproach: Fostering resilience by embracing a trauma-informed approach to elementary education. *Journal of Aggression, Maltreatment & Trauma, 30*(1), 118–137. https://doi.org/10.1080/10926771.2020.1737292

Wentzel, K. R., Battle, A., Russell, S. L., & Looney, L. B. (2010). Social supports from teachers and peers as predictors of academic and social motivation. *Contemporary Educational Psychology, 35*(3), 193–202. https://doi.org/10.1016/j.cedpsych.2010.03.002

Werner, E. E. (2000). Protective factors and individual resilience. In J. P. Shonkoff & S. J. Meisels (Eds.), *Handbook of early childhood intervention.* (2nd ed.; pp. 115–132). Cambridge University Press. https://doi.org/10.1017/CBO9780511529320.008

Wright, T. (2007). On Jorge becoming a boy: A counselor's perspective. *Harvard Educational Review, 77*(2), 164–186. https://doi.org/10.17763/haer.77.2.r230j143345x8750

Wright, T. (2010). Learning to laugh: A portrait of risk and resilience in early childhood. *Harvard Educational Review, 80*(4), 444–464. https://doi.org/10.17763/haer.80.4.w18726475585x5t2

Wright, T. (2013a). "I keep me safe." Risk and resilience in children with messy lives. *Phi Delta Kappan, 95*(2), 39–43. https://doi.org/10.1177/003172171309500209

Wright, T. (2013b). Revisiting risk/rethinking resilience: Fighting to live versus failing to thrive. In *Reconceptualizing early childhood care and education: Critical Questions, new imaginaries and social activism—A reader* (pp. 183–192). Peter Lang, International Academic Publishers.

Wright, T. (2022). Teachers' fears as barriers to supporting young children experiencing homelessness [Unpublished].

Wright, T., Nankin, I., Boonstra, K., & Blair, E. (2019). Changing through relationships and reflection: An exploratory investigation of pre-service teachers' perceptions of young children experiencing homelessness. *Early Childhood Education Journal, 47*(3), 297–308. https://doi.org/10.1007/s10643-018-0921-y

Wright, T., & Ryan, S. K. (2014). Toddlers through primary grades: Too scared to learn: Teaching young children who have experienced trauma. *YC Young Children, 69*(5), 88–93.

Wright, T., Taub, A., Fetter, A., & Shumpert, J. (2017). *MMSD 4K: Pathways to resilience for children and families experiencing homelessness.* Madison Metropolitan School District.

Yoman, J. (2008). A primer on functional analysis. *Cognitive and Behavioral Practice, 15*(3), 325–340. https://doi.org/10.1016/j.cbpra.2008.01.002

Index

Aarons, G. A., 2
Academic development, for traumatized children, 156–157
Acknowledgment, praise and, 160–161
Adler, N. E., 100
Adrenaline, 101
Adversity, 18, 20, 107–110, 113
 and learning, 118–137
 trauma and, 14–16
Affirmation, as anchor of emotionally responsive teaching, 157–165
Ake, G. I., 2
Alfonso, V. C., 153
Alink, L. R. A., 102
Alisic, E., 105
Amaya-Jackson, L., 2
Ambler, A., 77
Analysis, problem-solving and, 124–127
Anchors, of emotionally responsive teaching
 affirmation, 157–165
 connections, 152–155
 instruction, 155–157
 safety, 140–152
Andreou, E., 100
Annalakshmi, N., 80
Anxious caregivers, 121
Areba, E. M., 147
Arseneault, L., 77, 153
Artelt, C., 44
At-risk discourse, 80–86
Attentiveness, in classroom, 134–137
Authenticity, 157–158
Autonomic physiological response, 12, 100–101
Ayoub, C. C., 24, 74, 77, 78

Badness, inner, 116–118
Baeza-Velasco, C., 147
Bakermans-Kranenburg, M. J., 99
Barnett, M. L., 56
Battle, A., 100
Beers, S. R., 102
Behavioral management strategies, 136
Bergin, C., 100
Bergin, D., 100
Berryhill, J., 47
Best, K. M., 80, 81
Bettini, E., 56
Biopsychosocial model, 18–21
Blair, E., 43, 66
Blank, M., 98
Bonanno, G. A., 108
Boonstra, K., 43, 66
Bosson, J. K., 99
Botsoglou, K., 100
Boyce, W. T., 100
Bremner, J. D., 102
Brewin, C. R., 108
Brief stress, 107–110
Briere, J., 102, 118
Brindis, C. D., 118
Bruno, P., 56
Burnout, 178–181
Burt, K. B., 156
Burton, B. A., 80
Busette, C., 50
Bush, N. R., 100

Caregivers, 121–122
Cash, E., 108
Caspi, A., 77, 153
Castellvi, P., 147

Castle, S., 56
Catterall, J. S., 147
Challenging behaviors, 150–152
Chandler, S., 2
Chapman, S., 118
Chopik, W. J., 77
Christian-Brandt, A. S., 56
Chung, D., 57
Cicchetti, D., 77, 78, 102, 105, 118,
    134, 147
Classroom environment, threat in,
    105–106
Cloitre, M., 118, 149
Coatsworth, J. D., 153
Cohen, J. A., 101
Cole, S. F., 118, 123
Collie, R. J., 47
Communication
    emotional, 121–124
    skills, language and, 118–120
    social, 121–124
Compassion fatigue, 178–181
Complexity, developmental,
    76–79
Comprehension, reading,
    127–130
Connections, as anchor of emotionally
    responsive teaching,
    152–155
Costabile, A., 113
Coster, W., 118
COVID-19 pandemic, 46
Craig, F., 113
Craig, S. E., 115, 116
Critical reflection, 31, 176–178
    as essential practice, 62–65
Culp, R. E., 118
Culturally responsive pedagogy (CRP),
    30–31
Cummings, A.-L., 115
Curriculum, engaging, 134–137
Czaja, S., 105

Daignault, I. V., 102
Danese, A., 77
Daniels, M. L., 118
Darwish, D., 153

Daup, M., 108
Daviss, W. B., 101
De Bellis, M. D., 97, 102, 108, 131
Deep thinking, framework for,
    16–21
    biopsychosocial model, 18–21
Depressed caregivers, 121, 122
Development
    children, threat and, 99–100
    complexity vs. outcomes, 76–79
    defined, 75
    and emotionally responsive teaching,
        33–36
    pathways, 71–79
    of shared perspective, 8–11
Dewitt, E., 55
Diament, M., 57
Didaskalou, E., 100
Distracted caregivers, 122
Doba, K., 115
Dodge, K., 153
Dörfler, T., 44
Dubrow, N., 147

Earls, F., 131
Egeland, B. R., 153
Eisenberg, M. E., 147
Eklund, K. M., 81
Elizondo, S., 50
Ellis, C. G., 101
Emotional communication,
    121–124
Emotionally responsive ethic (ERE),
    39–40
Emotionally responsive teaching (ERT),
    139–140
    aims of, 37–39
    anchors of. See Anchors, of
        emotionally responsive
        teaching
    benefit to children, 172–175
    defined, 24–30
    development and, 33–36
    essence of, 30–33
    goal of, 25
    healing and growing through,
        181–183

metaphor to illustrate, 26–27
paradigm/ethic, 29–30
responsiveness of, 25–28
as teaching with awareness of
    context, 175
Emotional responsiveness,
    25–28
Encouraging language, 119
Engel, G. L., 18
Enriching relationships, 38
Epinephrine, 101
Eslinger, J. C., 47
Esquivel, G. B., 153
Ethic, 29–30. *See* Emotionally
    responsive ethic (ERE)
Ethical impulse, 38
Executive functioning, 130–134
Expectations, self-fulfilling,
    43–46
Experiences, restorative, 32–33
Expressive language, 119

Falvey, E. C., 118, 149
Fang, Z., 43
Fear, 12
    teaching from, 58–62
Fearon, R. P., 99
Fetter, A., 72
Fischer, K. W., 24, 74, 77, 78
Fisher, H. L., 77
Fleischer, A., 101
Ford, J. D., 12, 101
Ford, T. G., 56
Forster, M., 147
Fredrickson, B. L., 132, 160
Fromewick, J., 47
Furrer, C. J., 80

Gadd, M. G., 118, 123
Games, 133
Garbarino, J., 147
Garcia, V., 57
Garmezy, N., 80, 81
Garrett, P., 81
Garvert, D. W., 118, 149
Gatzke-Kopp, L., 153
Giordano, K., 57

Golem effect, 44
Gonzalez, A., 47
Goodness, 39
Gregory, M., 118, 123
Grigsby, B., 47
Groff, J. Y., 105
Gutiérrez-Rosado, T., 147

Haines, E. R., 2
Haley, A. D., 2
Halliday, M. A. K., 119
Heard, feeling, 40
Hebert, M., 102
Henn-Haase, C. M., 118, 149
Henschel, S., 115
Herman, J. L., 12
Herrenkohl, T. I., 2
Heuristic, 120
Holistic, emotionally responsive
    teaching essence, 30–31
Homelessness, 17–18
Hong, S., 2
Hope
    teaching from, 58–62
Hopelessness, 12
Hormones, 101
Houtz, J. C., 153
Howes, C., 153
HPA-axis, 101
Humanizing, school environment, 39
Hypothalamus, 101

Igelman, R., 101
Imaginative language, 120
Imberman, S. A., 56
Inequities, systemic, 13
Ingram, B. L., 108
Inner badness, 116–118
Instruction
    as anchor of emotionally responsive
        teaching, 155–157
    care and, 173–174
Intimidating language, 119
Intrapsychic phenomenon, 17

Jaffee, S. R., 153
Jeon, S., 56

Joireman, J. A., 115
Jones, N. D., 56

Kaniasty, K., 108
Karing, C., 44
Karwowski, M., 44
Katz, C. C., 2
Kelly, D. J., 118
Khan, C., 118, 149
Kidd, P., 12
Kim, J., 43, 66, 102, 105
Kindlon, D., 131
Kira, I. A., 12
Knocke, K. E., 2
Knowledge, 166
Knowledge, skills, values, and resources
    (KSVR), 165–168
Koenen, K. C., 77
Koplow, L., 24
Kostelny, K., 147
Kwon, K.-A., 56

Ladson-Billings, G., 24, 30, 158
La Greca, A. M., 108
Lai, I., 56
Language
    and communications skills,
        118–120
    intimidating *vs.* encouraging/
        expressive, 118–120
    seven roles, 119–120
Lapsley, A.-M., 99
Larson, S., 118
Lawrence, H., 118
Lawrence-Lightfoot, S., 24
Leahy, K. E., 77
Learning, 156
    adversity and, 118–137
    and submission, 55–57
    teaching and, relationship between,
        40
Lelli, C., 2
Letts, D., 118
Lewis, S. J., 77
Limonero, J. T., 147
Linney, J. A., 47
Liu, J., 153

Llistosella, M., 147
Loeber, R., 153
Long, J. D., 156
Looney, L. B., 100
Losada, M. F., 132, 160
Lu, P., Oh, J., 77
Lubeck, S., 81
Lucke, C. M., 24
Lynam, D., 153
Lyytinen, H., 81

Mackintosh, M.-A., 118, 149
Malchiodi, C. A., 2
Mannarino, A. P., 101
Maraganore, A., 24, 74
Marcionetti, J., 77
Martin, A. J., 47
Massat, C. R., 102
Masten, A. S., 24, 80, 81, 153, 156
Mathiason, M. A., 147
McFarlane, J. M., 105
McKeating, E., 57
McMorris, B. J., 147
Meaningful work, 38
Mental flexibility, 131
Mental health, 20
Messy lives, children with
    as context for development,
        11–13
    shared perspective, development of,
        8–11
    teaching, 7–21
Mezzacappa, E., 131
Moffitt, T. E., 77, 153
Montirosso, R., 113
Murray, L. K., 101

Nakkula, M. J., 24, 43, 62
Nandrino, J.-L., 115
Nankin, I., 43, 66
Narrative materials, organizing,
    127–130
Naveed, M., 49
Needham, T. L., 115
Negative experiences, 20–21
Nelson, K. M., 24
Nikulina, V., 105

Noam, G., 24, 74
Nurmohamed, S., 44

O'Brien, J., 44
O'Brien, J. G., 118, 123
Obradoviæ, J., 100, 156
O'Connor, E., 77, 78
Orange, A., 47
Ott, L., 115
Outcomes, developmental, 76–79

Paley, V. G., 24
Paradigm, 29–30
  shifting, 65–66
Parasympathetic nervous system, 101
Pardo, C., 147
Park, Y., 56
Patel, S. V., 2
Pérez-Ventana Ortiz, C., 147
Perrotta, G., 14
Perry, B. D., 14, 123
Perry, D. L., 118
Perry, N. E., 47
Peters, M. L., 47
Pezard, L., 115
Physiological responses, 13
  autonomic, 12, 100–101
Pitzer, J. R., 80
Play, 133
Positive identity, 38
Powell, B. J., 2
Praise, and acknowledgment,
  160–161
Problem-solving, and analysis,
  124–127
Protection, 141–152
Public school system, 51–55
Pygmalion effect, 44

Rabovsky, S. J., 56
Racusin, R., 101
Raine, A., 153
Rappolt-Schlichtmann, G., 24, 77, 78
Rausch, T., 44
Ravitch, S. M., 24, 43, 62
Raya, P., 24, 74
Reactivity, 44, 131

Reciprocal transformation, 31
Redding, C., 44
Reiser, J., 101
Relationships, 31, 152–155
  enriching, 38
Representational language, 120
Resilience
  defined, 81
  reframing, 79–86
Resources, 166
Responsiveness, 25–28
Restorative experiences, 32–33
Reynolds, C., 153
Rice, M. L., 118
Risk
  at-risk discourse, 80–86
  reframing as resilience, 84–86
Rist, R. C., 43
Ristuccia, J., 118, 123
Rivera Rodas, E. I., 56
Rizzato, V., 113
Rogosch, F. A., 77, 78, 102
Roisman, G. I., 99
Rossier, J., 77
Routines, 133
Rowe, W. G., 44
Russell, S. L., 100
Ryan, S. K., 105

Safety, as anchor of emotionally
  responsive teaching, 140–152
Saito, J., 118, 149
Santacrose, D. E., 56
Schedules, 133
Schooling, social inequity and,
  48–51
Schore, A. N., 118
Schultz, L. H., 24
Scott, C., 102, 118
Seen, feeling, 40
Seifert, H. P., 2
Self-concept, shift in, 112–118
Self-control, 131
Self-doubt, 9
Self-fulfilling expectations, 43–46
Self-regulation, 130–134
Selman, R. L., 24

Sephton, S. E., 108
Shaffer, A., 153
Shaffer, E. J., 76
Shared perspective, development of,
    8–11
Shifting paradigm, 65–66
Shift in worldview, 112–118
Shonk, S. M., 102, 134
Shumpert, J., 72
Siegel, D. J., 102
Simpson, D. M., 108
Singh, I., 24, 74
Skills, 166
Skinner, E. A., 80
Sleeter, C. E., 80
Social climate, of classroom, 154–155
Social communication, 121–124
Social inequity, and schooling, 48–51
Sorrels, B., 123
Spetz, J., 118
Stallworthy, I. C., 24
Stamperdahl, J., 100
Steele, W., 2
Stouthamer-Loeber, M., 153
Streeck-Fischer, A., 105, 134, 150
Stress, 97
    brief, 107–110
    toxic, 96, 100, 102, 107–110, 112
    traumatic, 97–98
Stress response, 100–106
Stressors, 13, 109
Strunk, K. O., 56
Submission, learning and, 55–57
Suldo, S. M., 76
Supporting teachers
    importance of, 24–25
Supportive learning environment,
    149–150
Surviving vs. thriving, 87–88
Swadener, B. B., 81
Swann, W. B., 99
Sympathetic nervous system, 101
Systemic inequities, 13
Szumski, G., 44

Taliaferro, L. A., 147
Taub, A., 72

Taylor, A., 153
Tenuta, F., 113
Terr, L. C., 14, 108
Thinking, deep
    framework for, 16–21
Thomas, J., 101
Thompson, D. J., 108
Thompson, T., 102
Threat
    and children's development, 99–100
    in classroom environment, 105–106
    embodied experience of, 95–100
    impact of, 97–98
Thriving, surviving vs., 87–88
Torppa, M., 81
Toth, S. L., 77, 78, 147
Toughness, 15, 57
Toxic stress, 96, 100, 102, 107–110,
    112
Trabacca, A., 113
Traditional instructional models,
    111–112
Trauma, 12, 13, 107–110, 112
    and adversity, 14–16
    language of, 97
    redefining, 91–110
    usage of term, 96
Traumatic events, 108
Traumatic stress, 97–98
Treacherous times, teaching in, 47–57

Ueland, B., 1
Understanding, 39

Valencia, R. R., 44
Value/valuing, 40, 166
Van der Kolk, B. A., 12, 98, 100, 101,
    103, 105, 108, 134, 149, 150
Van Dillen, T., 97, 102, 108
Van IJzendoorn, M. H., 99
Verbrugge, B., 2
Vermetten, E., 102
Vlachou, M., 100
Vulliez-Coady, L., 115

Wall, C. R. G., 147
Wallace, D. L., 118, 123

Watkins, R. V., 118
Watson, K., 105
Watts, C. L., 24
Weissbecker, I., 108
Wentzel, K. R., 100
Werner, E. E., 147
Widom, C. S., 105

Wood, W. J., 56
Working memory, 130–131
Wright, T., 2, 43, 66, 72, 79, 81, 83,
      100, 105, 147, 153, 173

Yates, T. M., 153
Yoman, J., 152

About the Author

Dr. Travis Wright is a nationally recognized expert on school-based support for children who have experienced trauma. Blending developmental, clinical, and educational perspectives, Wright studies how schools influence social–emotional and identity development for children navigating challenging circumstances and how best to prepare teachers to meet the needs of these students.

Currently, Dr. Wright is an associate professor of counseling psychology and early childhood education at the University of Wisconsin–Madison (UW–Madison), where he is also faculty director of the Morgridge Center for Public Service. At UW–Madison, Wright founded and directs the BASES (Building Academic, Social, and Emotional Supports) Project, a research–practice partnership with the Madison Metropolitan School District focused on increasing school-based supports for young children experiencing homelessness and building the capacity of schools, teachers, and families to better meet the needs of these students. The BASES Project has provided over 8,000 hours of direct support to more than 400 homeless children in the past 7 years. During the 2015–2016 academic year, while on leave from UW–Madison, Wright served as the deputy chief of early childhood education for District of Columbia Public Schools, where he oversaw implementation of one of the nation's largest Head Start programs. Previously, he worked as a school-based mental health counselor, public school teacher, and early childhood educator in Washington, DC, and Boston, MA. Dr. Wright is licensed as a professional counselor in the state of Wisconsin.

Wright completed his doctorate in human development and psychology and a certificate of advanced study in school adjustment counseling at Harvard University and was a Phi Beta Kappa undergraduate at the University of Tennessee, Knoxville. He has received numerous academic and service awards for his efforts, including the American Educational Research Association's Early Career Award for Child Development and Early Childhood Education Research.